Education on the move

Educational reforms: experiences and prospects

Unesco

Published in 1979 by the United Nations
Educational, Scientific and Cultural Organization,
7 Place de Fontenoy, 75700 Paris
Composed by Malvern Typesetting Services Ltd, Malvern, U.K.
Printed by Duculot, Gembloux, Belgium

ISBN   92-3-101669-5

Preface

A group of senior officials responsible for educational reforms in Member States met at Unesco Headquarters from 24 to 28 October 1977 to discuss major problem areas of educational reforms in the 1970s and 1980s. The meeting was organized in accordance with a decision taken by the General Conference at its nineteenth session and the present publication is an outcome of that discussion. Participants had been invited to present papers with a view to eventual publication, but, in order to extend the areas covered so as to include problems concerning the implementation of educational reforms, the Secretariat sought contributions from additional authors.

This publication is intended for educational planners, administrators and decision-makers who are confronted in their daily work with the demanding task of bringing about changes in education in order to adapt it to the requirements of modern society. Those directly involved in specific activities dealing with the implementation of educational reforms, such as the development of suitable curricula, administrative and pedagogical supervision, teacher training, school mapping, introduction of modern technology, etc., will also find its contents informative.

Unesco would like to thank the authors, who have spared no efforts to review their original texts, thus producing the final versions as presented here. It is hoped that their contributions will stimulate further discussion on the subject and thus serve the cause of education throughout the world.

It should be noted that the views expressed in the individual studies are those of the authors and do not necessarily coincide with those of Unesco. Furthermore, the designations employed and the presentation of the material in this publication do not imply the expression of any opinion whatsoever on the part of the Unesco Secretariat concerning the legal status of any country, territory, city or area or of its authorities, or concerning the delimitation of its frontiers or boundaries.

Contents

Introduction

The present publication includes studies presented at a meeting of senior government officials, as noted in the Preface, along with additional studies supplied by other eminent writers. It is divided into three parts. Part One is devoted to the problems of educational reforms and particularly to the translation of policy options into concrete action. It is itself subdivided into two sections: the Working Paper of the Expert Meeting, prepared by the Secretariat in the form of an annotated agenda for use by the participants at the meeting; and the Final Report adopted at the end of this meeting. Part Two is devoted to a number of particularly important aspects of the problems raised by educational reform. Lastly, Part Three consists of several case studies. These are based on experiments in educational reform carried out in a number of countries, situated in various parts of the world and differing widely from each other, socio-economically and culturally.

It was intended that this consideration of the application of reforms should be related to the mid-term appraisal of the United Nations Second Development Decade and to the objectives of Unesco's Medium-Term Plan. These reflect the programme of action for the establishment of the new international economic order which should, in the words of resolution 9.11, adopted at the nineteenth session of the General Conference, lead to

a new human order based on freedom, justice and equity, removal of inequality among nations and peoples, mutual understanding, co-operation in mankind's major common tasks, and the participation of everyone in welfare, education, knowledge and culture.

It is well known that the mere expansion of the existing education systems has exacerbated, rather than attenuated, differences in the level of educational attainment between different countries, and often within one and the same country. As a result, a new approach to these problems is emerging which, it is hoped, will open the way for more detailed studies leading up to the formulation of a strategy for the Third

Development Decade in this field. Participants in the meeting were accordingly called upon to formulate recommendations as to the directions future programmes in the field of educational policy and planning should take. These recommendations are included in the Final Report of the meeting.

In order to grasp the full meaning of this document and its practical implications, the list of questions to which the participants in the meeting of experts were invited to reply in their written contributions is needed:

What should be the nature of an international strategy for the Third Development Decade in education and what might be the implications of such an international strategy for educational reform?

How can educational reform gain recognition as an instrument in the service of an international strategy to mobilize human resources, in view of the economic, social and cultural dimensions of the new international economic order which is to be introduced?

How can the approach to problems associated with democratization lead to reforms which are consistent with a particular transformation of political, economic and social life, and how can the planning of these reforms be combined with decentralization of discussions, decisions and responsibilities?

How should the strategies on which the educational reforms of the next decade will be based tackle the problems of the rural world and set about reaching those requiring education in the poorest regions?

How can reform of the educational system help in attaining the aims of a strategy designed to increase autonomy and reduce factors making for dependency in the development of a country?

How can the requirements of endogenous development and those of co-operation between developing countries both be met by the joint elaboration of educational strategies and reforms?

How should the reforms of the next decade link education with the world of work, in view of the changes to be made in the international division of labour, in the conditions and organization of production and in the structure of employment?

What are the implications for education of the transfers of technology likely to take place in the course of the next two decades?

How can international technical co-operation and the various forms of technology transfer assist in the implementation of educational reforms and vice versa?

The first conclusion to emerge from reading the particular studies included here is a difference of opinion as to what is meant by educational reform. Hence the need to reach a certain measure of agreement on the definition of this concept. It is common practice to present as a reform innovations in detail—to do with teaching methods, for instance—as well as radical changes affecting at the same time educational ideology, objectives, strategies and priorities: in short, all the factors related to educational policies and planning. However, it is generally accepted that reform implies major structural changes, and that it therefore constitutes a political option. Reform, when considered as an integral part of the overall process of social transformation, involves significant changes in general educational strategy, and decisions concerning it are the responsibility of the national authorities or legislative bodies.

Another finding to emerge from the studies is the general preference for comprehensive educational reforms rather than isolated and fragmentary innovations introduced here and there in the educational system. This policy trend was specifically emphasized by the Director-General of Unesco at the Conference of Ministers of Education in African Member States: 'It should always be remembered that innovation is not an end in itself but is to be seen in the context of a coherent reform.'[1]* Many governments during the past twenty years in fact chose reform as the most appropriate means of ensuring the modernization, renewal and growth of the educational system.

However, certain contributors stress the modest results achieved by so-called 'fundamental' reforms. Under what circumstances and in what socio-economic context does reform constitute the most effective method of promoting change in the field of education? A good number of the studies provide examples showing how necessary it is to have favourable conditions within society as a whole as a prerequisite for reform. Education is not an isolated activity, but a part, both dependent and dynamic, of the social system.

How long will it take to bring about an educational reform? A few years, a decade, or one or more generations? In fact, one can see educational reform as the long-term, integral development of a process made up of several stages. Some people tend to view educational reform as evidence of social contradictions or conflict, while others see in the process a natural quest for balance between education and the social, economic and cultural context. In the latter case, reform is nothing more than a process of gradual change. These proponents of evolution maintain that there are stages of growth through which every educational system must pass. In several of the studies, it is clearly shown that preparations and experimentation for reform may last for one or more decades.

*Numbers in text refer to notes at the end of each chapter.

Very different situations, sometimes scarcely comparable, are analysed in the case studies presented in this publication. It would seem possible, in this connection, to discern three scenarios, namely, (a) relative equilibrium, (b) gradual change, and (c) radical change. Since this is true both of the whole social system and of the educational system, we can combine the two systems as variables in a matrix in which the specific reforms each country has envisaged for its own educational system could be assigned an appropriate place, for example, as follows:

		Predisposition to social change		
		Status quo and cumulative change	Moderate reforms	Radical social change
Predisposition to educational change	Maintenance and incremental adjustments	1.1	1.2	1.3
	Moving equilibrium educational reforms	2.1	2.2	2.3
	Radical change of educational object-ives and policies	3.1	3.2	3.3

Do the different examples of reform throughout the world have points in common? It seems that one can reply in the affirmative, at least for the great majority of cases. First of all, in analysing what has to be changed, those concerned frequently accuse the system of social elitism and of being ill-adapted to employment prospects or to culture. Next, quite naturally, we often find as an introduction to the reforms common objectives intended to correct those distortions. This has made it possible for the Working Paper and the Final Report to be arranged under three headings: democratization; due regard for cultural identity; and relationship to a comprehensive employment policy.

Unesco has always studied with interest experiments in educational reform and disseminated information concerning them. Although there is not a sufficient number of case studies to justify drawing general conclusions, nevertheless some lessons can be learnt from the experience already acquired:

In order to be successful, reforms must embody new ideas and original solutions.

Reforms often fail because they are not ripe for action, and are seen as
too violent attempts to disrupt the normal order of things.

The priorities adopted are not always clear and do not take into account
the margin of change which is politically acceptable at a given
moment.

The necessary resources are not available.

Certain preconditions are not fulfilled as regards decentralization, local
initiatives or the participation of students, parents and the local
community in planning and carrying out the reforms.

The all-important role of the teaching or administrative staff was not
sufficiently borne in mind.

Lack of measures for shifting bureaucratic inertia.

Particular attention must be paid to integration of the formal and non-
formal educational subsystems. This raises another difficulty. What do
we in fact know about what has actually been done in various parts of the
world in regard to non-formal education? Has this contributed substantially to the development of education, especially in the developing
countries? What are the prospects, therefore, in this field?

The idea of reform as gateway to the future leads quite naturally to
that of prospective studies. Directed towards profound reforms, they will
most probably be a major component of long-term educational planning. If these studies are to result in a truly international effort to
promote equality in educational development, they can be extended to
include all Member States, grouped, not according to population or
wealth, but according to their stage of educational development and the
extent to which they have embraced the spirit of reform. The aim of
these studies should be to draw up, not a model, but scenarios and
different options. Later the time-scale applicable to such studies could be
considered. The viewpoint of the countries for whom these studies are
intended should be borne in mind, so as to avoid imposing standards,
goals or, *a fortiori*, external models on developing countries without
having consulted them. This is why studies in futurology must take into
account each country's own situation. Solutions must not be proposed or
imposed in the name of agreement on principles. True principles are
above particular cases. It is for each country to define its future in its own
terms, above all as regards educational reform.

Where educational reforms are concerned, the future is necessarily
the field of action, but such action will be more firmly based if we
consider what the future could and should be. A distinction must be
made between the identification of aims, the expression of values and the
'history' of the future.

It will also be necessary to attempt to steer our way in the light of the
present situation as well as the goals set up and values recommended and

to vary the solutions according to various logical categories — the desirable, the possible and the probable.

NOTE

1. Conference of Ministers of Education in African Member States, organized by Unesco with the co-operation of the Organization of African Unity (OAU) and the United Nations Economic Commission for Africa (ECA), Lagos, Nigeria, 27 January to 4 February 1976; *Final Report*, p. 61 (Unesco ED/MD/41).

Part One

Documents of the Expert Meeting on Major Problem Areas of Educational Reforms in the 1970s and 1980s (Experiences and Prospects)

Background[1]

The main characteristics of educational reforms during the 1970s: national experiences and general tendencies

During the last twenty years, profound changes have taken place in the general picture presented by educational institutions throughout the world, and these have not always been the result of action taken by the authorities with a view to adopting or introducing changes in the educational system by legislative means, in other words of a 'reform' in the generally accepted meaning of the term.

First of all, in most countries the scale of education has changed, albeit at different levels of education in different countries and regions, and public expenditure has increased to an extent that would even recently have seemed unthinkable. Between 1960 and 1975, total school enrolments rose from 320 to more than 550 millions, while the number of teachers doubled.[2] The new scale of education, which was due to population growth, the extension and lengthening of the period of school attendance as well as an unprecedented increase in educational activities designed for adults, has consequences which warrant more systematic examination, as regards systems administration and control, the composition, training and attitude of the teaching profession and the relations of education with its physical and social environment. Indeed, many reforms have been undertaken with the short-term objective of remedying the confusion caused in a rigid system by a rapid increase in numbers and expenditure.

At the same time, in many countries there have been important shifts of emphasis in the organization and content of training — shifts towards modern mathematics, science subjects and, to a lesser extent, technical courses — while education in the human sciences has expanded by leaps and bounds in higher and sometimes secondary education.

17

Out-of-school forms of training and vocational retraining, both on a permanent and an occasional basis, have multiplied to such an extent that it is sometimes necessary to reconsider the aims and the scope of the initial period of training.

We thus begin to get a clearer idea of systems of lifelong education — not yet fully developed — which include initial training, adult education and use of the media, and which cover all age groups. Although this phenomenon is more obvious and to some extent more clearly measured in quantitative terms than in the past, its implications in terms of the allocation of resources and of teaching methods are still far from clear. It would perhaps be better to focus our attention more on the definition of indicators of 'modalities' which draw attention to the good points of new forms of education (user participation, expansion of the scope of education, decompartmentalization of subjects, role of manual skills in the development of the personality) which could be used as a basis for reforms of and adjustments to the initial period of schooling.

Sometimes one has the impression that this trend consists of a gradual and not always very logical juxtaposition of various types of educational system, which are organized on a different basis, which either compete with each other or have opposing objectives, and, even worse, which are so specialized in their appeal that they may reinforce discrimination between social and geographical groupings instead of combating it. It would probably be useful to determine to what extent and under what conditions such diversity is a stage in evolution towards a broader and more diversified system and to what extent it can be reconciled with the requirements of a democratic society.

However, despite the importance of these changes, one cannot but be struck by the continuity of educational systems whose basic rules have become more flexible without undergoing any radical alteration and by the relatively few changes in teaching equipment, the basic educational way of life and the process of learning, still being coloured by national customs and traditions, even in countries where the traditions are imported. When observed at the level of the actual situation of education, the boldest plans for reform appear to have been remarkably transformed or attenuated in their effect.

In very many countries the rapid succession of reforms — affecting curricula, objectives and diplomas — has made the idea of continuing reform commonplace, but it has also shaken the naïve belief of the public at large in the immutability of the structures and values of the educational system. In the wake of the radical and often constructive criticism which was echoed in the report of the International Commission on the Development of Education (*Learning to Be*),[3] a certain disenchantment with the reforming spirit seems to be appearing here and there, a preference for pedestrian views and stabilizing measures. Perhaps this should be seen as the effect of a better understanding of the difficulties of self-imposed change and of the political gauntlet to be run when vested interests are challenged. Perhaps it should also be seen, at least in certain countries, as the effect of a prolonged economic crisis in which unemployment among youth has made the relation between education and employment even less clear than it was and in which resources are dwindling and innovation is losing its impetus.

Nevertheless, the political significance of educational institutions has perhaps never been so clearly stated, nor the political responsibility of education so vigorously asserted. As the ever-increasing proportion of public money in expenditure on education becomes more evident, national authorities seem compelled to give an ever more detailed justification of the policy or rather the plan which they propose to their citizens or submit for their approval. It is hardly surprising that the definition and implementation of an educational policy is seen as an attribute of sovereignty, whether acquired or regained, or that external interference, however well-meaning, is not suffered gladly. It is naturally when reforms are being made—that is to say when planned action is being taken to change the 'course of events'—that a national policy or a medium- or long-term project in all its originality will be formulated more clearly, demonstrating the link between practical measures and values. The corollary is that in many cases the debate, whether dispassionate or animated, on the wisdom of the measures proposed or adopted soon moves to the level of ideology or even of political confrontation. Thus the same methodological or structural measures may be assessed in radically different ways by the protagonists, and even by the teachers themselves, according to circumstances of time or place.

Interesting though this trend may be, it seems to call for the clarification of three points, which are important for different reasons: first of all, what new forms can the debate on reform be expected to take, since that reform is immediately associated with a projected type of society in which each citizen, and not only the specialist, feels himself involved? This question goes beyond what was until recently called public information or the technique of overcoming resistance. In the second place, in many countries there is a tendency to universalize reform, to present it as a calling into question of basic principles and to make it part of a supposedly coherent overall plan to transform social relations. Experience tends to justify this attitude, for it has been observed that a reform which is limited in scope often sets off a chain reaction whose effects can spread throughout the system, to such an extent that there would seem to be little point, in the context of this agenda, in drawing a clear-cut distinction between overall and partial reform. The question which then arises is: do we really possess tools for analysis which would enable us to approach the question of education in its entirety in a given society today, and, if not, what research is required to improve the tools we have? Can we today move from empiricism to ideology, from social practice to its theoretical justification, from the paths of learning to the form of society? Or should the frontiers of un-certainty, and thus of the risks involved, be more clearly established when reforms are undertaken? And does not the shrinking of these frontiers require a much more sustained effort of observation, study and analysis, for which invaluable material will be found in the considerable experience of the last few years?

After this brief survey of the subject, in which national experience and even regional differences have of necessity been ignored, certain questions may perhaps be considered:

Future reforms will be applied to systems whose scale and, in some cases, whose form has changed, and which are still undergoing the resulting transformations. Will not the machinery of reform be affected by its application to such a changing situation?

Can the blunting of the reforming spirit which is observed in educational practice be lessened by wider previous concertation, by the multiplier effect of reforms outside education or by more sustained attention to supporting machinery?

Would it be helpful to undertake a systematic survey of the reforms promulgated in recent years in order to arrive at an empirical assessment of regional and world trends?

Are there any criteria which might help us in assessing the advantages and risks involved in temporarily allowing several different educational systems to exist side by side, and how should they be interrelated within an overall system of lifelong education?

What research would make it possible to strengthen the link between educational practice, the organization of educational systems and the theories on which both these are based?

The main problems facing the translation of policy options in education into practical action

Some reforms have no effect and others have effects which are unforeseen or even contrary to the original intentions; in other cases again, the internal dynamism of reforms re-creates, in some other part of the educational system, the very imbalance which they were designed to redress; finally, there are some effects which appear to have no cause, or at least for whose existence no recognized determining factor can be found; they are the result of some outside initiative, some adventitious movement, which spreads like wildfire throughout the system. There are several obvious and familiar reasons for this state of affairs, others which are less so and might call for some analysis and others which, although considered obvious, need to be looked at again.

Perhaps it should be accepted that in education, as in other areas of social life, good ideas do not always come first to those with the authority to propagate them. It may be that systems which are operated on a more pragmatic basis, which have fewer regulations and are more receptive to individual initiative are better suited to continuing reform than those which bring a ponderous hierarchical machine into operation when any change is introduced. It may be — and this is a question which is worth going into — that the greatest changes in education and real progress are not the result — or not only the result — of deliberate reforms. This was true of Gutenberg, and it is true of certain technological or social mutations, of unexpected influxes of funds, of sudden cultural or linguistic changes and even of teaching ability. Education policies have something in common with seamanship — they sometimes have to sail with the wind. In education as in legal affairs, custom may in time become law. It would no doubt be useful — for the helmsman — to investigate the origins and the spread of these movements and actions which have such far-reaching consequences.

The difficulties encountered when translating a planned reform into practical action occur from the very beginning, if the beginning is the choice of an option. A policy option is as firm in what it discards as in what it retains. First of all it discards the impossible, which is defined by various restrictions. Financial restrictions do not cause much discussion; they merely establish a limit. But human restrictions are much more local. In an area which, in the last analysis, concerns all the population and in which results can only be achieved through the efforts of those who study — and their efforts, like the knowledge to be acquired, must be pleasurable — policies must be accepted by consensus.

Consensus means listening, and not merely taking a decision. Persistent resistance to reform, whether that of the teacher, that of the student or that of the rural population, is sometimes a way of voicing an opinion when the debate did not take place at the proper time. Perhaps the choice of educational policy is more a matter of decoding a consensus than of imposing it. In the last analysis, it is by sounding out the impossible and other possible choices — for there is always more than one way of arriving at one's destination — that good reasons can be advanced for an option which makes what it rejects as clear as what it accepts.

The preamble to the text of many reforms makes one think that objectives are often identified with values. The appeal to values is used to fill in the gap of uncertainty when the actual choice is made. But a working system cannot be deduced from values. The examination of human rights does not lead to the formulation of systems; it serves as a measuring stick for them. The objective of an education policy is something different; it is the result anticipated, the declared conclusion of a course of action whose various stages, methods and instruments are clearly defined. How can a reform be operational if its objective is not operational? These considerations incline one to the view that a policy is not only a statement of objectives, but that the decision made must include a choice of systems, methods, resources and instruments, which are by no means extraneous to the objectives. Experience of reform has shown that a system which is elitist in its structures may in practice contradict the objective of democratization, that the way in which textbooks are produced can throw a reform off course and that adoption of a certain type of educational technology can increase dependency.

A reform is a progression towards a target, which fascinates by its very nature, but it is also a point of departure. This leads us to a consideration of what some will call tactical problems. How can one state be replaced by another while the machine is in operation, while pupils are in the classroom, while buildings are being erected and the budget is being adopted? Such problems are neither trifling nor unimportant. The tactics of the clean sweep or the short cut have recently been tried in several countries. It would be interesting to see whether or not such action introduces a new factor which can help in the solution of the tactical problems associated with educational reforms.

The first tactical decision concerns the choice of the point or points at which the reform will come into operation. It calls for detailed knowledge of the different parts of which the system is made up and of their interactions. In a school system a reform is always threatened from both before and after it is introduced, whereas the reform of a particular branch of education is threatened on its flanks. A reform of adult education can be emptied of its content by the school system or by the absence of employment outlets or follow-up. Recent history offers numerous examples of this type of difficulty, and should lead to immediate consideration of the repercussions which even limited reforms are likely to have in the remotest parts of the system. It may be judged useful to consider in some detail the special and no doubt crucial role played by the universities and by higher education in general in bringing about the success or failure of any large-scale reform. Higher education, with its dual function of training and research, is the corner-stone of the educational structure. It defines and at the same time embodies the highest standards of academic knowledge, and is partly or wholly responsible for the training of teachers and educators. Its principles inevitably exert an influence, if only as a term of reference, on all education, however elementary or informal. It also represents a capacity for the organization of research which reformers certainly require.

Many reforms have been trimmed to a surprising extent as the result of caution, an excessively pyramidal image of education and in some cases the influence of technical assistance. One is familiar with the fate of pilot classes or model establishments which came into being because the need for preliminary testing was realized and which long afterwards inexplicably survive as a reminder of the embryo stage of a reform long since defunct. One is also familiar with teacher-training institutes in which the impetus of reforms which were more ambitious at the outset has gradually worn itself out. This relegation of reforms to the sidelines brings us to one of the most difficult aspects of their introduction: how can one avoid both the disadvantages of excessive slowness and the dangers of undue haste? Education has its own time-scale, which is based on the time needed to learn and the units into which this is divided by the structure of the system. These must not be interfered with. But the duration of a reform, the time between its beginning and its results, is affected by further constraints, of which the timetabling of expenditure, the slowness of research, the fickleness of public opinion and even ministerial instability are by no means the least. This question leads in turn to another, that of the control actually exercised by the promoters of a reform over the system to which it is applied. Might it not be useful to analyse this control and the conditions under which it is exercised at the outset in order to avoid attributing to the implementing authority the supreme power of the authority responsible for promulgating a reform?

There has been some controversy recently as to whether society must be changed before education can be changed, or vice versa. Rather than trying to decide whether the chicken or the egg came first, it would perhaps be useful to analyse in some detail the external obstacles with which reforms may have to contend, going down to grassroots level. These obstacles are of at least two orders. Some arise from contradictions between the social and cultural environment — social customs, the organization of production, communication, social relations — and the models implicitly or explicitly proposed by the educational system. Whether it sees itself as conformist, traditional or militant, it is better that education should be aware of the ways in which the society to which it belongs hinders it or supports it. Other obstacles are the result of an often inevitable lack of synchronization in the development of different economic and social sectors, even when changes are operated under a highly integrated overall plan, for example between the construction industry and the school-building programme, between technological equipment and technical training, between fluctuations in employment and those in the number of diplomas awarded, and so on. These add to the cost of a reform, and the extent to which they can be tolerated should not be overestimated.

Cost-effectiveness studies are now an accepted part of educational reform and educational strategy. It is surprising that unforeseen events and undesirable external influences are not examined as carefully. Reform, like failure to reform, always involves risks on account of the large number of hypothetical factors which it brings into play, but any alteration made to a social institution involves a special kind of risk: until such time as the transformation is complete the system will be more vulnerable than usual to external hazards. Shortage of equipment, a sudden reduction in public funds, economic crises, all these things will be more keenly felt by an education system which is out of its routine, half-way through a reform. Rather than leaving the situation to be dealt with by the trouble-shooters, as some, all too easily, resign themselves to doing, it would perhaps be better to take measures whenever one is carrying out a reform which will, as far as possible, make it catastrophe-proof. Here again, one wonders if the answer lies not in rigid organization but in the support of individuals, the decentralization of responsibilities and greater self-reliance on the part of education, which would make it possible for the substance of education to be extracted at any time from a particular environment, a particular task or even a particular event.

The role of planning and administration in the implementation of educational reforms

School education, like agriculture and the State budget, has an annual rhythm, which is largely responsible for the repetitive administrative methods of the systems. On this level, the changes affecting education are not readily perceptible and are difficult to control. With the development of long-term economic and social activities, government departments—education departments later on than others—have gradually adopted the practice of planning for several years. In this new perspective, changes become visible and also interactions, and the idea of exerting an influence upon them by means of a global and integrated plan of action becomes attractive.

The twofold function, which has been more clearly marked in the recent past, of ensuring the coherency, in the medium and long term, of the different stages and sections of a complex action, and ensuring or restoring cohesion between sectoral actions that are subject to different factors and influences has induced government departments to employ new means, i.e. those that provide the data, plans and modifications needed for the execution of a large-scale project, from the preparation of decisions to their execution and measures to regulate their individual repercussions. It remains to be decided what part of this function should become an integral part of administrative practice and what part, in accordance with the principle of the division of labour, should be the responsibility of specialized units situated at different points in the administrative apparatus, which will vary from country to country. Nevertheless, experience — in educational matters and of reforms — seems to indicate that certain forms of organization neutralize the function of planning or reduce its effectiveness by limiting it to one or other of its tasks.

Because it facilitates perception of changes in educational systems and shows how sensitive education is to other social sectors, planning can appropriately be applied to reforms — non-repetitive actions covering long periods — and promises them, though not necessarily providing it, the means for their globalization and their integration into a projected type of society. Planning, it might be said, promotes reforms by offering them the tools for achieving their ambition.

Consequently, consideration of the problems discussed earlier may lead one to ask the following two questions:

Do difficulties which arise in the implementation of educational reforms result exclusively from the continued survival of outdated practices in government departments, or are they also due to faults in the planning methods now applied?

Would not the changes in education and the aim of reform have repercussions on our views as to whether other methods should be used or even radical changes be made in educational administration and planning?

The first question will probably lead us to examine a number of points where we can see that the methods being used are in many cases incapable of attaining the aims of a department that practises forward planning. The second will incite us to examine the obstacles and contradictions hindering the renewal of education that may be caused by certain planning practices.

In the first place, a political decision often catches planning services by surprise, before they have provided the data or the various alternatives, accompanied by timetables and costs, that would make it possible to weigh the pros and cons more carefully before taking a decision. Educational reform has inbuilt risks which must be taken; why add to this lack of foresight, which, even when the plans are properly made, may cause innovative effort to degenerate into a disorganized application of the method of trial and error?

The study of comparative education and consideration of the experience of others in educational matters will reduce the length of our journey considerably. In the same way, comparison, on the regional and international level, of the principal systems indicators (costs, yield, efficiency) makes it possible to judge of their relative importance and to detect anomalies that would not be visible on the national level. The International Bureau of Education (IBE-Unesco) has undertaken a programme of collection, preparation and dissemination of information on reforms and educational innovation. Such a programme will probably be considered worthy of the full support of the national institutions that are both the source and the beneficiaries of this information.

In some cases, educational planning may tend to preserve, as a consequence of its economic origins and its long application to the linear expansion of systems, habits of operation that reduce the value of its contribution to reform. For one thing, in planning reforms it considers only questions of investments, whereas in many cases investment is not enough to influence flows (of students) or create jobs (for teachers); sometimes, indeed, it constitutes only a secondary aspect of a reform, and increasing recurrent expenditure may have a greater effect upon success. For another thing, some educational planners may neglect to deal with specifically educational aspects and modalities of introducing a reform — the preparation of programmes and the quality of their content, the various forms of teaching situation, the cultural gap between education and the environment — all of which are factors that cannot be expressed in monetary terms but about which more extensive information is available from the social sciences and the educational sciences.

Finally, in the last twenty years attempts to adjust education to employment have led to considerable disappointment, especially in the developing countries. If we made a retrospective study covering a number of years, we should probably see that the adjustments we failed to make by trying to subordinate one system to the other should be made at the level of educational and employment policies and perhaps with the aid of different structures for terminal training and access to employment.

The direction in which certain reforms are aimed and the introduction of certain educational strategies surely call for further improvement in the management and planning methods of educational systems which have now become incapable of achieving their objectives.

It was perhaps inevitable that in the first stages planning should have helped to reinforce the technocratic and often centralizing aspects of government departments, since it applied methods that were not fully understood. There is no question that in order to restore responsibility to decentralized bodies, steps must quickly be taken to disseminate at all levels and to everyone the knowledge of methods of controlling, even at the level of resources, the operation of educational systems that have become more complex and are increasingly bound up with the social and economic situation of the regions of the country concerned. Probably, too, measures should be taken to restore the homogeneity of the vocabulary used by those who give and those who receive an education closely related to immediate experience, that used by experts more familiar with overall systems and that used by the originators of other actions — economic, social and cultural — that intersect and combine with educational actions. National aggregates should certainly be the result of a social, as much as an arithmetical, operation if the technocratic aspect is to be subordinated to democracy.

It has been argued that the progressive relinquishment to the State of the major responsibilities in education has entailed strengthening the bureaucratic machinery, whose function is to administer extensive systems and enormous budgets by applying a multitude of regulations. An encroaching bureaucracy is sure to be drawn towards a self-sufficient form of organization which makes it unaware of anything other than the personnel, buildings and material for the production, financing and supervision of which it is responsible. The effect of this double tendency is, on the one hand, to weaken educational creativity, which though often regarded as a deviant phenomenon yet makes a vital contribution to reform, and, on the other hand, to increase the burdens of systems which do not use the educational resources located outside the margins of their administration. It may also slow down the development of diffused, more flexible educational programmes such as the organization of rural educational activities, educational broadcasts, functional literacy teaching and certain vocational training courses which come under different management and in which the government department is called upon only to provide an educational stimulus for personnel not under its management, messages that circulate outside its networks and activities it does not finance.

An insidious temptation to revert to old habits and to reduce the scope of the proposed change is inherent in the very methods used in planning the most innovatory reforms. To a large extent, the changes introduced into a system by reform are, in the nature of things, without precedent, at least in any form already sanctioned by the administration. But, in order to make proper provision for the time required, the costs and the mobilization of personnel and means, the planner must draw up a new scheme of segments of action, each of which is seen to be identical with or analogous to a practice that is known. It is a different game, but the same cards are used. Let us suppose that our object is to train teachers of a new type, who are capable of playing a more active role in the life of a rural community. The first idea that comes to mind concerning their training is to build a new teacher-training school, modernized of course, but we may not realize that by assigning the candidates to long periods of residence in it we are really segregating them — and that is the opposite of what we are trying to do. Television is used, but it disseminates — only in a more attractive form — messages that reproduce the classroom situation and the distinction — often an artificial one — between subjects. It was a long time before cars were made that did not look like carriages. A sustained effort of imagination is needed if reform is not to follow the pattern of the old system. The same danger is found at the level of evaluation, where, because we have no measuring instruments suited to the new objectives, we continue to use the yardstick of previous achievements in assessing effects and results.

Because of all these questions, and perhaps others which have arisen in the participants' experience of reform, they will probably wish to recommend the study and testing of administrative practices and of planning procedures and methods that are more likely to attain the aim of many reforms which are based upon the belief that initiative, concerted effort and acceptance of responsibility are not only the end result but the very condition of a new kind of education.

Essentials for the coming decade

In inviting the participants in the meeting on educational reforms to discuss actively and independently some ideas regarding what must be done in the coming decade, the intention was to make it clear that the shape of the future depends on the sovereign decisions of States, particularly because of the national options which determine their desires for reform. It is nevertheless true that the future of nations, and the future shape of national education systems in particular, will largely depend on the success of efforts to eliminate, in relations between countries, the dependence that is part and parcel of the present forms of the division of labour, the unequal allocation of resources and techniques, and cultural domination. Educational progress and reform are seen to be an integral part of the new world order, in which new principles and forms of international co-operation will be established.

Three imperatives seem to emerge from the concern felt by many countries, and they are among the focal points in the most recent formulations of educational policies: the democratization of education; the modernization of education, with due regard to cultural identity; and the links between education and productive work. All three of these call for future-oriented studies, whose usefulness and purpose could be debated in the course of examining this item of the agenda.

At first glance there is nothing new in these problems, which bring to mind past debates. But we must not repeat old formulae, but rather try to see how our aim in these three vectors of reform should be profoundly changed because of the progress achieved by education. We must certainly raise our standards; in other words, we must accomplish more and find the means to do so, but perhaps we must also do something new in a different way, which might result in more profound changes in educational tools and systems.

Democratization of education

The Second Development Decade has been characterized, in particular, by a marked expansion of the base of the school pyramid, which is due to the increased access to education as well as to demographic growth. Even if one were to succeed in reducing the growth rate of the population slightly by around 1985–90, the demographic growth during the next decade would still lead to an increase in the numbers of school-age children, a parallel increase in the demand for non-formal education and a growing diversification of those making use of educational services (even if the concealed demand for professional retraining, cultural promotion and social mobilization is not taken into account).

The inevitable effect of this accelerated growth of the demand for education is that more educational goods and services are produced, chiefly owing to a rapid rise in the number of school places available, which often takes place prior to the training of skilled teaching personnel, the setting up of an adequate infrastructure of buildings and equipment, and the establishment of educational industries and facilities for producing educational materials. Consequently, despite the progressive movement towards mass education, a climate of *relative penury*, qualitative shortage and persistent inequality continues to exist alongside the increase in supply.

The fact that certain courses of instruction have become more generally accessible leads to the disappearance of the advantages but recently associated with the skills that this instruction confers, which is annoying to those who have just gained access to them. It is not that there are no more such skills, but they shift towards branches that are hard to get into and are constantly moving towards the top of the system.

Given that scarcity is, in part, the cause of the selectivity of the systems, the chances for promotion and democratization would probably be increased if it were possible to provide a genuinely 'affluent' education — large-scale, diversified and available on a lifelong basis — and to make education fully accessible to all those who want it. There are two ways of attaining this goal; they are not incompatible, and should perhaps be followed simultaneously.

First, a greater effort should be made to ensure that technical progress and the lessons of industrial organization are applied to education. Wherever the industrial organization of production and distribution has made it possible to produce certain goods at low cost and to make them readily accessible, it has, at the same time, established consumer equality in relation to these products. Education, or the 'industry of education' as it has been called, has for the most part maintained a small-scale mode of production and an organization of distribution linked to the physical presence and the spoken word of the teacher — of the skilled professional. Even when modern and refined instruments have, at great expense, been placed at their disposal, the 'craftsmen of education' have often reduced to nothing their multiplier effect and their potential productivity by using them in an amateurish way and treating them as mere accessories. Surely this persistent use of outdated forms of educational production is one of the reasons for its high cost and therefore for the penury of educational provision and the limited availability of broad and democratic educational opportunities.

In effect, conventional systems in themselves have no machinery capable of correcting the disparities bound up with the social cost of education, which is heavier for those who are most in need, and with the unequal allocation of educational resources between urban zones and rural zones and between countries and groups of countries. All sorts of additional fellowship systems, compensations and transfers, whose effect is slow and often unsatisfactory, have to be tacked on to them. The standardization and mass production of equipment and buildings, the adoption of advanced communication techniques which make it possible to reach the entire population, the instant transmission or the storage of information, which enables better quality information to be disseminated — all this has contributed towards the surprising increase in the availability of education in disciplines and at levels until now reserved for a minority, and will probably do so even more very shortly.

A second path has been opened up by the development of lifelong education structures which make it possible to offer a second or even a third chance to anyone who has been unsuccessful in the initial stage of education and to promote the diversity of the paths to culture, which now extend throughout life. But it must be recognized that a lifelong education system cannot properly be said to offer these opportunities unless the education available to adults is abundant and diversified, unless it is easily accessible and unless the rewards it offers in the form of diplomas and job opportunities are recognized as equivalent to those available in the initial education system.

There is, however, a third possibility, which is much more difficult and involves even more radical reforms. The persistent inequality in the chances of promotion reveals a contradiction: in many conventional systems, and in spite of reforms, promotion is governed by a system of classification and criteria which in the final analysis recognizes only academic qualifications that have not been tested against the cultural, social and economic objectives of a society which is struggling for its *own* progress. Such a system unconsciously produces the élites of another day or another society, while it leaves untapped vast resources of knowledge, culture and excellence which are allowed to filter through the examination screening process.

The result is a waste of human resources and an increase in the cost of education which is all the greater because education lives in its own world, indifferent to the resources of the human and physical environment, drawing from its own tradition or even importing from outside its language, tools, code, personnel and even the image it gives of the society which nourishes it. Besides this, an artificial collusion — by no means guileless — grows up between the academic criteria of excellence and the distribution of social power within rigid hierarchies. Thus the development of a type of schooling which was meant to be democratic may end up by reinforcing or even reproducing relations of dependency and domination within society, providing them in addition with the justification of diplomas and skills.

Consequently, the prerequisites of a truly democratic system of education are syllabuses that are judiciously planned and consistent with the needs of the environment and the aims of society, an internal organization from which hierarchies and unjustifiable powers are progressively eliminated, and also, outside the educational field itself, the redistribution of vocational, social, cultural or political functions, whose prestige and advantages are judged less by academic standards than by the usefulness of the services provided.

The modernization of education with due regard to cultural identity

Many educational reforms explicitly include the modernization of education systems among their objectives, and this is commonly taken to mean the extension and updating of scientific and technical programmes, the introduction of new teaching equipment and the adoption of computerized management techniques and of teaching methods based on the latest information provided by the human sciences. More education — in a modern form — is seen as the indispensable basis for the rapid modernization of production techniques and a means of expediting and controlling the transfer of advanced technologies, engaging, on equal terms, in international competition and, lastly — a most important goal — taking an active part in scientific research and, before long, influencing the development of a humanism which claims to speak for all mankind.

In other cases, reforms — indeed, they may be the same ones — inspired by the belief that education should faithfully reflect the cultural identity of each country, are directed towards the content of education, a body of knowledge built up in the context of other environments and other cultures, whose linguistic medium, principles and memories annihilate the riches and the creativity of vigorous cultures all too long regarded as unimportant and archaic. The resurgence of national languages, traditional modes of aesthetic expression and even 'appropriate' technologies, while expressing a desire to attach the tree to its own roots, at the same time constitute an assertion of the endogenous character of social change, a realization of the need for self-reliance, and a desire to curb interference and pressure from without, the effect of which is to eliminate all differences between one way of life and another.

It can scarcely be denied that these two trends actually run counter to each other in several ways, and it is true that, in some cases, they have given rise to extremist and conflicting strategies. Those who advocate the first strategy insist that ushering in modernism is to take the most direct way towards eliminating penury, and that modern methods will enable the personnel required for accelerated development to be trained and productivity to be improved so that natural resources can be turned to account at the national level. Those who advocate the second strategy take the view that it is only by standing on his own feet that man can progress, that it is better to teach everyone to read in their own language than to teach a few to read in a foreign one, that it is better to be poorly paid for one's own work than well paid for working for someone else and, finally, that the concert of nations, even if all discords were removed, would still be polyphonic.

It is not, of course, intended either to exacerbate or to settle out of hand an argument in which the final word rests with history, but merely to note that it is a central issue in the processes leading to the establishment of a new international order and that this twofold trend reflects what are perhaps the greatest challenges of the contemporary era. It consequently concerns every country, and education in every country.

For while science purports to have universal designs, it is also willing at present to be confined within centres of excellence hedged about with secrecy; it leads man not only to contemplate the infinite spaces, but also to place satellites in them, not all of which are there for the purposes of telecommunications, and the technologies to which it gives rise are seldom without commercial trimmings which are, in various ways, sources of pollution. Nor should modernity be confused with its setting, its accessories or the fripperies that may accompany it. The distinctive mark of the modern peasant is perhaps not that he sits perched up on a tractor, but that he possesses the tools to do his own work, organize his community and communicate with the society to which he belongs; and science, as much as will, is needed if he is to be able to use those tools.

Of course, most reforms are compromises between extreme positions, and it is probably worth examining them so as to see in what way they lead to progress and where the pitfalls lie. So far as the language of instruction is concerned, some reforms set a boundary between target-groups, e.g. the mother tongue for adults in rural areas, and the administrative language for school pupils — or between one level of education and another — a widely spoken language being gradually substituted for national languages when science and technology begin to be systematically taught. Other reforms maintain, at least for a while, a bilingualism which gradually establishes a language barrier between disciplines: science education on the one hand, and, on the other, the teaching of literature, the arts, civics and religion. These are of course stages, sometimes short stages, but when they are prolonged they may create new inequalities in the first case, and in the second, as has happened elsewhere, they may lead to 'disenchantment' with technology and work coupled with a folklorish attitude to leisure and art.

Many countries are therefore engaged in an in-depth review of the programmes and methods of scientific and technological training, covering all the stages in the education system from elementary education onwards and including the modification of scientific research policies. The development of a scientific outlook is something far removed from the rapid assimilation of a hastily formulated body of knowledge. Technological training is not merely the rapid acquisition of manipulative skills. A scientific outlook and skill are required even in the use of familiar techniques and languages and in the immediate environment. They develop through confrontation, which is not artificial but real, with more accurate instruments, more diversified tools and more complex machines, under the very conditions in which they are integrated into the work of society.

Viewed in this way, education leads to the reinstatement of entire areas of traditional experience as subjects of scientific investigation and as fields for the application of science; it is intended to re-establish, at grass-roots level, a cultural continuity between the 'empiricism' of tradition as it is experienced and the mastery of scientific method. It also leads to the re-establishment of the ever precarious harmony between a policy of investment in technology and an education policy, thereby ensuring that the hand is not like a serf wielding tools without knowing how they are operated, and that the mind does not dip into various sections of the sciences without knowing what tools have been used in them or which ones they have produced.

At the same time, there certainly is a need—though not in the way in which the school usually sets about it—not so much to develop art education as to set aside time for the development of the artistic faculties, to encourage familiarity with the instruments used in art, its heights of achievement and its representatives, to arrange encounters which stimulate creativity, to avoid arresting its progress by a misplaced respect or removing all vigour from it by allowing it to be used for commercial purposes, and, lastly, to encourage it not merely to contribute occasionally to the modernized setting of urban life, but to invade it, to confront it, to let people hear and see that tension, that teeming welter of memories, moods, hopes and determination which is expressed by a national, popular, living culture.

Education and productive work—education in relation to a comprehensive employment policy

School-attendance figures have mounted and still continue to mount, while at the same time, and often as a result of official action, young people are not able to find employment for some time. In cases where the demand for adult education is encouraged by legislative provisions which reduce the number of working hours and enable workers to alternate periods of paid leave for the purposes of training with periods of training or further training, more wage-earners are taking adult-education courses. There is a sort of *de facto* mutual exclusion between educational activity and productive activity: when one is being pursued, the other is suspended.

This also affects content: general education is still marked by traditions that die hard, according to which, in the past, the specific object of academic knowledge was the 'clerical' or liberal professions; it developed outside the pale of the 'menial' occupations. In the practice of an occupation, even one of those formerly known as 'the liberal professions', there tends to be less and less opportunity for self-teaching, owing to the demand for productivity and specialization.

Vocational training, whether at school or on the job, lies at the crossroads between general education and occupational activity; it is designed to help pupils move from one status to another which is entirely different. Torn between two often conflicting variables — that of the flow of pupils and expectations and that of the kind and number of posts offered — vocational training courses become longer or more diversified, heavier or more flexible.

For twenty years now the trend has been more and more in the opposite direction towards re-establishing meeting-points or even a tacit agreement between education and working life. There is more in this than the tradition of do-it-yourself or of the school garden, which is still vigorous in certain places, or of putting a classroom in industrial space-time. The object is, by means of co-operation between professionals and educators, on the one hand to integrate into the general education experience that everyone receives of productive activities as they really are carried on and, on the other, to modify the definition of tasks and the hierarchical specialization of decision-making and organizational functions involved in day-to-day working life so that the practice of an occupation regains its power to stimulate workers to reach a higher standard of education. The success or failure of this undertaking is certainly bound up with its twofold dimension, and education and employment must be reformed in conjunction.

This trend can be illustrated by a number of recent reforms. They are not unprecedented, for they may be seen as the product — sometimes remote and highly diversified — of large-scale innovations introduced in the last two decades. The first of these was polytechnical education, which incorporated into the initial education provided for everyone the technology and practice of renewal types of productive work as practised in industry and agriculture. The second was functional literacy, which has shown that, in a community concerned with controlling its progress in respect of technology and organization, it is possible to devise a programme for learning the basic techniques of reading, writing and arithmetic which are directly integrated into the fabric of social life and productive work. Lastly, various attempts to 'ruralize' primary education have helped to bring back the idea that pupils may learn from the work that adults do in the neighbourhood of the school. The most recent reforms comprise many variants which cannot be listed here. Some relate to elementary education, others to the period of secondary education and others again to the education of the different age groups in one community. However, we may recall some of the goals of these reforms, the relative importance of which varies from one country to another.

One goal is to bring back the practice by everyone of manual work which is indispensable to the country's development, so as to ensure that an education centred on books does not encourage the notion that such work is reserved for those with scant knowledge. Another is to make educational institutions create resources and not merely be objects of expenditure, by organizing them as part-time production units. Yet another is to link education and community village development closely together by means of a training centre, open to all age groups, which, while providing an elementary education, at the same time will give technical instruction which will be immediately applied in productive work. Many reforms allow for the coexistence of general education of the conventional type and the practice of productive work for educational ends. Others go further, being designed with a view to eliciting from production and the tools of production, from the organization and episodes of social life and from the links with the physical environment which are forged by both productive work and social life, the elements of a new type of general education programme. This last goal itself, perhaps, represents the cultural essence of these reforms.

The widespread implementation of these reforms presents tremendous problems of financing, equipment, organization and human resources: the priorities are not the same as in the past — tools may be more important than buildings; the custodians of knowledge are not necessarily teachers — they may be craftsmen, workers and farmers; training programmes are drawn up in the field, instead of in commissions; school timetables and training schedules are governed by the rhythms of production.

Most of these reforms are too recent for them to have given rise to the desired changes. As we have seen, they cannot of themselves bring about more than a partial change. But at least they are an attempt to provide an instrument which lends itself more readily to the objectives of an integrated policy of social change and development. Their effect is that education is no longer planned on the assumption that there will be a certain employment structure, an irresistible urge towards gainful employment and subsidies to the tertiary sector which, in many countries, correspond neither to the constraints nor to the demands of economic development.

However, it must be acknowledged that none of these reforms by itself can be expected to settle effectively the problem of the adaptation of education to employment. Moreover, it is true that the assumption underlying these reforms is that one of the difficulties encountered by any employment policy is the unsuitability of the content of the methods and structures of educational systems.

Unfortunately, however, policies designed to ensure full employment come up against other obstacles and other difficulties. First, the unemployment and underemployment from which so many countries suffer can no longer be regarded as a residual phenomenon which, inadmissible though it may be, is due to the imbalance between the overall supply and demand for labour and between the specific supply and demand for workers with different levels of qualifications. The phenomenon perhaps derives also from the socio-economic system within which it appears.

It is no doubt a direct consequence of dependence and of the economic strategies adopted by countries, with their underlying social options. After all, do not some States assert that all categories have the right to work, and do they not take the necessary steps for that right to be exercised? Is not continuing to speak of unemployment as a structural problem tantamount to resigning oneself to treating it as such? Despite unemployment assistance policies, is it not tantamount to regarding underemployment as the price to be paid in order to limit an inflationary spiral which governments cannot control? To admit that the unemployed are a constituent part of the labour structure is to believe that the role they perform is perfectly consistent with that structure.

Prospective study and research for educational reform

Discussion of earlier agenda items and consideration of the changes which have taken place over the last twenty years and of the fate and the fruits of the major reforms will have paved the way for the following questions: With a view to future reforms, what benefit could be derived from large-scale prospective research covering vast areas, a variety of educational situations and all the educational structures — or at least the main ones — operating concurrently in societies in our time?

If such an undertaking is thought worth attempting, what assistance could be provided by previous studies, already numerous although of recent date, such as those devoted to the future of education in a limited geographical area or to world economic development over the next few decades? What horizons should be set for such a study? Should research be organized according to geographical areas or groups of countries, and if so, what criteria should be used in establishing these? Should education as a whole and its organization be studied from the beginning, or should one concentrate on certain areas defined according to type of education (for example, technical education), its recipients (for example, adults) or even particular components of the system, such as buildings, teachers or techniques for the production and distribution of educational material? When the various plans are being drawn up, how should one identify the structural or *ad hoc* connections between educational subsystems and the great parameters of social, economic and cultural change and the roles which these connections will play? Finally, how should such research be organized, and what contribution could Unesco and its various institutions make towards it?

The aim should hardly be a prediction, or even a large-scale, long-term plan, but rather a sketch, with several variations, of areas of probability and of the domain of the unlikely. It would necessarily be based on retrospective studies, as described above, and would call for considerable improvement of the conceptual framework by means of which we today identify the structure and mode of operation of educational systems and of learning processes, especially by referring to a number of enlightening analogies. Prospective studies conducted in such a way and on such a basis would provide the reformers of the future with a better knowledge of the way in which deliberate action affects educational institutions, and those responsible for policy and planning with a frame of reference less influenced by passing enthusiasms and fashions.

When setting the horizon for such forecasts, several different time-scales will probably have to be considered simultaneously: the time-scale of the process of education itself, which varies, within limits, according to the organization of the system, its scope and its various extensions; the time-scale for the planning and full implementation of important changes; and, finally, the period during which the social and physical environments register the repercussions of the reform, which will in turn create boomerang effects calling for further adjustment of the system.

While it may be considered useful for the purpose of this investigation to draw a distinction between areas or groups of countries, the criterion of geographical proximity may not be thought decisive in all cases, and other forms of categorization may perhaps emerge, depending on the consideration given to the level of development of the systems, demographic factors, the environment, resources, and historical, cultural or political affinities. Perhaps different methods of categorization will have to be used, depending on the aspect under examination, always allowing for major innovations which sweep through all national systems in a very short time, and of which the recent reform of mathematics teaching is a good example.

Some types of education, such as vocational training or medical training, seem to enjoy sufficient autonomy within the system to deserve a separate prospective study. Some components of the system, for example the architecture of educational premises, evolve under the pressure of trends which are not all connected with teaching, but in which demographic factors, the nature of the materials, the evolution of urban life, of transport facilities and of the building industry play a dominant role. Here again, however, the interactions between the parts of which the educational systems themselves are made up must be taken into account, even if each part develops under the influence of different factors. In this way it may be possible to shed light on some of the many links, once these have been defined on a more empirical basis, that connect the educational system to society which, in a variety of ways, produces the system, while at the same time the system itself reproduces the habits, aims and divisions of society.

New dimensions of international co-operation for the support of educational renovation

Discussion of previous items will in many cases have led to a definition of machinery for co-operation with a view to conducting the research required for the implementation of reforms. This section has a different purpose: first, to find new forms of international concertation and co-operation which are entailed by the movement to reform and renovate education, within the historical framework of efforts to establish a new international order, and, second, to find ways of making progress towards this end.

THE EMERGENCE OF THE NOTION OF SOLIDARITY AND MUTUAL AID

International co-operation for the renewal of education has for a long time been linked with the very existence of Unesco; in fact it has come to be one of its *raisons d'être*. For a long time it was dominated by the idea of the 'transfer' of resources, techniques and knowledge, and this idea of transfer is still a useful and fruitful one, albeit in a new context. During the second decade, however, things gradually began to be seen in a new light, with the emergence of the idea of collective self-reliance, to which the non-aligned countries attributed crucial importance as early as 1974, at their fourth summit conference in Algiers, and in the Lima Programme on solidarity and mutual assistance. 'The Heads of State or Government of non-aligned countries reaffirm their belief in the concept of collective self-reliance.' This solemn declaration, which opens the Action Programme for Economic Co-operation adopted at Colombo in 1976, at the fifth summit conference of non-aligned countries, is also a feature of the Economic Declaration in which the Heads of State or Government state their 'firm belief that only a confident spirit of collective self-reliance on the part of the developing countries can guarantee the emergence of a New International Economic Order'.

The Heads of State and Government themselves make it quite clear in their declarations that this concept is closely linked with both structural reforms and international co-operation:

Collective self-reliance implies . . . preparedness on the part of developing nations to follow internally the discipline required of them by . . . the process of growth with social justice, at the focal point of which will be eradication of unemployment and poverty . . . for in order to satisfy the basic needs of the population . . . *structural changes* will be required.

The Heads of State follow this statement up with

. . . most importantly, self-reliance means willingness to explore and pursue the immense possibilities of *co-operation among the developing countries them-selves*. . . . The need of the hour is to develop a common will and evolve suitable mechanisms to fully utilize complementarities, resources and capabilities.

This is why there are sections of the Colombo Programme devoted ex-plicitly to co-operation between developing countries in respect of employment and human resources and of education and training, as well as sections on scientific and technological development and on technical co-operation and consultancy services. The conception of international co-operation for the support of educational reforms revealed in these pages is a very exacting one. Mention is made of the organization of special programmes of co-operation for the training of technical per-sonnel at all levels in plants, technical colleges and universities; ex-pansion of the system of fellowships and of exchanges of teachers, researchers and other specialists; the exchanging of expertise relating to the development of national education policies to serve basic needs, including joint education strategies relevant to the objectives of developing societies; the establishment of joint projects in education, the training of personnel and the production of teaching materials; provision for the periodic exchange of information between the countries con-cerned on subjects of common interest, etc.

Such statements deserve to be borne in mind, for there should be awareness here from the beginning that the consideration of new dimensions for co-operation is being undertaken primarily in response to the clearly expressed wishes of the countries themselves. Unesco, for its part, has reached an identical conclusion in respect of education. In its resolution 9.21, the General Conference at its nineteenth session declared itself

convinced that the progress still to be made [by the developing countries] will depend at one and the same time on the mobilization of their own capability and potentiality devoted to development, on the transfer of resources, in terms of quality and quantity, that the international community will supply to the developing countries, and on the will of Member States to increase co-operation among themselves, particularly at the regional level and between developing countries.

SOME PRIORITY AREAS IN WHICH NEW FORMS OF INTERNATIONAL CO-OPERATION SHOULD BE INTRODUCED

Industries supplying the needs of education

Reliance on foreign countries for various teaching aids essential to the educational process is indeed a major problem. Their production in the developing countries themselves would enhance their collective self-reliance in respect of manufacturing industries, replacing the present world distribution of labour by arrangements more favourable to the developing countries. The new production capacities should be divided among the developing countries, thus providing each with a market covering several States. What is needed, therefore, is a tightly controlled industrial policy designed to organize and direct the market without going so far as to abolish it. There will be above all a need for concerted action to encourage the *rapprochement* and regrouping of the countries concerned, which alone can counterbalance the power of transnational undertakings.

School buildings

Here, too, a major problem arises, which is connected with the durability of school buildings constructed of long-lasting materials: in the wake of the rapid expansion of the conventional educational system, more schools were built in two decades than in the previous two centuries. Thus, at a time when teaching practices are undergoing radical change, when educational policies are in the process of rapid evolution and when the idea of lifelong education is calling the traditional view of educational premises into question, these new buildings may, on account of their lack of adaptability and flexibility, block future development over a long period and seriously compromise the possibility of the renewal of education.

It is, therefore, understandable that architects should have sought radically different solutions: in the first place, the use of local building materials and techniques makes for much lighter buildings, which could easily be pulled down and replaced by others. In the second place, progress in the prefabrication of 'compatible components' and 'construction systems' (whereby a variety of modules can be assembled) has recently led to a system of generalized compatibility known as 'open industrialization', which considerably increases flexibility in the use of the premises and freedom of design. This is why Unesco can now allocate its resources, modest though they are, for the adaptation of educational premises to the needs of modern teaching methods, of educational technology and of different cultures, and, above all, for consultation on the standards to be observed, so as to ensure that industrially produced components can be adapted to the diversity of educational systems and national legislation.

Innovation networks

Innovation networks are the most important of the new arrangements which Unesco promotes and which facilitate co-operation at regional and subregional level. The innovation networks system is very flexible, and lends itself to change. The networks consist of a number of national institutions from different countries, the idea being to increase exchanges of experience between them. Such networks can readily be established in a wide variety of geographical and political contexts. The Asian prototype, the Asian Programme of Educational Innovation for Development (APEID), is unquestionably a success; Africa has also established a network which reflects the African situation; Latin America in its turn is about to set up a network in the Caribbean, while a number of European States have expressed the wish to establish a similar structure.

Standards

It should be noted that mutual consultation on standard-setting involves relatively few restrictions. It does, of course, represent one step further towards solidarity than the network system, because it implies from the beginning that the governments accept an initial constraint, that of engaging in mutual consultation leading up to a consensus, and also because the rules worked out by common consent eventually impose a further series of constraints. However, it does not in any way imply the adoption of common policies, the use of the same materials or a communal system: its structure is similar to that of a club which makes no demands on its members other than the acceptance of certain rules.

Mutual consultation between a limited number of countries which have agreed to adopt the same rules involves in the first place some standardization of sizes and measurements in order to ensure that the material produced complies with the requirements and specifications laid down by each of the club members. Such standardization does, however, allow for some differences in the specifications laid down by the different countries which, far from having to renounce their sovereignty for the sake of solidarity, find in fact that standardization of measurements increases their independence and their freedom of choice in respect of equipment and teaching methods.

Mutual consultation on standards is, moreover, the first step towards organizing a common market. Even more than the free movement of goods within a customs union or their protection by a common external tariff, the elimination of non-tariff barriers resulting from divergent practices in the different countries and from the use of different technical standards within the same economic area would be an important step towards the gradual reorganization of markets and of orders, which is the only way to increase production of a series and to share detailed studies. Mutual consultation on standards leads naturally to consultation on products with a view to channelling the requirements of these countries towards a limited range of materials which are compatible with the various groups of innovatory models chosen in each country.

Programmes of concerted action

To move another step in the direction of solidarity, programmes of concerted action are the third type of arrangement which should be drawn to the attention of Member States. They form the basis for all the systems of regional co-operation which involve a diversification of roles in accordance with a division of labour agreed upon in advance by the firms concerned. These include:

Concerted action in research and development. A network structure may thus be transformed into a chain of national projects, each covering the whole region.

Agreements between industries (or governments) with a view to encouraging the manufacturing industries of the various countries to specialize in complementary lines, in a voluntary reorganization of industrial structures within that group of countries (like the Andean Pact of Cartegena).

The formation of consortia bringing complementary firms in different countries of the same region into a federative type of organization in order to carry out a large multinational project (in the building and public-works sector, for example).

Concerted action in the field of training which combines training abroad with training in the national educational system in various ways: it may, for example, be advisable to take advantage of facilities for specialized higher training which exist within the region or of opportunities for vocational training which migrant workers may be offered in the host countries.

Community structures

When regional co-operation reaches a high degree of solidarity and interdependence, the system of community structures and joint organizations is to be preferred; it calls for complex consultation machinery leading to the joint management and use of these systems of resources. The following examples of this formula can be given, which are all based on the same principle:

Data banks. These involve the pooling of information and of facilities for its automatic processing.

Audio-visual programme banks. The pooling of this educational 'software' can enable all the parties concerned to increase their educational potential, sometimes to a considerable extent.

Co-operatives for the production of teaching materials. The pooling of production capacities can result in the formation of one or more large community production centres, thus making a definite break with craft methods of production. A co-operative structure could be the beginning of an industrial type of organization of educational activity.

But it is obviously not enough to enumerate possible fields of application or machinery which could be used to organize mutual assistance through mutual consultation and interdependence. We must also discuss the fundamental question of how to initiate a process which leads far beyond mutual information and the polite comparison of theories to the establishment of machinery for co-operation which can then be converted into effective institutions. The similarities which arise from the educational situation and from the operation of convergent strategies or even of very similar practices must first be recognized — probably in a more limited area than the region — then tested — on the territory on which new guidelines and practices are worked out — and then strengthened — by forging the tool of co-operation in specific areas. It is true that teachers have frequent meetings, but often not to improve their familiarity with the profession and not at the time when the agreements which are a feature of other sectors — of industry, for example — could easily be formed. Other kinds of meetings are needed — meetings of some of those responsible for reforms in the various countries, for example — and also far more working visits to the field and exchanges of staff down to the lowest practical levels. Unesco can allow its information to be used to further attempts to establish similarities, it can find new ways of encouraging the holding of meetings and the organization of visits whose programme and follow-up would be decided upon by their promoters, and it can seek support for the establishment of institutions which would have no official connection with it. Its programme invites it to do these things, provided the countries concerned manifest the desire for them to be done.

NOTES

1. These reflections of the Secretariat do not presume to give an accurate account of the rich and diversified educational reforms throughout the world; nor do they

provide a systematic analysis. They were merely intended, as part of the annotated agenda, to stimulate creative discussion at the meeting.

2. See *Unesco Statistical Yearbook 1975*. These figures do not include China, the Democratic People's Republic of Korea or the then Democratic Republic of Viet Nam.

3. E. Faure *et al.*, *Learning to Be. The World of Education Today and Tomorrow*, Paris/London, Unesco/Harrap, 1972.

Final Report, adopted at the Expert Meeting

1. Introduction

The meeting of experts on Major Problem Areas of Educational Reforms in the 1970s and 1980s (Experiences and Prospects) was held at Unesco Headquarters, Paris, from 24 to 28 October 1977. This meeting (Category VI) was organized in accordance with the Programme and Budget of Unesco for 1977–78 approved by the General Conference at its nineteenth session (para. 1016).

The purpose of the meeting was to provide the Director-General with suggestions and advice concerning the orientation of Unesco's future programme as regards the implementation of educational reforms. The participants reviewed the various aspects of educational reforms, particularly the problems involved in translating policy options into concrete action. The participants made recommendations to the Director-General of Unesco regarding the content of future research and study programmes, bearing in mind the new approach towards problems that emerged from consideration of the implementation of reforms. The agenda of the meeting is printed above (see 'Background').

The participants serving in a personal capacity came from sixteen countries. Seven representatives came from Unesco established offices away from Headquarters (five), the International Institute for Educational Planning (IIEP) (one) and organizations of the United Nations system (one representative). In addition, ten observers designated by Unesco Member States (six), Regional Development Banks and Funds (two), international non-governmental organizations (one) and research institutes (one) followed the proceedings of the meeting.

At the opening of the meeting, Mr Harold Foecke, Deputy Assistant Director-General for Regular Programme Activities, welcomed the participants on behalf of the Director-General and outlined the background and the terms of reference of the meeting.

Mr Boris Kluchnikov, Director of the Division of Educational Policy and Planning, introduced the working document prepared by the Secretariat and presented a synthesis of major findings and recommendations of the papers prepared by the participants. He drew the attention of the participants to the differences in understanding of what is an educational reform and invited the participants to focus their attention on major long-range and comprehensive changes in educational ideologies, objectives, policies, structures and priorities.

The participants, who met in plenary sessions and in four working groups, elected the following officers:

Plenary: Chairman: Mr S. Moberg (Sweden). Vice-Chairmen: Mr A. Razafindrakoto (Madagascar), Mr Mandour Al Mahdi (Sudan). Rapporteur: Mr W. Platt (United States of America).

Working Group I: Chairman: Mr J. Pliya (People's Republic of Benin). Rapporteur: Mr C. Fitouri (International Bureau of Education — IBE).

Working Group II: Chairman: Mr P. J. Mhaiki (United Republic of Tanzania). Rapporteur: Mr C. Picon (Peru).

Working Group III: Chairman: Mr M. Haak (German Democratic Republic). Rapporteur: Mr A. Remili (Democratic and Popular Republic of Algeria).

Working Group IV: Chairman: Mr J. Fiser (Czechoslovakia). Rapporteur: Mr R. Carneiro (Portugal).

The plenary sessions and the working groups examined the main working document of the meeting prepared by the Secretariat. In addition, general and case studies prepared by participants and which served as background documents were made available to the participants of the meeting.

2. *Conclusions*

Overall objectives of reform in education should include measures to guarantee education for all as a basic human right and the alignment of social and educational reforms to guarantee meaningful employment.

The meeting noted the projected increase in the number of school-age children during the next decade and also an important increase of adults in need of more and better general and specific knowledge. This must inevitably lead to an accelerated growth of the demand for formal and non-formal education during the 1980s. Towards this background education was considered as one of the basic problems of mankind.

THE MAIN CHARACTERISTICS OF EDUCATIONAL REFORMS DURING THE 1970s: NATIONAL EXPERIENCES AND GENERAL TENDENCIES

Even within the meeting's 'profound and comprehensive reforms' it is useful to distinguish between (1) educational reforms, which are major improvements within existing systems, and (2) reforms of education, which are transformations in goals and objectives generally linked to social or political changes outside the education system. Both types of reform need attention in the 1970s and 1980s: it can be argued that while the 1960s and early 1970s saw considerable progress in the first type of reform, with only a few but notable exceptions was there actual implementation of the second type. None the less it would appear that consciousness of the imperative for education to make its full contribution to societal development and to a new world order is rising among educational and political leaders, as well as among different parts of society, suggesting that educational reforms can and must move more rapidly in the 1980s.

The meeting noted that social and economic changes are an essential condition for the success of reforms in education but also that there are no simple automatic connections between social and educational change nor between availability of resources and effective reform. Favourable preconditions for reforms in education include political commitment supported by broad public participation and resources—human as well as financial and material commitment, and will can sometimes surmount part of the shortages of resources. The absence of revolutionary social or political orientation need not inhibit profound and important reforms in education, including those inspired by international undertakings such as Unesco's 1974 Recommendations concerning 'Education for international understanding, co-operation and peace and education relating to human rights and fundamental freedom' and the 1976 Recommendations adopted at the General Conference concerning 'Unesco's contribution to the establishment of a new international economic order'.

While objectives and obstacles to reform of education often differ between developing and industrialized countries, there is value in international co-operation in this field. In part this value derives from lessons which can be learned from comparative experience, and in part from the urgency of an evolution towards a more equitable world order in which learners everywhere have a stake.

It was concluded from the discussions of the main characteristics of educational reforms in the 1970s that major reforms in the 1980s should give attention to further means of integrating in- and out-of-school education and to the creation of environments which facilitate learning as distinguished from the more conventional autocratic teaching systems. Further efforts at democratization will need to lessen education's preoccupation with sorting out a few winners and many losers; instead learning should be designed for maximizing the realization of all human potential.

In spite of difficulties or sometimes failures in reform efforts, the meeting was aware of the significant contribution many successful reforms made to the progress and development of education during the 1960s and 1970s.

THE MAIN PROBLEMS FACING THE TRANSLATION OF POLICY OPTIONS IN EDUCATION INTO PRACTICAL ACTION

The meeting agreed that the Secretariat working paper and the country case studies prepared by several of the meeting's participants provide rich analyses of problems and obstacles encountered in translating planned reforms into practice. The discussion gave particular attention to the following, not all of which affect every country: the failure to design an operational strategy for introducing, implementing and correcting the reform; the danger of conflict between democratization and the maintenance of conventional standards; inadequate financial and material resources; the lack of clarity in objectives for reform; the stranglehold on reform exercised by the examination system; the possible alienation of children and parents when reforms are too ambitious or not adapted to local conditions and when children are educated while educational opportunities are not available for the illiterate parents; the neglect of, or inadequate training for, the whole range of personnel responsible for aspects of implementation, such as teachers, administrators, evaluators, etc.; the neglect of components such as educational technology and changes in organization; imbalances between political will for reform and professional competence to effect changes; inappropriate institutional framework; the lack of linkage between education and work.

It was noted that embarking on reform in education brings with it uncertainties, side-effects, and paradoxes which require flexible and pragmatic management and continuing evaluation and correction. For example, the very success of a reform in primary education creates new problems in secondary education; quantitative change at certain scales becomes qualitative change; personnel at operational levels and the population directly concerned are often in an as good or even better position to be aware of and adapt to difficulties than are planners and policy-makers—their views and participation must be provided for flexibility.

THE ROLE OF PLANNING
AND ADMINISTRATION IN THE IMPLEMENTATION
OF EDUCATIONAL REFORMS

The meeting discussed at some length the manifold changes in occupational requirements for planners and administrators deriving from
the emphasis on reforms in education likely to occur in the 1980s. Not
only will their professional competencies have to improve in appropriate
ways, their earlier neutrality will probably have to give way to participation in and commitment to the values and motivations inherent in
the reform being planned and managed. A practical consequence of this
is that at initial stages of reform planners must discuss with political
leadership the ideology and aims of the transformations being undertaken outside and within education. Such an approach will require
new working relationships with policy-makers and political leaders,
teachers and all the educational personnel without whom reforms cannot
become practice.

The reforming and planning of education will need to interact and
collaborate with research in and out of education and planning for social
and economic transformations in all sectors. Accordingly, educational
planning must be closely integrated with economic and social planning.

The planner helps invent the future by expressing aims, objectives
and strategies in potentially operational terms. None the less, modesty
and pragmatism must guide the planner in carrying out these responsibilities. Maximum effort should be made to render planning processes
as democratic as possible. Still, it must be realized that the responsible
leadership must take decisions regarding reform. Over-insistence on
total consensus is likely to yield only stagnation rather than the
achievement of reform.

ESSENTIALS FOR THE COMING DECADE

The meeting noted that three problem areas were of capital importance
for most Member States: the democratization of education; the
modernization of education with due regard to cultural identity; and the
reinforcement of linkages between education and productive work. In
each of these main problem areas, it was emphasized that two issues
deserve particular attention: the bridging between formal and non-
formal education on the one hand, and the transition from teaching-
based to learning-based educational processes. A fourth problem area,
namely the promotion of prospective study and research for educational
reform, was also dealt with. The four problem areas were considered in
separate working groups and the conclusions which follow are those of
the groups.

A. The democratization
of education

For most countries, the democratization of education remains a basic objective for the 1980s with regard to both the universal provision of education and the effective reduction of existing disparities between regions and countries as well as between the sexes, ages and social categories and groups. Democratization implies that equal opportunities for all are actually provided, as regards access to and success in education, any kind of elitism being banned.

The structural reform of educational systems can alone facilitate the achievement of these objectives. This reform is itself contingent upon the structural reform of society, the radical transformation of the teacher's role and the complete overhauling of the structures, methods and content of education. The integration of the social and educational policies of formal and non-formal education, the use of all available educational resources and the participation of various social categories in the process of educational planning and administration can all help to bring about the democratization of education.

Cultural identity should be defined and promoted as a precondition of efforts to democratize education. Special attention should therefore be paid to the institutions of higher education as the main 'productive factor' of knowledge and thereby a most significant authority in supporting cultural identity.

B. The modernization of education with due regard
to cultural identity

One of the major problems which newly independent national States are facing is how to protect the endogenous character of educational development simultaneously with its modernization — how to establish a unified educational system relevant to all strata of society, national in character but free of xenophobia and promoting international understanding and co-operation in our interdependent world.

Modernization of education is directed towards a global and coherent effort to achieve the realization and updating of social dynamic change in a given society. This modernization of education implies therefore a permanent and dynamic flux of creativity leading to innovations and reform and it does not necessarily mean the adoption of concepts and technology which are foreign to endogenous environment. Modernization of education in this sense is a form of reinforcement of the cultural personality.

It was underlined that education is a part of culture and is consubstantial to it, and that education exists because culture exists. In fact, it is through education that transmission, re-creation and generation of new cultural values are possible. In the light of this, the concept of integral education has a profound meaning.

It was considered that the key problem was the enhancement of culture, and in this context the importance of the use of the mother tongue as a medium of instruction and education has been stressed. The importance of national languages for reasons of nation building was also recognized.

C. Education and productive work—education in relation to a comprehensive employment policy

Efforts to democratize education should not be confined to democratizing knowledge, but should also and more particularly concentrate on the know-how without which the recipient is unable to take his or her place in the production system.

It was considered that training and vocational and technical education as now organized do not always meet the needs of the economy nor provide for workers' advancement. Attention was drawn to the following shortcomings: there is no co-ordination between the various parts of the training system; training is not linked closely enough either with the rest of the education system or with the working world; there are too few teachers with experience of production; there are restrictions due to the economic and social context (economic or technological options, control of means of production), lack of sufficient information to meet the economic and social requirements.

As a result, there are considerable uncertainties about the policy to be adopted as to the organization, content, methods of training and means to be used in vocational education. The international community should, in the next ten years, pay increasing attention to the reforms to be introduced into this subsystem, especially as regards production and research, in view of the strategic contribution of know-how to the establishment of a new international division of labour and the finding of a response to the essential needs of the peoples of the world.

D. Prospective study and research for educational reform

The importance of the role Unesco should play in supporting and undertaking prospective studies as a major asset in providing frames of reference for future educational reform and planning was strongly underlined. Adequate resources must be made immediately available to foster co-operative research work at various levels—international, regional, subregional, national—ensuring an effective participation both of the developing world and of the major stake-holders in the educational process.

Substantive issues related to the main purposes and consequent selection of key areas for prospective analysis should follow the criterion of overall relevancy to the different clusters of member countries in their growing concerns on the future of educational renewal and improvement.

The meeting endorsed the above-mentioned conclusions presented by each of the four groups.

NEW DIMENSIONS OF INTERNATIONAL CO-OPERATION FOR THE SUPPORT OF EDUCATIONAL RENOVATION

The meeting particularly commended to all interested in reforms in education the portions of the Secretariat working paper dealing with both the conceptual basis for international co-operation and the several promising modalities of concertation. It was agreed that international co-operation related to educational reform must be an integral part of the new international economic order and that it must be inspired by, and contribute to, the international strategies for the Third and Fourth Development Decades.

International co-operation should counteract tendencies for educational reforms to be conceived and carried out in national isolation — tendencies which derive legitimately from the sensitivity of the links between education and cultural and societal renewal. The coming United Nations Conferences on Technical Co-operation among Developing Countries (TCDC) and on Science and Technology Applied to Development provide an environment for continuing international collaboration within the context of collective self-reliance.

As highlighted by prospective United Nations studies on the future of the world economy, educational reforms should be seen as an essential part of the internal structural changes, together with changes in international relations, which are preconditions to the sustained accelerated growth to be achieved by developing countries during the next decades. Further prospective studies should be elaborated on the regional and subregional dimensions of the United Nations world models so as to shed light on the complementarities to be taken into account in strategies of educational development in relation to growth in collective self-reliance.

The meeting took note that education's relative isolation can also be overcome by involving education in multi-sectoral activities, such as those for training, job entry requirements, mass communication, etc., and in regional and subregional agencies for co-operation in research on aspects of development and training.

Clearly, an international dimension of education and educational reform is that of preparing students more adequately for performance in an increasingly interdependent world.

3. Recommendations

A. GENERAL RECOMMENDATION

The meeting's umbrella proposal is to recommend that the Director-General of Unesco ask the United Nations to take up education as one of the major problems of mankind in its cycle of major United Nations conferences.

B. UNESCO PRIORITIES FOR THE CO-OPERATION WITH MEMBER STATES

The meeting recommends that, in the light of the trends and need of the coming decades, Unesco give the highest priority to the following essentials:
(a) the democratization of education;
(b) the modernization of education with due regard to cultural identity;
(c) the development of links between education and productive work;
(d) the undertaking of prospective studies;
(e) education for international understanding, peace and universal human rights.

The meeting suggests that Unesco also encourage its Member States to accord these essentials a similar priority in their educational reforms.

The meeting suggests Unesco offer good offices to developing countries and to bilateral and other agencies of co-operation in educational development, for the effective mobilization of technical capacities critical to collaborative efforts in the above priority essentials.

C. RECOMMENDATIONS FOR UNESCO ACTION

To achieve these essential aims, as indicated above, priorities for Unesco's operational actions relative to reforms in education during the 1980s are as follows:
(a) In preparation for a major prospective study, conduct studies at a world level of illustrative education reforms completed or in progress. Such a survey should involve participants in the reforms, including the teachers and learners themselves, so that they contribute as subjects, not objects.
(b) Orgnize a limited number of 'Country Reviews' of major reforms in education. These should be well prepared in advance by host country nationals and by a small team of outside experts. Participants in the review should be policy and professional personnel from a limited number of countries which are considering or undertaking educational reorientations similar to those of concern in the host country.

(c) Since transformations in education are complex phenomena, Unesco and its National Commissions should encourage fundamental research on the several processes of reform from conception through implementation, including the micro-studies which will illuminate adoption and diffusion practices in real social systems.

(d) Co-operate upon their request with developing countries which are undertaking major reforms by offering to mobilize the external financial resources to permit reforms to become more systematic experiments from which the host country and perhaps the broader educational community can learn. These resources could cover the incremental costs of pre- and post-studies and measurements, of continuing evaluation, and of the use, where appropriate, of the strategy of planned variations. Expertise for carrying out such systematic experiments can be drawn almost entirely from institutes in developing countries themselves.

(e) Organize cross-national studies of the relation of examination systems to reforms in education, including means by which appropriate modifications in examination and diploma structures may be planned and implemented with participation by those most directly involved.

(f) Unesco should play a role in supporting and undertaking prospective studies as a means of providing frames of reference for future educational reform and planning. Adequate resources must be immediately made available to foster co-operative research at various levels — international, regional, subregional, national.

(g) Unesco should co-operate with other agencies within the United Nations system in search of information and experiences. It should survey work already produced and draw on existing networks, private as well as public, having accumulated relevant knowledge and experience. Finally, Unesco should appoint a panel of experts and leading personalities in prospective studies as applied to education who can provide sustained guidance to the development of Unesco's work.

(h) Conduct prospective studies on the international dimensions of democratization in the context of lifelong education, placing emphasis on the reduction of educational disparities between nations and regions, and its implications regarding the infrastructure needed for the production and distribution of educational messages.

(i) Through disciplinary seminars and publications, facilitate means by which educational planners and administrators can stay in touch with the rapidly advancing state of the art in planning techniques used outside education for prospecting alternative futures, for preparing scenarios and their probable consequences, etc.

(j) Organize informal meetings bringing together specialists important in the planning, implementation and/or appraisal of reforms in education from several countries, probably on a regional basis, so that free-wheeling and unofficial exchanges of approaches and experience can take place.

(k) Concentrate more of Unesco's training efforts through its Regional Offices and the International Institute for Educational Planning (IIEP) on the planning, implementation and appraisal of reform and innovations in education.

(l) Unesco should, as part of educational planning, promote and contribute to the dissemination of studies on the national policies for cultural development and on policies, experiences and studies of multilingual education, and assist Member States in training of professional and non-professional personnel to permit their participation in the elaboration of multilingual programmes.

(m) The meeting considers that education reforms should take into account the conditions and needs of communities in rural areas where, in a number of countries, a majority of youth and adults are living. It is therefore recommended that Unesco encourage innovative studies and experiments in order to meet the specific demands of such population groups in appropriate educational forms and contents while providing them with equal opportunities of access to and success in the educational system.

(n) Co-operate with other United Nations agencies in undertaking a study of the educational dimensions of a more equitable international division of labour and of the educational implications of the objectives and targets adopted by the major United Nations world conferences. This work could examine, together with the International Labour Organisation (ILO) and other agencies, the role of vocational education and training in the mobilization of the human potential.

(o) Co-operate with ILO and other agencies in evaluating alternative patterns of vocational education and training (including the use of part-time teachers otherwise engaged in production) and alternative approaches and contents (both in formal and non-formal systems), keeping in mind the need for a growing mobility between education and work.

(p) Co-operate with ILO and other agencies in promoting case studies of educational experiments intended to enable the workers to take part in the management of means of production and to play their role in the development of the society.

(q) Education systems, particularly in developing countries, tend to get caught up in a dilemma between equalizing access to education on the one side, and making the content of education relevant to the needs of the majority on the other, when the selection function of education, particularly in relation to employment, takes heavy precedence. Unesco should encourage studies in order to move towards a resolution of this dilemma.

(r) Considering the significant impact of good co-ordination both internal and external and at any stage and level of management, the meeting recommends that Unesco should emphasize the fact that co-ordination must be regarded as an indispensable element for any educational project and especially education reform projects, it being understood that education as a national task implies the participation of governmental and non-governmental agencies.

(s) Unesco should link considerations of reforms in education to the growing efforts to strengthen co-operation among developing countries themselves, with particular reference to the forthcoming United Nations Conference on Technical Co-operation among Developing Countries (TCDC). The co-production of building components and of teaching aids, equipment and materials by developing countries on a collaborative basis would offer a splendid illustration of collective self-reliance.

(t) Unesco should further promote education for international understanding as an important means for strengthening the ethical foundations of a new international order based on solidarity and equity.

Part Two

Specific aspects of problems relating to educational reforms

Planning educational reform

by Roberto Carneiro

Man and society

Educational reform in the 1970s and 1980s is closely associated with the future of man and society in the twenty-first century. Once under-standing the future is recognized as a national and scientific activity, a heuristic approach leading into participatory forms of educational policy planning may increasingly emerge.

Man and society, assumed as reference co-ordinates of an educational trajectory, lie well beyond a mere abstract concept, an intangible philosophical creation or a lifeless mathematical average. Recognition of legitimate differences between cultures, beliefs and social organizations, added to striking disparities in welfare and in access to education, present today's social scientists with the initial ingredients to design alternative spectra of the days to come.

Because fundamental options dealing with culture and civilization are at stake, the issue is essentially normative, or at least quasi-normative, since learning from the experiences of others is an asset to be taken into account. Proper international co-operation can increasingly tear down national barriers and narrow development gaps.

Planning educational reform signifies tracing, in a quasi-normative way, the shape and contours of the future. This involves four major activities:[1] (a) goal identification and specification; (b) anticipatory consequential analysis; (c) value-shift assessment; and (d) sketching processes and means.

A great deal of emphasis will be attached to foreseeable goals and values, since these may have major consequences for the substance of educational reform. Some main goals with obvious potential impact on the content, methods and processes of education are: (a) construction of a lasting pluralistic democracy in the concert of nations; (b) deeper humanization of society and better personal development; (c) improved quality of life in its multi-dimensional aspects; and (d) a new international order whereby the freedom, dignity and development of nations and peoples are increasingly protected and supported.

A firm understanding that democratic pluralism is a basis on which the organization of modern societies must rest has a direct influence on the content and organization of learning. Analysis of curricula in force in typical monolithic or totalitarian structures reveals what should not happen. Successive schools of thought in modern pedagogy have underlined with vigorous arguments the principles of a democratic education, while actual classroom practices remain persistently conservative. Tolerance and mutual respect are corner-stones of the full exercise of the personal freedom which the school ought to enhance. A special place should be reserved for civic education. This is designed to provide future citizens with an understanding of the functions of government and society, thus ensuring future policy-makers of an alert and informed electorate. It should also act as a catalyst in terms of active participation in society, provide non-biased information, knowledge concerning alternative social patterns and mastery of the instruments necessary for a truly responsible engagement in full citizenship. Further democratizing access to the benefits of education and culture will play a leading role in the preparation of the competences required by society and in the adequate development of the individual.

Cross-combination of items (a), (b) and (c) above would underline the future relevance of positive discrimination policies in favour of disadvantaged groups, such as those in the poorer rural or urban areas, minority ethnic or linguistic groups, the handicapped, illiterates, migrants, etc., or of increasing lifelong educational opportunities to compensate for former imbalances of the system and to meet the growing aspirations of the adult population.

Increased possibilities for substitution and the changing conditions affecting the division of labour, implicit in the goals above, presume a radical reformulation of the relations between education and working life, with a strong emphasis on the problems usually associated with first employment. Further research into these areas will certainly be needed.

Thus, ideas can flow and alternative policy options will emerge from a serious and continuous effort directed to the future. Detailed assessment of the divergent schools of thought about the future, their principles, methods and results achieved, could be a good start toward a concerted programme to discover creative and comprehensive ways of fashioning a new era in the evolution of education.

New challenges in educational planning

A scenario of global values and its subsequent expression in terms of an adequate educational set of goals is only a beginning. There remain the problems of resources, of means and of the organizational infrastructure to achieve the overall aims: and these entail a need for policy definitions. A new set of problems then arises: how to deal with issues related to the management of the system and its reform. This introduces a science — or perhaps merely a practice — which is still in its infancy. The key concepts involved, and their interplay, are worthy of careful analysis.

Adequate research and development must be provided to throw light on methodologies, build theories, conduct experiments, carry out pilot-scale tests, monitor changes, evaluate trials, develop ideas, probe innovations and compare systems. The allocation of resources, choice of methodologies, definition of trends and co-ordination of efforts in educational research, both at intra- and international levels, pose formidable problems. Despite the voluminous publications and prolix journals which attest the widespread work currently conducted in educational research, and despite the engagement of international organizations in the exchange and dissemination of findings and results, these latter, with few exceptions, exert little or no influence on policy thinking and reform.

Policy-oriented research is struggling to survive in a hostile environment, where decisions are often subject to personal dictates, ruling fashions, vested interests or sheer empiricism. To make use of available conventional wisdom, eagerly offered by external consultants or organizations, is often much safer and more comfortable and immediate than to spare time, effort and resources in search of the best solution for each problem. Moreover, the pressure of interested parties, or of time constraints on the introduction of changes, can result in the sacrifice of a rational approach to short-term result-warranted action.

The reverse may also be true. The researcher in his fairly well-funded ivory tower, whether university department or laboratory, progresses at his own pace, often indifferent to the crying demands of realities and to the requirements of the planners or of politicians. In short, compartmentalization is the general rule in education, and the institutional arrangements of most administrations are strikingly incapable of promoting dialogues between those engaged in different parts of the same general field.

Discontinuity, however, does not end here. The educational planner, the person who theoretically is placed at the very crux of the process of change and innovation, is limited by a multitude of difficult dialogues. In particular, those with the decision-makers, whose priorities often conflict with the technocratic approach, may be dramatic. The time is gone when the planner sat tight and awaited clear-cut policy orientations for appropriate 'technical' treatment, or else would be expected to serve on a tray, for superior decision, a set of nice and tidily worked out alternatives. While linearity sometimes occurs, the planner increasingly finds himself at the heart of a much more complex situation, demanding an effective mastery and integration of values, techniques, policy guidelines, resource constraints and impatient claims which inevitably conflict.

Not surprisingly therefore, some of the classical tools used and misused in the planning of education have failed to serve when the quantitative expression of planning is being replaced by a more comprehensive view. While there is still need for specialization, and a balanced use of cost-benefit, social-demand and manpower-forecasting methodologies, a new form of bridging is needed: that between the quantitative macro-economic mechanism and the qualitative micro-educational approach.

Two factors contribute to this need. First, there is the emergence of a 'second generation educational planning' school of thought, integrating a strong emphatic view on the dynamics of interrelations between research, decision-making and planning. Second, there is the importance already attached by renowned training agencies to the qualitative aspects of education such as the preparation of planners: curriculum development, teacher education, policy planning, lifelong and recurrent education.

The institutional framework within which the planner works is a determining factor in making his dialogues easy or difficult. A review of the modes of operation of planning agencies within governmental frameworks could throw light on the discussion needed on this matter.

Crucial are the planner's relations with the executive bodies which have the difficult responsibility of coping with changes while administering the system. Separating institutionally the study and planning of reforms and their implementation causes a great deal of misunderstanding and conflict; while a large part of this can be avoided by adequate organizational arrangements, the remainder must be resolved by the ultimate arbitration of the decision-maker.

In countries where overall development plans, spread over a number of years, are organized, the planning-implementation structural tensions usually reach several degrees of climaxes, such as rating of objectives, priorities for reform and allocation of resources. Control over funds available for development programmes is the main source of opposing views. Giving the planners an effective grip on planned funds contributes to a better co-ordination, an easier evaluation of programme implementation rates and corresponding revisions and a firmer management of cross-departmental efforts. However, the planning unit then grows into an operational body and often appears as the major brain trust at the disposal of the Minister, who must seek to avoid misuse of power and its possible degeneration into a cryptic autocracy of technocrats.

On the other hand, withdrawing budgetary control from the planning sector strengthens the executive officers against the planners' attempts to co-ordinate reform activities; planning loses its practical interest and the unit degenerates into a planners' retreat. In any circumstances, and particularly in the absence of comprehensive plans for a period in which continuous planning activities result in concrete programmes and instruments of action, institutionalized channels of intercourse are indispensable.

Review of the planner's role in the light of educational reform entails due consideration of two further matters. First, the upsurge of unprecedented demands on the part of different groups of vested interests, such as families, teachers, students and communities, for a stronger voice in the planning of change results in the rise of spontaneous participatory forms of planning in several contexts. Second, the educational and training policy unfolds through, and overlaps with, virtually all other sectors of social activity and organization, and the resultant effects and reactions are difficult to anticipate.

A multi-sectoral and horizontal approach requires a special sensitivity to constraints within institutions or governmental departments to permit a desirable degree of concertation in objectives, programmes, efforts, resources and attitudes. The problems extend beyond the traditional confrontations attending budgets and funding policies. They revolve around delicate and burning questions such as the national pluri-departmental human resources development policy in the context of a specific economic situation, or the planning of local/regional-based integrated development. These examples illustrate different types of policy-matching to be pursued: the first, among planning officials and bodies of separate state departments; the second, among the local/regional planning services and national sectoral bodies.

Planning thus occupies a key strategic role in the search for a new balance of powers between central and local administration, and awareness that education is inextricably interwoven with the entire structure of social development must be reflected in the methodologies and exercises employed when shaping its future. Growing complexity, increased awareness of its role, and the pace of transformation in an ever-changing system make of the planning exercise an eminently interdisciplinary activity in which the orthodox one-shot ballistic models have been replaced by cybernetic networks having recourse to refined feedback and controlling mechanisms.

Educational reform in Portugal

Recent educational trends in Portugal illustrate some facets of the foregoing rather theoretical exposition. The Revolution inherited an educational system affected by the contradictions of a collapsing regime. Between 1970 and 1974 the Establishment allowed a gradual implementation of important educational changes to modernize social institutions, improve school attendance and provide the skilled labour force required by a diversified economy.

The approach was typically technocratic in the assumption that educational reform should occur, *grosso modo*, within the tight authoritarian rules of the prevailing social and political structures. However, advanced educational goals were clearly defined and ranked, educational research and planning was a flourishing activity and played a leading part in the reform movement, and the government was eager to promote broad public debate on its draft bills for reform. As a result, profound changes took place in Portuguese education.

Chief among these were: (a) a comprehensive reform bill approved by Parliament on 25 July 1973; (b) the extension of compulsory education in order to reach eight years of universal basic schooling by 1980; (c) the implementation of a unified secondary education as opposed to the two-branch classical and vocational system in force during the preceding twenty-five years; (d) the expansion and diversification of higher education, with emphasis on setting up short-cycle institutions and modern universities; (e) a strengthening of teacher education; (f) a reform of the central administration.

Thus, the April 1974 *coup* and the post-Revolution governments are faced with a changing educational system and a reform momentum in a particular sector without parallel in other areas of public concern. A first subsequent period comprising six provisional governments and five different Ministers of Education in two years (1974–76) has been unable to deliver a new educational order.

At the risk of oversimplification one could describe the educational results of this period as a combination of the following characteristics:

An on-going reform which the new Establishment strongly opposed on basic principles, but to which it was incapable of offering a sound alternative.

Fragmented and discontinuous changes in the educational system, some of far-reaching consequences, as a result of a new ideology in education. *Inter alia*, there were: substantial modifications in curriculum content; alterations in the primary education structure; the introduction of a year of civic service between secondary and higher education; and the establishment of democratic school governing boards.

Disrupting internal conflicts, revolving around politically biased pressure groups in the power structure of the Ministry of Education and in the schools, making unfeasible any clear-cut or stable definition of priorities, guidelines or orientation.

A weakened administration, progressively stripped of its most experienced staff and increasingly unattractive to the most able young professionals.

Serious labour confrontations involving the teachers and the Ministry.

Moreover, it became evident that any lasting educational effort required a substratum of institutional stability and social/political organization which the Revolution was failing to provide. On the contrary, two years of devastating political struggle, as always faithfully mirrored in the educational arena proper, crippled the system and emphasized the crying demand for a sustained educational development to be sought under the constitutional governments to come.

A number of favourable environmental aspects however, merit specific reference, including: (a) the irreversible drive in Portugal towards a more effective participation in education by citizens, institutions and interested groups, as part of a new democratic framework and of a move in the direction of overall decentralization; (b) the atmosphere of change, which surrounds major rapid social and political advances and which should be used to foster adequate educational innovation; (c) the increased general awareness of the role of education in the consolidation of democracy and pluralism in Portugal, as well as in the rediscovery of a renewed cultural identity. Heavy responsibilities were to rest on the shoulders of coming administrations.

Two further years (1976–78) have gone by since the constitutional bodies were set up. The approach of the first constitutional government[2] towards education is typically a reactive one, reflective rather than assertive. The key preoccupation is to counterbalance the excesses allowed during the former revolutionary period and to reinforce legality in schools. Law, order, stability, rehabilitation, effective management and, on the whole, a *functioning* school system seemed to be the overriding concerns. The Ministry of Education and Culture of the second constitutional government[2] openly lists educational reform as one of the priority tasks in the next few years. In a vast, ambitious and challenging programme, the government priorities in education up to 1980 are to: approve a new reform bill for the educational system;

expand pre-school education; reorganize upper secondary education on broad diversified and pre-vocational lines; set up and regionalize short-cycle higher-education institutions; reform teacher training, both initial and in-service, and organize a national curriculum-development network; improve school facilities and teaching/learning equipment; support special education; launch new adult education and literacy activities; strengthen vocational training opportunities for young people in search of their first employment; and decentralize and reformulate the system of educational administration.

There seems to be a sensible emphasis on the qualitative aspects of education rather than on setting high quantitative targets. Other than small-scale sectoral reforms, two short-term activities are fundamental. First, there is the preparation of a new reform bill which should clearly set out the essentials of Portuguese education in the 1980s, including educational objectives, the structure of the school, pre-school and out-of-school system and methods and processes. Second, there is the preparation of the next Development Plan (1979–84), during which the foundations of the projected educational system should be laid. This latter exercise will have to draw on precise qualitative and quantitative planning in a general setting of economic recovery, budgetary austerity and social reform.

To decide on where to go and how to get there is above all necessary to provide consistency to a government's charter of intentions, the most common criticisms of which underline the lack of operational priorities and of a clear implementation plan.

Eventually, no doubt, the government will have to dedicate greater attention to certain problems, at present absent from or insufficiently dealt with in its programme, especially: structures and management of educational innovation; training and research in the educational sciences, within tertiary education; co-ordination of vocational training agencies; non-formal education; development of poorer areas (rural, suburban areas, etc.); and community development activities.

By and large, fundamental education remains a core issue for a country which has set its eyes on Europe, betting on a medium-term economic and political integration vis-à-vis the European Economic Community, and which must seek to offer the Portuguese people a quality of living compatible with their cultural heritage, legitimate socio-economic aspirations and neighbouring standards.

A series of related questions should then find appropriate answers. Supposing that a full six-year compulsory schooling system can be established by 1980, what should be the next target? Should it be eight or nine years of basic education by 1985? How can a policy of raising the school-leaving age be combined with one for early childhood care, within a restricted budget? In the presence of overwhelming evidence of the inefficiency of the primary and middle schools, what steps should be taken and what subsequent resource allocations should be made? Curriculum development, teacher training and support, new teaching-learning methods, and others, are to be strengthened and encouraged: in what manner and through which priorities? Adult literacy programmes should form part and parcel of a fundamental education concern. How should they be linked to other training programmes and what quantitative targets should the government set according to its resource availability and technical competence?

Correct answers will call for prospective studies, including careful technical weighting of research data, developmental and evaluative work, and detailed planning and programming. On the other hand, the government is increasingly conscious of the political need to build its educational policy on a broad supporting consensus. Both activities will have to draw on a solid institutional basis to conduct the technical work and to encourage a constructive dialogue.

The Research and Planning Bureau (GEP)[3] of the Ministry, set up in December 1972, was soon transformed into the 'think-tank' of the educational sector. Heavily staffed — around 110 people, roughly half clerical — it was initially organized into seven units corresponding to major concerns of the reform thrust. Three were research-oriented (Pedagogic Studies; Policy Research; Professional and Vocational Education), three planning-oriented (School Mapping and Site/Facilities Planning; Macro-educational Planning; Programming, Implementation and Control of Development Plans), and one dealt with Information and Documentation. Remarkably, GEP has resisted the sweeping post-Revolution changes and the turmoil of rapidly changing provisional cabinets. Today, its original structure, which has since seen the addition of a Nucleus of Statistics (planning) and a Nucleus of Evaualtion (research), calls for urgent reformulation to adapt it to a new educational context and set of priorities, as well as modifications in public planning objectives and procedures.

There has been a notorious lack of institutional channels for a systematic dialogue between the administration, vested interests and the community at large. The government has promised to set up a National Board of Education (Conselho Nacional de Educação) to advise the Minister on policy issues and ensure broad representation.

The government must tackle the problem of overcoming an existing educational void immediately. Persistence of such a situation would threaten the principal aspirations of an idealistic Revolution and endanger a brighter situation for the Portuguese in the coming decades. These can be achieved only through democratic leadership, professional competence, dialogue, mutual respect and confidence among the administration, teachers, students, families and communities, national mobilization and solidarity, centred on a worthy project for reconstruction.

International co-operation

At the heart of the concept of education one finds the essential principles of exchange, communication and learning. In these fields, processes are as important as end products, and methods as formative as content. Thus, particularly in monitoring educational reform, international co-operation assumes the form of a give-and-take operation, a two-way learning experience.

Some strategic or instrumental aspects of multilateral co-operation in educational reform are as follows:

Systematic studies and critical appraisals of planning structures and mechanisms in different countries, including analysis of the corresponding institutional frameworks and interactions with the administration machinery.

Improvement and redefinition of a body of educational indicators, conceived as a meaningful set of measures of a system's performance, and rate and direction of change. Serious attention is required for qualitative dimensions which escape the traditional stereotyped measures, in order to provide basic tools adjusted to the control and evaluation of educational reforms.

Strengthening of regional and national networks serving educational innovation and policy research. Special stimuli could be given to co-operative research projects based on decentralized teams and subjected to periodic seminars and confrontation symposiums, allowing for free and open discussion of results. Unesco could play a leading role in the association of parallel institutions and groups, across both national and continental boundaries.

Facilitating access to a constantly reviewed pool of official information on reform trends in different countries, making use of simple and expeditious forms of communication such as newsletters and bulletins.

Broadening the scope and intensifying the provision of training opportunities for professionals — other than planners — strategic to the development and success of educational reforms, such as evaluators, administrators, curriculum specialists and developers, teacher trainers, field agents and officers, and systems analysts. The choice of training programmes and exchange priorities in staff development should consider both the multiplier effect and the degree of specialization sought, as they relate to local facilities and resources. Whenever possible and convenient one should aim at fostering decentralized national or supranational efforts and initiatives.

Allowing increased specificity in assistance and expert consultancy services to countries, through careful selection of the areas and programmes appropriate for more sustained forms of support. The main options should rest on the major needs of the country concerned, with due regard to the role and specificity of other international agencies.

NOTES

1. W. L. Ziegler, *The Look-out Function in Education*, CERI/OECD, 1972 (17 p.).
2. The first constitutional government, with a Socialist minority Cabinet, remained in power between August 1976 and January 1978; the second constitutional government, a Socialist/Christian Democrat coalition, took office in January 1978.
3. GEP — Gabinete e Planeamento do Ministério da Educação e Cultura.

Educational reforms and bureaucratic phenomena

by Thierry Malan

Images of administration

If you put the following question to teachers in a school, 'What does educational administration represent for you?', you can expect to receive among others, the following replies: 'they are people who have no under-standing of education, who don't know the realities of life in the field'; 'it's concerned with everything except teaching'; 'it's something which clearly must exist since there are special premises for it, distinct from the teaching premises'; 'it's a necessary evil, against which one is powerless to act'; 'it's the head of the establishment'; 'it's a source of embarrassment and conflict'; 'it's a faceless machine for producing paper: you only know it through the hierarchy and cold, remote texts having little application to everyday reality, sometimes self-contradictory'.

Taken as a whole, the administration will be seen as something rather negative and restricting. It is remote, formal, communicating mostly in writing; at the same time it is embodied in members of the hierarchy who are known, but with whom communication is difficult because the exact extent of their powers is not known, and therefore all the more potentially threatening. This frequently negative view of the administration explains why it is seen as an obstacle in the way of change rather than as a necessary instrument to implement reforms.

It fulfils functions deemed necessary, but whose existence and need are really only recognized when something goes wrong: in other words, it is only thought to be working well when it is not noticed. The restrictions which it imposes will often be seen as a sign of ill-will rather than as the ex-pression of impartial realities which are imposed on it: for example, when the distribution of activities and population in different regions of a coun-try is very uneven, and the teaching personnel's wishes in regard to postings do not correspond to school zoning requirements and cannot all be met.

The relationship between teaching and administration

The frontier between what belongs to teaching and what belongs to administration is not always clear in education, setting aside what is obviously the domain of teaching — classroom work — and what is obviously the domain of administration — for example, keeping the accounts of the establishment. There are numerous intermediate domains, for example the appointment and movement of teachers; the choice of teachers in accordance with their teaching capacities is the concern of specialists in teaching, while the organization of staff transfers and postings is an administrative operation. Similarly, school architecture conception requires the co-operation of architects, technicians, educational experts, administrators and financiers.

Moreover, all educational activity has its administrative side: a teacher changing establishments and moving from a post where the pupils' records are filled in by a supervisor to a post where he has to do this task himself will feel that he is undertaking a new job, quite different from his job as a teacher, and more administrative in nature. A colleague in his new establishment, who has always done this job himself, will not always have the feeling of doing something specific, 'separable' legally from his task as a teacher. If a language teacher who has learnt to work a tape-recorder and magnetic tapes, and is responsible for keeping a list of them and sometimes for repairing them, is suddenly given a technician to help him he will feel relieved of administrative tasks and techniques to the advantage of his teaching, whereas to begin with the former were but an extension of the latter. Among teachers who are interested in their pupils' careers and who get involved in various related activities, such as sitting on boards, counselling and completing files, some will feel they are doing 'administrative' work and will then complain about the increasing bureaucracy of the educational system, while others will see it as an educational act, complementary to their job as teachers, and would not want to see it taken over entirely by specialists.

In other words, all those working in the educational system, with different responsibilities and to a varying degree, engage in 'administration' in the broadest meaning of the word; if they do not do so at all, they thereby help to increase the bureaucratic weight of the educational system, if only, for example, by being insufficiently abreast of their own personal administrative situation. Beyond a certain threshold of quantitative and qualitative development, some tasks, mere extensions of educational tasks, become true administrative tasks and techniques, especially when it becomes necessary to call on specialized personnel; but educators cannot wash their hands of them completely without running the risk of lessening their own effectiveness.

Administrative structures and educational agents

At all stages of the educational system, relationships between the various agents involved are partly determined by the structures within which they operate. In a very centralized system, where few decisions rest with the head of the establishment and his academic or administrative council, the various partners in the life of the establishment — different categories of teachers, headmaster and administrative staff, parents — are not in control of all the factors which would allow them to settle among themselves their day-to-day problems. For that reason, a great deal of their energies will be spent on their relations with the hierarchy, or with similar groups in other establishments, rather than on comparing their problems and points of view in their own establishment, since this would only make them realize their own impotence; all this will result in problems of communication within the establishment itself, and the risk of increasing divergence of interest between the different groups.

In ministries of education, former teachers who have moved to careers in administration work together with professional administrators, often those who would be able to work in fields of activity quite other than education. Certain positions in the hierarchy are reserved, in practice or by right, to one or the other; each body keeps a careful watch on the origins and qualifications of those who are allowed to join it; they also keep a watch on the number and the quality of the posts reserved for them. This partitioning between professional bodies leads to various difficulties, for example, artificial distortion within the organizational chart, so as to ensure posts for certain people or else to ensure the exclusion from certain functions of people who might have the right qualities for the new tasks entailed by reforms, but who do not fulfil the administrative conditions required for the corresponding positions.

To this must be added the fact that for certain projects — rural development and the development of schooling in rural environments, for instance — it is frequently necessary to adopt structures which transcend the usual administrative partitioning, and to this end to appoint project leaders accepted by the various bodies which could lay claim to the management of these projects.

Within the teaching body itself, the division into disciplines can be a source of inflexibility in the application, and even the conception, of a reform. Thus all teachers will agree that a certain number of teaching hours per week for the pupils must not be exceeded; but when it is a question of rearranging existing timetables to give more room to one discipline, or to allow space for a new one, each group will keep a careful watch that its own timetable is maintained, or even increased: for decisions in this area have considerable effect on the future of teachers in the discipline concerned, their numbers, prestige and material status in relation to the others.

In the same way, one of the great themes of recent university reforms has been multidisciplinarity. The various groups of teachers approve of this aim in general as a means of tackling problems which cannot be studied by means of any one existing discipline (e.g. town-planning, protection of the environment, education, public health); moreover, many scientific discoveries are made by the convergent approaches of several disciplines, and by the gradual creation of new disciplines. But when it comes to the practical implications of the principle of multidisciplinarity, people tend to shy away; it would entail an organization of teaching units and of teachers' work by areas of activity and by the problems of society, and not merely by disciplines, but it is through the disciplines that reputations and careers are most often built; the man who escapes the usual criteria for promotion in his own discipline in order to explore other fields with teachers and researchers in other disciplines runs the risk of being less well-known and valued than his colleagues who have stayed in more traditional fields. As long as new fields do not constitute disciplines on their own, no one can be certain of promotion who devotes himself to them entirely, while that is just what would be needed in order to consolidate these new fields of activity.

Central planning and administration

Education plans have long been overall plans, often drawn up at the same time as plans for economic and social development; they are generally seen as more important for their broad policy guidance rather than for a detailed analysis of ways and means, as much with regard to financial resources (how will education budgets develop in relation to other budgets?) as with regard to human resources (for example, will the country have at its disposal enough qualified teachers to be able to implement the planned objectives within the time-scale proposed, or again, can the building industry actually construct the premises needed to carry out the reforms?).

These plans have an essential function at national level: they make it possible for all development agents to engage in far-reaching discussion and keep each other informed of what is going on and they acquaint the various social and occupational groups (and public opinion at large) with new conceptions of education and enable them to pool their problems and often to evolve joint methods and solutions.

But they can also have 'perverse' effects: in general they go hand-in-hand with social dynamism, and raise certain hopes. If these hopes are disappointed by the practical difficulties of implementation, they can create scepticism and make the work of planning harder for several years, even with the best-qualified people. The plans represent an ideal which can have a most discouraging effect if there is no spelling out of the concrete means of approaching it, that is, of bridging the gulf between it and reality; the existence of this gulf can only reinforce the influence of centralized administration at the expense of decentralized systems.

In any case, this relative disillusionment as far as all-embracing plans are concerned has led planners, preceded by systems analysts, first, to place more emphasis on the connection between plans and budgets; second, to try to define 'strategic' operations from which one could hope for particularly far-reaching effects on the system as a whole, and third, to attempt to modify the behaviour, especially the administrative behaviour, of the various agents involved.

There is then often a hidden conflict between political leaders, planners and administrators: the first will complain about the conservatism of administrators: administrators will invoke the utopian nature of the planners' suggestions, in particular their lack of realism in financial matters. Planners will tend to rely on the work of educational research in order to find principles of action and supporting arguments for their proposals: administrators will find this work too remote from their own preoccupations and will want to see researchers taking a greater share of responsibility in the choices to be implemented, which researchers will refuse to do, for considerations of professional ethics. Finally, researchers will complain that they only see administrators taking interest in their work when there is political urgency to resolve certain difficulties in the educational system, then turning their backs on it once this urgency is over, even if the problems in question are still not solved.

Implementation of plans and reforms by central authorities

Planning documents and proposals for reform often become stakes in interdepartmental battles and discussions. Thus a Treasury department, anxious to limit public expenditure, will use as an argument for refusing or delaying proposals for implementation the fact that they often involve policy documents which are not yet binding; it can also refuse new proposals by saying that they did not figure in the plan.

Once the plans and proposals for reform are adopted, there follows a phase during which the administrative department concerned adapts and spells out the objectives. It will already have taken part in the work of drawing up the reforms, either because it holds much of the essential information, or because it will have wanted to arm itself in advance against surprises imposed from without, or because, as a result of being responsible for the implementation of the reforming measures, it will have been associated from the beginning with formulating the proposals. The administrative department or authority concerned will view the reforms from a different standpoint to that of the planners, even if it happens that the two functions, planning and administration, have been fulfilled by the same people. It will try to translate the proposals for reform into terms acceptable to itself, in order, that is, to avoid changing its own organization and the status and division of tasks between its professional bodies too much; it will try above all to lay down work-rules which are sufficiently simple and stable to be effective, even if this causes some people to fear that the aims of the reform will be changed in character. The authority also decides when the various texts and measures bringing the educational reform into effect are to come into force: during this phase of the work, less open and accessible to the public gaze than that during which the reforms are discussed and adopted, the pressure of public opinion will often have eased off and the authority will therefore have more freedom of action.

Researchers, politicians, planners, central administrators, local authorities and families do not all experience educational problems at a similar tempo nor from the same viewpoint, which often leads them to say, when they meet, that they 'don't speak the same language'. Researchers study the problems they think important, free from the pressures of political expediency and the institutional restrictions which affect administrators. Planners live in the medium term, administrators live with annual budgets, in the short term or from day to day. Central administrators and planners discuss new reforms or new methods of management when the local administrators are scarcely beginning to assimilate and apply reforms and methods which the former are already considering abandoning. Families want more stability in the flood of successive reforms which confuse them and multiply their problems as to direction and choice, and therefore their risk of making a mistake; at the same time the expression of their dissatisfaction helps to speed up the movement towards renewed reforms, even when the means which would allow them to be effectively implemented are not available.

Local administration and the decentralization of decision-making

At the local level, the internal difficulties experienced by central authorities are not always clearly understood. Local administrators are very much aware of the contradictions apparent between decisions taken by different central departments, or between declarations of intent and the measures put into effect. Some therefore who have, for example, seen discussion reopened after a few years on an innovation which was beginning to work well in their institution once a lot of initial problems had been sorted out, may be tempted to be very cautious and reserved in the application of new directives: they will wait a while to see whether others are following them.

In order to bridge this gap between national officials, local officials and users, educational policies often provide for administrative reforms which allow greater decentralization or deconcentration of decision-making. In the case of decentralization there is a devolution of jurisdiction and resources to authorities legally independent of the central power. In the case of deconcentration, there is a transfer of responsibility to local authorities who continue to be hierarchically dependent on the central power. In practice, the two methods have the common effect of bringing the power of decision closer to the officials who best know the realities of the local situation. One important difficulty in decentralization policies is the problem of their coherence: it is difficult in fact to define areas of decision pertaining solely and entirely to national, regional or, as the case may be, local policy. In most cases all levels of decision-making will be necessarily involved, and decentralization can further accentuate the complexity of the process; it would be more true to say 'appears to accentuate', for in a very centralized decision-making process those responsible for implementing the decisions, as well as the users, though excluded from the process, maintain the essential power of their inertia; this can block a reform just as effectively as its rejection during official proceedings. For example, the power of deciding on the creation of a school in a particular area may rest with the mayor, but his powers will almost always in fact be shared. For the school to be built and then to be able to function, a large number of criteria and decisions must be harmonized: technical standards — type of buildings, interior structure, size of classroom, safety measures — financial norms, powers of decision — in regard to the purchase of land, choice of building contractors, school zoning, curricula to which the premises must be adapted, appointment of teachers, etc.

Decentralization can therefore give rise to many practical difficulties, when, as is very often the case, the most important powers are vested in different authorities; a single veto can prevent the exercise of other powers, for example a refusal to finance a project presented by a municipality because it does not conform to technical standards recommended at national level, or again, a refusal to allocate teachers, recruited and paid by the central authority, if the school project is not negotiated with it on points which legally rest entirely with the municipality. Thus what is decentralized in principle may often be recentralized in practice if the aims pursued by decentralization are not sufficiently clear to all parties, and if the distribution of resources, and people's behaviour, are not modified as a result.

Autonomy of establishments

Like decentralization, autonomy is frequently demanded, but it is not a clear notion: autonomy is made up of numerous educational, administrative and financial elements, in respect of each of which an establishment will be more or less autonomous, almost always without being completely so. The principle of autonomy is thus often evoked in a very general way in discussions between universities and ministries of education, but its application varies a great deal according to which of the establishment's different functions is involved, whether it is a question of defining the contents of courses, their duration and pass procedures, of awarding degrees and diplomas, of recruiting teaching staff, of determining conditions of entry for students and the amount of enrolment fees or of distributing resources between the various units making up the establishment. On all these points the absence of complete financial autonomy can limit considerably the effect of such autonomy as is possessed in the teaching field. The responsibility for recruiting teaching staff, for example, is an essential element in the responsibility for organizing teaching: this power is usually shared between the central authority, the establishment and the teaching body itself, whose members have great personal autonomy; this limits by an equal amount the autonomy of the establishment itself.

It follows that the central authority may be tempted, in order to continue to exercise sufficient control over the whole university system, to make use of the ambiguities of this principle, sometimes by sheltering behind the principle of autonomy to avoid taking embarrassing decisions, sometimes by invoking its limits in order to put a brake on certain initiatives: progress in autonomy may therefore very well be accompanied, as a result of the reactions it provokes, by a return to centralization.

Administrative decentralization and training

As the relationships between central authorities, local authorities and educational establishments move in the direction of greater decentralization, new working conditions are created; they call for a change in the behaviour of all parties. Central authorities often find it hard to limit their activities to laying down general guidelines which allow a sufficient margin of initiative to the local officials. These authorities include members who, having exercised responsibility in local authorities and establishments, sometimes have difficulty in adapting their methods when working at central level: they may tend to work with too great attention to detail. For each function in the administration of a complex system such as education there must be corresponding types of behaviour suited to the responsibilities involved: new officials often take a long time to adopt such behaviour and they transfer to their new functions the attitudes which brought them success in their previous positions, attitudes which may prove to be inappropriate. Conversely, at local level, officials can find themselves granted a power of initiative whose extent they are not immediately aware of; they therefore try to get from the central authority more cut-and-dried directives which limit their initiative, and this can strengthen the centralizing reaction.

It is therefore not enough to define the aims of educational reform; we must make it possible for the various agents of the educational system to modify their behaviour so that they can evaluate sufficiently precisely what must depend on them and what must be done by others, and so that they may have the opportunity to develop their scope for action in their new roles; it follows that training in administration, whether geared to professional administrators or to all those in the educational system who have to engage in 'administration', must not only be a general and technical training, but must also aim to make its recipients clearly aware of the new links between education and its environment created by the reforms, and of the possibility of developing these links still further.

Educational reform
for interdependence

by William J. Platt

The generation now in the classrooms of the world — the generation which will inherit the earth as the calendar turns to the twenty-first century — will be tested in life by a situation which did not confront any of its predecessors; it has no choice but to learn to cope with global interdependence; it is the first generation which must do so to survive.[1]

Interdependence among societies and nations has been around a long time. Trade, which is based on economic and technological specialization, is as old as recorded history. Cultural enrichment through travel, through the diffusion of art, music and literature, through communication, is part of nearly everyone's heritage, while the advance of science owes much to international exchanges. In the realm of political interdependence, alliances, ententes, treaties — even intergovernmental organizations — pre-date this generation, sometimes by centuries.

However, such interdependence differs from that of the future; the partial and largely self-serving 'dilettante' forms which have obtained hitherto will cease to exist: today's generation will have to practise the real thing.

'Dilettante' interdependence — tolerant and intolerant systems

'Dilettante' interdependence has meant choosing those aspects of inter-societal and international relations which seemed advantageous and agreeable to our own ethnocentric outlook. We could, for example, purchase raw materials from a developing country without granting it access to our consumer product markets. We could be active members of international organizations and yet ignore their channels of co-operation or conciliation when domestic politics were sensitive. We could call for

81

ecological conservation while allowing or even encouraging practices which polluted rivers, seas or the upper atmosphere. When awkward or unfamiliar (i.e. foreign) accommodations were the price of attaining the next stage of interdependence, or even when they were the price of equity within the existing one, we would withdraw into our sanctuary, claiming that the sensitive issue, no matter what its effects on others, was of domestic concern only, permitting no external interference.

We have been able to postpone coping with true interdependence because most complex systems, when operating at levels well below capacity, can tolerate considerable abuse. For example, traffic violations on a lightly used road network rarely cause serious obstruction, but when the network is operating at full capacity, a single violation or accident may clog the whole system.

'Dilettante' interdependence has been almost viable when systems were tolerant, in a world of apparently endless frontiers within which each nation pursued its own unilateral policies, population was not pressing on available land and resources, and people were not ready for common definitions of justice and of human rights. But these conditions have changed. The world is finite. It is already crowded and is rapidly becoming more so; its population is expected to increase from today's 4,000 million to 7,000 million by the year 2000. Some degree of minimal interdependence will therefore become inescapable.

Subsystems of minimal interdependence

Minimal interdependence will need to embrace the connected subsystems of global security; of global economic relations — including energy and resources supply and use, food supply and use, and co-operation for development; and of global justice and human rights.[2]

Arrangements for interdependence in each of these subsystems are both rudimentary and changing, but this is no excuse for the practice of education to continue to neglect these arrangements until the subsystems have matured. The search for a new world order should be brought into every classroom, so that those who must live with the consequences of the inevitable interdependence will acquire a sense of its dynamics and of the give and take necessary to put it into effect early in life.

The United Nations Organization was established in 1945 primarily 'to save succeeding generations from the scourge of war'. To this end, a considerable peace-keeping and conciliation machinery was set up. In practice, however, more reliance for international security is placed on the threat of national military force. Beneath a nuclear sword of Damocles of the super-powers, mutual distrust becomes self-reinforcing;

countries spend 163 times as much on armaments as they do on all United Nations development and peace-keeping activities.

When governments do, occasionally, turn to United Nations arrangements for peace-keeping, it is usually as a last resort after unilateral efforts fail. If it is not to atrophy, the peace-keeping apparatus — the only existing institution of universal participation — should become an avenue of first, not last, resort.

Despite elaborate arrangements to facilitate international economic interdependence, present enormous inequalities between rich and poor are widening rather than narrowing. Poverty, undernourishment and disease condemn hundreds of millions of people to a subhuman existence. The food–hunger balance is precarious: world grain reserves declined from 105 days' supply in 1961 to 31 days of reserve supply in 1976.

The United Nations Environment Programme (UNEP) reports that in much of the world fertile soil is being degraded, contaminated or lost, and that many of these processes are self-perpetuating and irreversible. Unequal access to energy and other non-renewable resources has, until recently, been disregarded. Succeeding generations are being exploited through the depletion of such resources and through the pollution of rivers, of seas, of the air and upper atmosphere, and even of space (by orbiting debris). We can no longer trust in science and technology to overcome any scarcity, owing to the laws of thermodynamics and other constraints. Hence we see the emergence of 'appropriate technology', a more modest and useful conception of the contribution of science and technology.

International co-operation for development is a key aspect of economic interdependence. The first objective of development of the Third World — that of political liberation from colonialism — has been substantially achieved. The United Nations system was instrumental in this process, implementing its Charter's commitment to the 'self-determination of peoples'. But the economic gap continues to widen. The slow but promising search for a new international economic order gives hope of a more equitable and mutually beneficial co-operation for development among developing and industrialized countries.

True interdependence can be practised only by observing global ethics and justice. Although the world has but the flimsiest machinery for this purpose, we have more understanding of the ethics and justice of interdependence than of other aspects of minimal interdependence. Part of improving justice depends on the new international economic order which is evolving. But already a magnificent edifice for judicial interdependence exists, deriving from the work of those who drafted the Charters of the United Nations and Unesco, and from the United

Nations 1948 Universal Declaration of Human Rights. These instruments anticipated the true interdependence to come.

The Universal Declaration of Human Rights begins:

Whereas recognition of the inherent dignity and of the equal and inalienable rights of all members of the human family is the foundation of freedom, justice and peace in the world. . . .

It goes on to assert that everyone is entitled to all the rights set forth in the Declaration

without distinction of any kind, such as race, colour, sex, language, religion, political or other opinion, national or social origin, property, birth or other status.

The Declaration's thirty Articles spell out rights which need to be translated into learning opportunities in all classrooms: everyone has the right to be free and not a slave; not to be arrested arbitrarily or tortured; to be equal in the eyes of the law; to have privacy and protection from slander; to travel abroad and return; to have freedom of religion, thought and expression; to engage in peaceful assembly and association; to choose representatives in free elections; to work; to a nationality; to seek and enjoy asylum from persecution; and to an education which 'promotes international understanding and tolerance'.

The minimal interdependence facing today's twenty-first-century generation is beginning to take shape, thanks to a number of inquiries that are now under way. In its series of reports labelled 'The Predicament of Mankind', the Club of Rome has made an important contribution to understanding the coming interdependence.[3]

Implications for education

The shift from 'dilettante' to a true minimal interdependence has significant implications for educational reform. First, it means continuing or even increased attention to the identity of self, family, community, province, nation, or region, since it is only on the basis of civic training for these levels that a student can acquire the understanding and competencies needed for world citizenship.

Second, education for interdependence does not imply a movement away from cultural diversity and pluralism in education. Interdependence is a manifestation of the division of labour in a cultural as well as in an economic sense, a differentiation not sustainable in a simpler autarchy. Conflict and confrontation may ensue from such division, but the common destiny of all humankind will be the theme for correlating diversity and pluralism and for resolving conflicts without violence. Thus, educational preparation for true interdependence will be more complex and differentiated than that for the 'dilettante' type.

Third, educational reform for global interdependence does not mean adding special courses to curricula on interdependence, international relations or inter-cultural studies. Instead, what is required is the integration and infusion of a global perspective into all parts of a curriculum.

Lastly, education for global citizenship and interdependence means education which is no longer ethnocentric and nationalistic, worshipping parochial military heroes, glorifying self-righteousness, and reinforcing dominance and dependency. It must also cease encouraging the 'conquest' of the environment, the belief in the providence of an unfettered science and technology, distrust of foreigners, and racism, aggression, and the oppression of minorities. Education should attend more to the future and less to the past; it should foster interdependence, not independence, and world, not national, citizenship.

Unesco Recommendation

In 1974 Unesco's General Conference of 135 Member States adopted the Recommendation concerning Education for International Understanding, Co-operation and Peace and Education relating to Human Rights and Fundamental Freedoms. Applying to 'all stages and forms of education', Article III begins:

Education should be infused with the aims and purposes set forth in the Charter of the United Nations, the Constitution of Unesco and the Universal Declaration of Human Rights.

The Recommendation advances the following objectives:

(a) an international dimension and a global perspective in education at all levels and in all its forms;

(b) understanding and respect for all peoples, their cultures, civilizations, values and ways of life, including domestic ethnic cultures and cultures of other nations;

(c) awareness of the increasing global interdependence between peoples and nations;

(d) abilities to communicate with others;

(e) awareness not only of the rights but also of the duties incumbent upon individuals, social groups and nations towards each other;

(f) understanding of the necessity for international solidarity and cooperation;

(g) readiness on the part of the individual to participate in solving the problems of his community, his country and the world at large.

The Recommendation specifies the kinds of civic and ethical behaviour and attitudes which derive from the principles of interdependence. These latter should 'become an integral part of the developing personality of each child, adolescent, young person or adult by applying these principles in the daily conduct of education'. The Recommendation deals also with: how the various sectors and stages of education can each infuse international and inter-cultural dimensions into education; ways and means of preparing teachers; needed reforms in the production, dissemination and exchange of equipment and materials; and stimulation and support of research and experimentation.

Incorporating as it does the other ethics instruments of the United Nations, the Recommendation is a remarkable consensus by the world's member governments on what education should do to support basic human rights and global interdependence.

Education for peace and the new world order

In promoting peace,

The task of education is to develop a global patriotism, to inspire commitment to a larger world community; and to teach behavioural skills that can imagine, analyse and evaluate future possibilities and probabilities, or in short, the strategies of survival. [4]

Material resulting from widespread and fruitful inquiries into a new world order being conducted by the United Nations, the Conferences on International Economic Co-operation (the 'North-South' conferences), the Club of Rome, [5] and other bodies must be adapted for educational purposes. This quest spotlights fascinating contemporary events deriving from ancient historical roots and destined to have significant impacts on the world's future. For example, a report requested by the Club of Rome contains a rich and provocative interpretation of the struggle of developing countries to participate as full partners in the conduct of international affairs — magnificent material for education.

Educational methods and interdependence

Effective education for interdependence must include attention to educational methods, processes and structures as well as to content. Otherwise the former may operate against content. An authoritarian pedagogy would negate broad citizen participation at every level;

students segregated by race or ethnic background would have difficulty learning tolerance; instructional styles encouraging unquestioning and non-critical responses would make students easy prey to parochial dogma. An education system which is primarily a sorting process for identifying a few winners and many losers would encourage competition and concepts of superiority and dominance, and so work against collaboration for mutual benefit.

Further conceptions of development and change operate positively or negatively. The 'trickle-down' conception would not encourage participation because it places reliance on elitism, while the 'trickle-up' notion would encourage many centres of initiative and the formation of networks of communication, thereby supporting interdependence.

Students will master the results of educational reform for interdependence only by applying the skills and attitudes of inter-dependence — only by making the needed insights a part of their own behaviour. This suggests experiential learning through civic training, such as encouraging students themselves to deliberate on the rights of the child and of students. When reality cannot be brought into the classroom, simulations should be used.[6]

Education — leader or follower?

To ask that education seriously adopt reform policies which help prepare today's generation for a future which is already having an impact is to ask something which has always been difficult to implement. But this time, world survival is at stake, and all who dare to undertake the sacred trust to 'educate' must also implicitly take up the challenge to reverse the present situation, in which education more easily follows than leads, more easily mirrors the present and past than anticipates the future.

Conclusion

For mankind to survive on this fragile planet in the twenty-first century and beyond, today's generation has no choice but to practise true inter-dependence, instead of the partial and self-serving type which has hitherto been almost viable. Processes and institutions for a minimal interdependence exist in at least embryonic form. But they cannot continue to be abused by selective use and neglect; interdependence in a finite and crowded world cannot be as tolerant as it has been in a simpler era, when there was room for unilateral action and acquiescence in oppression.

Education should prepare people for world citizenship as well as for participation in their own communities and nations. In the 1974 Unesco Recommendation, many of the principles by which education can do this were adopted by representatives of 135 governments. Very substantial reforms are now required to bring educational practice up to the norms appropriate for real interdependence.

The future world order is now being reshaped within and outside the United Nations. These efforts, and the international debates to which they give rise, are the proper stuff of today's education. The generation which will bear the consequences of the reshaping should also participate in it. The task of the educator, then, is to institute the reforms by which content and methods of education will encourage students to acquire the understanding, competencies and attitudes needed for global survival.

NOTES

1. The convenors of the Club of Rome, Aurelio Peccei and Alexander King, are perhaps more emphatic: 'The possibility for mankind to emerge safe and even stronger from its current multiple predicaments does exist, but the possibility that mankind will do so is frighteningly slim. The situation can be turned around and human prospects made bright only by a supreme concerted effort by all peoples and nations, before it is too late' (Laszlo *et al.*, *Goals for Mankind*, New York, Dutton, 1977, p. xi).

2. This grouping corresponds to the main organs of the United Nations system, with the first arrangements assigned to the General Assembly, Security Council and good offices of the Secretary-General; the second assigned to the Economic and Social Council and the agencies of the United Nations; and the third assigned to the International Court of Justice and to the United Nations Commission on Human Rights.

3. For example, the Club of Rome's most recent study *Goals for Mankind* (op. cit.) compiles a 'world atlas' of contemporary goals, including a disaggregation of goals for each of eight major world regions and for each of the major world religions. It also offers a rough measure of the degree to which the goals of various segments of the population of the several regions represent globally responsible goals as distinguished from aspirations uninformed by global and long-term considerations. These and other analyses ease the task of the educator in giving form to the educational materials appropriate to today's challenge.

4. Quoted from the report of the Conference of the World Council for Curriculum and Instruction, 1974, *Education for Peace: Reflection and Action* (ed. Haavelsrud), Guildford, Surrey (United Kingdom), IPC Science and Technology Press, 1976 (see especially the chapter by Robert Kwaku Atta Gardiner).

5. The latest Club of Rome report sees us in the midst of a World Solidarity Revolution: 'We are in the midst of another revolution in consciousness today, activated by the spread of communications and technology. As formerly backward and isolated masses of humanity enter into the interdependent global community, they recognize the universality of human rights, and compare their lot with that of more advanced peoples' (Laszlo *et al.*, op. cit., p. 415).

6. An interesting example of a relevant simulation is the *Global Futures Game* (copyright Earthrise 1975) in which teams representing major world regions play out fifty years of interdependence, making policy decisions on population, food, technology and education. Imbalances result in the accumulation of 'world destruct points'.

Teachers' organizations and educational reform

by John M. Thompson

Teachers' support for reform

Teachers and their organizations have long sought reforms in the goals, content and methods of education. They have, however, been handicapped by administrative restraints, traditional concepts of education dominated by the examination system imposed by entry to higher education, and, in some instances, by a feeling that educational reform is not their business.

Indeed, teachers have frequently been criticized by others who wish to see their educational reforms introduced immediately and with a flourish, and who believe that the only reason their ideas do not work is because the teachers either do not want them to be effective or are incapable of putting them into practice.

While it is true that teachers have rejected — and will continue to reject — reforms which they consider educationally unsound, they have, in fact, introduced many reforms gradually, even imperceptibly, and without dramatic or instant change, by evolution rather than by revolution.

Teachers' organizations have sought changes in the goals of education in order to make education more relevant to contemporary times. In newly independent countries, they have pressed for changes which will foster national development — defined by the 1976 World Confederation of Organizations of the Teaching Profession (WCOTP) Regional Conference in Gambia as 'the ongoing process of deliberate change aimed at the improvement of the quality of life'. They have urged reforms which further the process of liberation from economic dependence on other countries or on multinational interests. The 1975 WCOTP Regional Seminar in Costa Rica concluded that 'the educational systems conceived within the limitations of dependency must be transformed in such a way as to permit at all levels the formation of a free and creative citizen, with a critical mind and a corporate spirit'.

Likewise they have pressed for educational reforms to improve both access to education and the chances of success on the part of all pupils and students, rather than reforms which serve only the interests of the small minority which goes on to higher education. The 1977 WCOTP Assembly of Delegates in Lagos, Nigeria, discussed 'Compulsory education's social expectations' and, reiterating 'the inherent right of the youth of the world to participate in a free education system', specified that education must be compulsory for all 'because it is easy to deny such education on the grounds of economic conditions, geographic isolation, mental, physical or emotional disability, sex, race, creed or any other grounds for inequality'.

Teachers' organizations have pressed for changes in educational systems which will eliminate, or at least minimize, premature selection to the detriment of late developers, diminish the importance of examinations and result in more integrated systems, with consequent inplications for teacher education.

Changes have also been urged in the content of education and in the methods used to improve the learning process and the opportunities for pupils of all kinds of aptitudes and competencies, not just those with auditive/linguistic faculties and deductive intelligence. A more international content has been sought and more opportunity for the development of thinking and critical faculties. All too often, however, teachers have had little opportunity to change their methods because of restrictions imposed by the examination system, and because new methods frequently require costly new provisions both in schools and teacher training.

Sources of educational reform

Educational reforms have usually been effected by political decision, frequently under the impulse of a crisis, external to the education system, which it appeared might be settled by educational change. The October Revolution in the U.S.S.R. was followed by widespread change in the educational system and in the United Kingdom, major educational legislation followed the First and Second World Wars. The launching of the Soviet Sputnik provoked significant educational change in the United States. National independence has been the natural starting-point for major educational change in former colonies. Political revolution has always involved educational change to conform to the new philosophy.

While some educational reforms have had academic origins — e.g.

the new mathematics — and others have been brought about by individuals — e.g. Maria Montessori — large-scale educational reform under non-crisis conditions has been rare. The introduction of the comprehensive school in Sweden is a notable exception but the success of this was largely due to a long period of political stability which permitted meticulous planning and implementation.

In most pluralistic societies, political changes follow in too rapid succession for the development of educational change. While national teachers' organizations may see clearly the need for change, they are caught in the middle of political argument, and a crisis is then necessary to get the attention of the public. Failing this, there seems to prevail a sort of inherent conservatism on the part of the public and acceptance that things should not change too much at a time.

Overall and immediate reform needs political decision, the will to carry this out and a commensurate financial commitment. Since political decisions can be made only within the limits of what the public is willing to accept, sweeping reforms are the easier after revolutions or under a dictatorship.

International action is being taken to publicize situations calling for educational reforms. One example is the Unesco-UNEP (United Nations Environment Programme) Conference on Environmental Education, held in Tbilisi in October 1977. Another is the interest of the United Nations Fund for Population Activities (UNFPA) in the educational sector. However, there is some concern among teachers' organizations that such support for reforms is not accompanied by adequate financial provision for their implementation. There has been, for example, some suspicion that educational reform ideas promoted by the Organization for Economic Co-operation and Development (OECD) have been designed to save money more than to effect educationally desirable changes.

Teacher initiatives in reform

The contributions of teachers' organizations to the initiation of educational reform cannot be sharply distinguished from those of other parties concerned. Often, however, they are clearly substantial, as the few following examples will suffice to show.

The association of Swiss Teachers (Schweizerischer Lehrerverein) and the Syndicat National des Instituteurs (SNI-PEGC) of France both went into the publishing field in order to ensure that educational development was not influenced by political or commercially oriented texts. The Swiss Centre for Education World Diagrams, initiated by the

Association of Swiss Teachers, has produced over 100 large-scale world diagrams with accompanying booklets. Complementary to its publishing efforts, the SNI-PEGC has made extensive use of its weekly publication *l'École libératrice* to promote debate on new educational ideas.

Similarly, the need for educational materials relevant to contemporary needs has stimulated teachers' organizations in newly independent countries to foster book development. The Jamaica Teachers' Association promoted, initially with a commercial publisher and later on its own, the Jamaica Publishing House. The Ghana National Association of Teachers has developed, in co-operation with the Canadian Teachers' Federation, its book-development project with thirty-eight titles currently in production or about to be published.

The establishment of departmental committees, including representatives of teachers' and parents' organizations, to study the reform of education in France was a direct result of action by national teachers' organizations following the events of May 1968. This is not to say that teachers are satisfied with the outcome. In the field of nursery or early childhood education, the SNI-PEGC was very dissatisfied with proposals put forward in 1974 by the Secretary of State for Nursery Schools and mounted a campaign to ensure that these were withdrawn. To promote their own proposals and to make them widely known to parents and the public, the teachers prepared a film, *Soon We Will be Six*.

The Schools Council in England and Wales was established to provide greater opportunity for the channelling of teacher-organization initiative, especially in regard to curriculum development and examination reform. The Council works through some thirty committees or working parties with a total of about 1,000 teachers actively involved. As a result of the efforts of the teachers' organization, a widespread network of over 700 teachers' centres came into being.

In respect of the governance of the teaching profession, the Educational Institute of Scotland was the main initiator of the General Teaching Council, which registers all teachers and ensures a fully qualified teaching profession, governing its entrance requirements and disciplinary practices.

The management of schools is another area of educational reform in which teachers' organizations have been deeply involved. In Sweden, the teachers' organizations have pressed for greater union involvement in school management, parallel to the movement for greater worker involvement in the management of industry, the subject of recent government legislation. (It is indeed an open question whether the introduction of the comprehensive school in Sweden was the result of political action or the outcome of pressure by teachers' organizations.) In Yugoslavia, the teachers' section with the Civil Workers' Union has been promoting teacher participation in the self-management of schools.

Finally, teacher-organization initiative has played a significant role in the development of in-service training. From modest beginnings in 1962, an extensive programme has been promoted by national teachers' organizations in developing countries in Africa, Asia and the Caribbean, in co-operation with the Canadian Teachers' Federation and two Swiss teachers' organizations (Schweizerischer Lehrerverein and Société Pédagogique de la Suisse Romande). These teacher-sponsored projects have led directly to regular government-supported programmes being developed. A specific example is Gambia, whose government representative at the 1975 International Conference on Education referred to this initiative of the Gambia Teachers' Union.

Teachers' participation in reform

The Unesco General Conference at its nineteenth session held in Nairobi in 1976 declared that it

Invites all those concerned and, more especially, governments to pursue their efforts to bring the training of teachers into line with the demands of scientific and social development; to ensure that the position, remuneration and working conditions of teachers are commensurate with the importance that their work has for society; to encourage the participation of teachers and of their organizations in the preparation of educational reforms and innovations.

The WCOTP European Seminar held in Luxembourg in May 1976 specified that teachers and their organizations must play an important part in educational planning and in the determination of educational policy because:

(a) teachers have a far-reaching knowledge and experience of the needs of the situation and the life of educational institutions;
(b) the decisions taken about education affect the conditions of service of the teaching profession;
(c) no educational reform can be effective without agreement and collaboration of teachers.

Thus there is no disagreement on the theory of involvement in reform on the part of teachers and teachers' organizations. The problem lies with the practice. The delegate of the Caribbean Union of Teachers (CUT) at the WCOTP Caribbean Regional Seminar in St Kitts, in April 1977, stated:

Far too often have the so-called policy makers embarked on policies and programmes which we as teachers know are doomed to fail; far too often have they copied systems and innovations from the developed nations—innovations which have been sidelined by the developed nations themselves because they have proved failures or have become outdated; yet, when these programmes are thrown down the throats of teachers and the pupils they are to educate, and they meet with the expected failure, governments are quick to put the blame on the teachers and the institutions without realizing that these teachers should have been co-opted in the planning stages of the whole programme. It is time that we as educators let our voices be heard on all aspects of the educational development plans of our nations; it is time that we as teachers desist from accepting just consultative status but demand a status of full co-partners in the big business of education.

There is, indeed considerable mutual mistrust on the part of teachers and educational authorities. To some of the latter, teachers' organizations are concerned too much with conditions of work, or are too protective of their own traditions and interests, and are not concerned with educational reforms on their educational merits. On the other hand, teachers sometimes question the sincerity of governments' expressed desires for educational reform. For example, in Latin America the belief is widespread among national teachers' organizations that such expressions are not infrequently smoke-screens behind which old methods are maintained in order to support the existing political system. The great scepticism prevailing was expressed forcibly during the 1976 WCOTP Regional Seminar in Honduras. This identified as a major obstacle to reform 'the imposition by the Latin American governments of national and foreign conservative educational policies to serve the dominant class'.

Teachers and their organizations will not, of course, accept just any reform or support one merely for reform's sake. They ask that objectives be made clear, that means for achieving them be provided and that they themselves be involved in plans and find them acceptable before being expected to implement a reform.

If the beneficiary of reform is to be the individual, the emphasis will be on the learning process with the maximum freedom of choice and opportunities for self-development. If it is the State that is to benefit, the emphasis will be on the provision of the manpower necessary for its prosperity, with a place in society for everyone but with more limited freedom of choice. If a broad cross-section of the population is intended to benefit, the emphasis will be on provision of facilities for all to the highest level possible, with opportunities for general educational development transcending selection for higher education.

If the purpose is economy, reform will aim to achieve the best possible results within fixed limits of expenditure. A notable example of this was the mandate given by the South-East Asian Ministers of Education Secretariat (SEAMES) to its Regional Centre for Educational

Innovation and Technology (INNOTECH) group: the rationale of project IMPACT states that 'the focus of INNOTECH research should not be on ways to increase funding', rather 'ways must be found to increase the student–teacher ratios (perhaps to as much as 200:1)'. Unless it is clear which of these objectives, or which combination of them, is the target, a reform cannot be effectively planned and implemented.

Involvement in the process of reform requires special attention to the problems of the flow of information. For this reason, teachers and teachers' organizations took a particular interest in the 1977 Unesco-IBE International Conference on Education which devoted special attention to the theme 'The Problem of Information at the National and International Level which is Posed by the Improvement of Educational Systems'. The Recommendation adopted by that Conference specified that 'Teachers and their organizations constitute a very important group in the educational community and therefore their participation in educational information processes should be facilitated at every stage'.

Teachers' organizations, of course, offer an information transmission mechanism which is second to none. There are teachers in every corner of every country: when they are effectively organized in national, provincial and local bodies, these can play a most effective role in spreading ideas, attitudes and practices fundamental to effective implementation of educational reform.

Clearly, when given the opportunity for involvement, teachers' organizations must provide competent people to partner the educational authorities. This entails responsibilities both for teachers and employers. This is widely recognized by teachers' organizations. The 1976 Caribbean Seminar in St Kitts declared:

Teachers should equip themselves for consultation. Unless they acquire a deep knowledge of educational developments and study how these could be adapted to meet the needs of the country, governments are not likely to seek their advice and participation in the formulation of educational change.

The WCOTP European Seminar in Luxembourg in 1976 concluded: 'The employer should provide teachers with both information and concrete means necessary for exercising their rights regarding procedures in participation.' At the same time the speaker from the Syndicat National des Instituteurs de France (SNI-PEGC) emphasized that teacher participation 'is a responsibility that requires great intellectual and human qualities on the part of the person fulfilling it'. At the same seminar, the Danish Minister of Education noted that 'the significance of teachers' participation in the advisory bodies of education and planning is dependent on the contact which exists between the ordinary teacher and the teachers who are members of these bodies'.

National teachers' organizations in all parts of the world are concerned that their representatives on educational reform bodies should be of the highest competence possible. However, the best training for such involvement is involvement itself. Even if this should at times slow down the process of reform, the practical results will be of much greater significance.

The teachers' role

Teachers' organizations in all regions are deeply concerned with redefinition of the role of the teacher in the school of the future — as are Unesco, OECD and other intergovernmental organizations. The crux is whether the teacher is to be an agent of change or a preserver of the cultural heritage of society, a free agent or a servant of the school authority, State or otherwise. The attitude of teachers' organizations is determined in most cases by the nature of the society in which they operate and the confidence which their members have in the socio-political system. In some instances, the organization views itself as a major force supporting the political system, especially in one-party States; in others, the organization seeks forms of education which will promote the critical faculties and the capacities necessary to change that system. If educational reform is fundamentally a political decision, teachers will generally be viewed less as free agents than as agents of change determined by society.

There is much talk of the involvement of the resources of the community and of industry, of the use of specialists of various kinds and of para-professionals. Teachers' organizations recognize the value of marshalling such resources in order to improve the quality of education. They insist, however, that only qualified people should be entrusted with responsibility for the teaching-learning process. For this reason the representatives of teachers' organizations were particularly insistent at the 1975 Unesco-IBE International Conference on Education that the final Recommendation should state that 'this practice should be encouraged . . . provided that educational responsibility remains in the hands of qualified teachers'.

Teachers' organizations in Europe stressed this point in the conclusions of the WCOTP 1974 Regional Seminar on General, Vocational and Technical Education in Stockholm when they stated:

Only people having training of the same pedagogical quality should be considered as qualified to teach. It shall be for the school to decide whether it will make use of the services of individuals or institutions to assist in the educational programmes. Where the school so decides, this should be on the basis of retention by the school of control of the situation and should in no way detract from the responsibility of the teacher for the supervision of the teaching-learning process.

Teachers' organizations are pressing both educational authorities and their own members to see the work of the teacher as part of that of an educational team. The Asian Regional Conference of WCOTP in 1977 recommended that 'there should be supporting services for teachers including advisory, psychological and counselling services in order to assist teachers to carry out their duties more effectively'. It recommended further that 'in view of the fact that knowledge nowadays gets more specialized, teachers should work as a team so that they can not only benefit from one another but also assist each other in achieving the educational objectives'. The European members of WCOTP have asserted that 'in the perspective of working as part of an educational team . . . all teachers should be trained in demonstration and practical work in the subject in which they teach and should have opportunity during their training for similar experience in another subject area'.

Teacher education

No educational reform can be carried out effectively without a fully competent teaching force. Thus, teacher education is a major concern of all teachers' organizations. These seek adequate initial preparation, given by people who have themselves had recent classroom experience and integrated with continuing programmes of in-service education. Such education is of particular importance in respect of projected reform. Teachers' organizations have spoken of one year in five being needed for in-service training if teachers are to keep up with new methods and techniques, content and reform progress. However, as this would imply a substantial increase of perhaps some 20 per cent in the size of the teaching force, such a proposal is usually rejected on grounds of cost.

Teacher education to enable teachers to prepare young people for the transition from school to working life is the subject of particular concern in Europe, its importance being enhanced by the current youth unemployment problem faced in many countries.

Student and parent participation

Besides acceptance of the fact that teacher and community involvement is essential if educational reforms are to work, it is increasingly recognized that greater student involvement in the process of education is necessary if maximum learning is to be achieved. This is of particular importance in the 16 to 19 years age group. Raising the school-leaving age does not of itself provide educational benefits. The school programme for the additional years must be meaningful to the students, and for this their involvement is to be sought. At the 1975 WCOTP Assembly of Delegates in Berlin (West), it was agreed that, in order to educate students in the political process, teachers should 'establish appropriate structures and procedures within the classroom and the school to enable the participation of students in decision-making'. There is, however, considerable disagreement as to the extent of the student participation which is desirable.

The involvement of parents in the educational process is also much to be desired, especially in cases where major reforms are contemplated. Unless they understand fully what is happening and encourage their children, rather than criticize the work of the schools, there will be a resultant frustration to the detriment of reform. Parental opposition, for example, has in many countries been one of the major factors in the lack of reform of the examination system.

Reform areas

Teachers' organizations are increasingly recognizing that they should be concerned not only with school education or with the work of their members in the school setting. The Asian members of WCOTP have agreed that 'adult education should form a part of the syllabus of the teacher education colleges and teachers' associations should consider it their duty to foster and assist these programmes'.

Another area of educational reform to which national teachers' organizations throughout the world have given special attention in recent years is that of early childhood education. It is recognized that the formative years of the child's life from one to five play a major role in the whole of his or her subsequent educational development. This is especially true when the child is affected by physical, mental, cultural or environmental handicaps. Unless these factors can be compensated for in the early years, much of the effectiveness of educational reform at later stages will be lost.

Class size preoccupies teachers' organizations in all parts of the world. The demand has repeatedly been made for smaller classes, so that teachers can work more effectively. Counter argument is produced that numbers have been proven to be less critical than previously believed in respect of academic achievement and with present teaching methods.

These two qualifications of the argument are extremely significant. If reform of education aims to lessen emphasis on academic achievement in the traditional sense and consequently to introduce new methods, then the case for smaller classes will undoubtedly be pressed by teachers' organizations everywhere.

Measurement of educational achievement is still one of the major areas for serious study and reform and one to which national teachers' organizations will need to give increasing attention in the years to come.

Curriculum reform, away from the traditional subjects to issue-oriented programmes, is sought by many teachers and teachers' organizations. The citizens of tomorrow need to comprehend in their totality — causes, effects and solutions — the problems posed in respect of environment, population, water, energy and so on. There are no general answers as to whether this can be done within the traditional curriculum or whether the school programme should be re-oriented and if the latter, whether the examination or evaluation system should be changed. In the past, teachers' organizations have generally favoured revised use of current curriculum subject areas rather than introduction of new studies. However, the recent Unesco-UNEP Conference on Environmental Education called on 'Member States to include in their educational policies measures designed to introduce environmental concerns, activities and contents into their education systems', including a number of specific actions to fill the gaps that, despite outstanding endeavours, continue to exist in our present education systems.

The relationship between school programmes and working life after school is under very serious examination by national teachers' organizations. Educational reform to meet the contemporary needs of young people is being studied both in relation to the subject-matter content of the school programme and the general orientation of students in relation to their social and political responsibilities and their employment opportunities. The European approach was summed up at a WCOTP Seminar in Stockholm in 1974:

General education should provide all pupils with a balanced education including all elements and fields of human life. In this respect general technical education should, at all stages of education, form an integrated part of what traditionally has been regarded as general education. It should incorporate learning experiences that contribute to the development of the whole individual. As part of a balanced education all pupils should receive general education both for their own continuous development and as a preparation for adult life. Introduction to technology, practical work and manual skills must be included.

As a solution to the employment problem, the Director-General of the ILO has put forward the pertinent suggestion that the answer may lie in less education before entering employment and more in-service educational facilities later. In general, national teachers' organizations have opposed such an approach, believing that a sound educational base is needed by all if they are to have the potential to adapt later to social and economic change. There is, however, general recognition that education in the 1970s and 1980s must be related more directly to the contemporary needs of both individuals and society if the potentially devastating problems of an unemployed educated community are to be avoided.

The problem of teaching in rural areas was emphasized at WCOTP's African Regional Conference in Gambia in 1976 and in its Asian Regional Conference in the Philippines in 1977. The former summarized its views as follows:

Teacher institutions together with agriculture departments could devise programmes which would promote economic education at all levels. By these means, people will strive to attain that quality of life necessary for an economically stable society. This, we believe, lends itself to participation in diversified agricultural programmes such as cash crops which improve the earning and purchasing power of the individual in society and promote self-reliance.

A major area of educational reform which concerns very many teachers' organizations is that of increased opportunities for women and girls through education, e.g. facilities for access, encouragement to study all subjects without stereotyped orientation and career possibilities, through higher education or professional studies or in all types of industry and commerce. The WCOTP membership as a whole is currently discussing a major Policy Statement in this field to sum up teachers' policies which national teachers' organizations have advanced piecemeal over the years. These can be summarized as follows: (a) to work within the policy of the teachers' national organization to promote the development of equal opportunities for men and women; (b) to examine all resources used in the teacher's school, rejecting those which perpetuate undesirable emphasis on dominant or subservient roles of either sex; (c) to open all activities and programmes to both boys and girls; (d) to encourage children to enjoy being what they are — girls, boys, people — as opposed to fostering any idea that either sex is more desirable or inherently superior; (e) to work to ensure that the practices of the school are a model for the concept of equal opportunity.

In world-wide, regional and national meetings, teachers' organizations are urging that greater emphasis be placed on studies of an international nature and that in all subject areas the international implications be covered adequately. However, when national and international interests conflict, even potentially, the teacher is very exposed. Even the national teachers' organization can face serious difficulties in the defence of its members. If the school programme is truly to be reformed in this field, there is need for much greater provision for the defence of the teacher when he or she is handling the issues involved honestly and sincerely according to his or her conscience. Serious dialogue is needed between the teachers' organizations and the educational authorities, and very clear guidelines need to be worked out and respected.

Implementation of reforms

Teachers and their organizations are deeply concerned with the speed with which it is expected that reforms can be implemented — and also with the speed with which they are all too often changed. It is the development of human minds that is at issue and, for this reason, teachers' organizations insist that all reforms be properly tested before they are put into practice. The only exception comes when a newly independent country wishes for a rapid break with foreign forms of education.

A major problem in all reform lies in its application to the education system as a whole. Experimentation in model schools may show outstanding results but this may be due in large part to the dedication of a small group of teachers and specialists in a clearly defined community. This point was emphasized in the conclusions of the Unesco expert meeting on the Methodology of Educational Reform in December 1976 which noted that 'the need to resist "the lure of the spectacular" was stressed, as was the need to avoid organizing "model schools" whose results, achieved in special circumstances, cannot be generally introduced'. This viewpoint is widely shared by national teachers' organizations.

When the objectives of a reform are clear and the ways and means in which it is to be put into effect have been agreed, teachers believe that they should be given the maximum freedom to carry it out with the minimum of administrative interference. Bureaucracy can become the greatest obstacle to effective reform. Teachers' organizations in many countries consider that administration unnecessarily absorbs many resources which could more profitably be used in the classrooms.

Reforms may often be delayed by excessive institutional conservatism. The Report on the 1975 Unesco-IBE International Conference on Education notes that 'the practitioner within an institution . . . may come to attach more importance to consistency in the pursuit of his rational but artificial concept of professionality than to the diverse and possibly non-rational perceptions and needs of his client'.

A major contribution to the breakdown of false institutionalism is being made by international teachers' organizations such as WCOTP. The confrontation of ideas and concepts across national and regional boundaries causes all organizations to review their own policies and attitudes. This is a liberalizing process, the long-term benefits of which in promoting educational reform may in many ways be decisive. Juxta-position of different approaches by international teachers' organizations and their varying memberships—as has developed over the past three years—can play an equally significant role.

Conclusion

In summary, teachers and teachers' organizations seek educational reform in respect of goals, systems, content and methods. They seek to be involved in the political process of determining educational policy and at all levels of the evolution of programmes to put policy into effect. They are suspicious of reforms for the sake of reform or for the sake of political ends without sound educational merit. They wish to see clear goals for any projected reform and adequate financial means at the disposal of the educational system so that the reform can be implemented.

When they have been involved, when the goals are clear and when the means to bring about the reforms are available, teachers will accept responsibility for implementation. When these conditions are not met, they resent accusations of conservatism or of failure to produce the expected results. Educational reform can come about only through a true partnership of educational authorities and teachers' organizations, working together to achieve the goals set by society.

Perspectives of the implementation of educational reforms

by Lord John Vaizey

The background to the educational reforms and the possible and perhaps desirable evolutional trends of education in various parts of the world in the Third Development Decade needs to be spelled out. If we cast our minds back to the end of the Second World War, the educational scene throughout was radically different from what it now is. Indeed, it would not be going too far to say that the generation which has grown up in the period since the mid-1940s has seen more change in education than has any other generation to date. The educational changes have had several major characteristics. First, there has been the enormous increase in enrolments in formal schooling throughout the world. The numbers are obscure because evidence of enrolments even today is not as good as it should be, and data for the period around 1945 are particularly weak. Nevertheless, it looks as though total school enrolments may well have quadrupled in the period 1945 to 1975, and the number of teachers may also have quadrupled. Unesco has stated that between 1960 and 1975 enrolments nearly doubled and the number of teachers doubled. Of course, part of this growth was due to population expansion, but the major part has been the incorporation into the school population of groups that previously did not attend school at all. Thus, while looking back on the past, there are many criticisms to be made of the way in which education has developed, and its content and structure are not necessarily ideal, but the remarkable fact must be acknowledged that education has experienced a growth without parallel, and a growth far beyond that of many other aspects of society, not only in the advanced industrial countries of various political forms, but in all the developing countries as well, ranging from those with very high per capita incomes, like the Republic of Korea at one extreme, to those with very low per capita incomes, like some countries in Africa, at the other extreme. The evidence suggests that this rate of growth will be attenuated by the end of the century, for the simple reason that a large part of the population of the world is already receiving a formal education of some kind or other.

The next thing to which attention must be paid is the quite extraordinary rate of growth in facilities for education. The number of teachers has risen quite considerably, while at the same time facilities in terms of schools, ancillary buildings, books, equipment and so on have also increased beyond measure. In some countries this has meant that large sections of the population which previously had to make do with a very elementary education are now fully incorporated in the education system with facilities which are no less adequate than those of the most affluent and favoured sections of society. This applies to the United States, the Union of Soviet Socialist Republics and a number of Western European countries as well as to countries like Canada and Australia, and is applying increasingly to a range of countries at the top of the LDCs (less developed countries) with the highest gross national products (GNP) per capita.

Thus, while the expansion of student numbers has been the dominant characteristic of the education system, the education system has not at the same time seen a decline in the material standards of education. It has indeed seen a very remarkable advance in many areas. It is perfectly true that this advance has been much less adequate judged by contemporary criteria than would have been the case if it had been judged purely by the criteria which were dominant in, say, 1930. Nevertheless, it is no less remarkable for all that. It does, however, represent a gap between the expectations of the population at large and the realization of these expectations, which is a significant and potent influence. If one is right in assuming that, over the forthcoming decade and looking ahead over the next generation, the rate of growth of student numbers will be somewhat lower than it has been in the past, it seems highly likely that the rate of growth of facilities may well exceed the rate of growth of the population enrolled in schools; that is to say, the pupil/teacher ratio will improve and the facilities in the less well endowed school systems will also improve. Thus there are reasons to suppose that the material quality of education will also begin to change.

Thirdly, there has been a radical shift in the philosophy which underlies education in many areas of the world. From being a system which conceptually at least was concerned with producing a small élite which could fill the key roles in society, together with a basic primary education for such other parts of the population as were necessary to make the system, economic and social, run efficiently, the emphasis has shifted towards an adequate education for the whole population. This in itself is in many cases a radical change of the most dynamic and important kind. It implies, for example, no differentiation with respect to the social and family background of the student, and conscious efforts have been made in many countries to overcome the handicaps, both material and psychological, which are suffered by children who come from relatively deprived groups, whether those groups be racial or social or, in many cases of course, rural. At the same time there has been in most countries an affirmation of the principle of sexual equality which has implied a radical shift in the value systems of a number of countries. This again is not universal, since there are substantial numbers of countries where the assertion of sexual equality is not accepted at face value. Nevertheless, this fundamental change has occurred in many parts of the world. It might reasonably be supposed that this might be one of the major factors which will grow in intensity, and it is reasonable, therefore, to suppose that the pressure for high educational quality in some form or other for the relatively deprived social groups, for rural areas and for women will continue.

One reaction to this pressure has been for people to throw up their hands in horror and take the view that the world's material resources and organizational prowess are together insufficient to provide an adequate education for all the world's children in the foreseeable future. To an extent this is a truism since, after all, large sections of the population of the world live on the margin of subsistence and, faced with the dire needs of hunger and elementary health, education is not necessarily the top priority, at least in the short run. But, nevertheless, in the longer term it is surely unwise to take the view that the pressure for an adequate level of formal education will diminish. Indeed, in so far as deprived groups and women are successful in fighting for their rights, as enshrined in the Universal Declaration of Human Rights for example, it will automatically follow that they will press for adequate education. In these circumstances non-formal education, whatever its attractions, may well appear to be a somewhat less adequate substitute for formal education than might seem the case at first sight, since what is at issue here is not so much the relevance or worth-whileness of education *per se*, but the fact that what is needed is an assertion of the principle of equality of provision for people sharing common citizenship, whatever their backgrounds, race or sex. This is a pressure, therefore, which is likely to increase.

Next, the changing social and economic position of the world has meant a radical change in the content of education. No generation since the dawn of human history has lived through such a period of immense technological and cultural change as that which is now in its early fifties, and this technological change has two major characteristics which are all important. The first is that it is based on science and its application

106

through engineering to the day-to-day lives of everybody in society. This process, once begun, is irreversible. It is inconceivable that, in the absence of a cataclysmic destruction of the whole human race, the present level of technical achievement could recede, and in order to maintain the present level of technical achievement it is necessary to have an adequate education system for all levels of society. It is this more than any other thing which has affected the basis of education and will continue to affect it to an accelerated degree as the technological achievements derived from the scientific revolution of the sixteenth and seventeenth centuries and above all, from the scientific and technological innovations of the nineteenth and twentieth centuries, spread throughout the world.

The second characteristic of the cultural, social and economic change through which the world has lived has lain precisely in the point that the present dominance of a scientific and engineering-based technology has produced the first civilization in the history of the world which has been universal. Hitherto, civilizations like those of China, Greece and Rome, and those of what is now Latin America, have existed side by side with only minimal contact between them, such as the trade in precious objects. The world is now linked in a collection of manufactured objects and common intellectual understanding in a way which is unique, and this again means that those of the human race living in civilizations which feel themselves to be relatively deprived of these crucial artifacts and of the powers to manufacture them will increasingly make determined efforts to take part in the fruits, good or bad, of contemporary scientific civilization. These attempts may take many and varied political, economic, social and cultural forms, but nevertheless they all require a sophisticated degree of understanding of the way in which modern technological processes work, and of the background, scientific, mathematical and intellectual, which lies behind them. It is to this degree, therefore, that the world is likely to find itself increasingly involved in the instruction of whole populations in the cultural and social requirements of the modern world. It is on this basis that phenomena like lifelong education as well as the widespread development of formal education systems have to be seen in a total world perspective, and it follows therefore that the development of the scientific revolution and its working out in the most minute detail will require a most intensive effort concentrated on the change in the curriculum and methods of teaching in all educational systems.

This again has taken place on a basis which is, so far as the present author knows, without precedent in the history of the world. The incorporation of new populations, of many more girls and women, of people of hitherto racially different backgrounds, has meant that the system has had to adapt itself culturally and socially in order to accept new criteria, both of excellence and of adequacy, while at the same time the relevance of the system to the prospect for employment and for working life has become absolutely dominant. There have been many civilizations where the major purpose of education was purely to maintain the traditional culture or religious forms, whereas the development of the education system therefore has to be seen in the context of a radical change in the constituency which is being educated, and also in the content of education, which is extremely important. What is interesting is that the reaction has on the whole been extremely positive to the development of education in these fields, and it is in this sense that there has been a very rapid succession of reforms of great importance, and this has followed the enormous development of new systems and structures in education, which will continue without cease to be an important feature of the modern world, and of education in particular. At the same time, it must always be remembered that one of the major functions of education is the inculcation in the students of the traditional values of the societies in which they are to replace the older generation which is ultimately responsible for instructing them, and the process of perpetual change through which the world has been living in the past few decades, together with the transition in educational structures, has itself been a profound and destabilizing influence. It is not without significance that many of the most disturbing political and social tendencies of the age have had their origins in educational institutions and among students. It follows therefore that, in contrast to the tendency towards perpetual change and reform within education, there is a powerful pressure for stability, a stability which people necessarily seek, both personally and socially, and which is indeed the characteristic of the good society. It may well be, therefore, that in future, or at least in the next decade, the changes will be less radical in form than those which have been seen in the past quarter century, though in spirit they may well be more permanent, more lasting, and more radical in nature. The instability of structures which has led to the development of such concepts as lifelong education and to the importance of non-formal education, and in some countries to the replacement of the traditional secondary school by the comprehensive school, may be replaced by a more profound shift in the attitudes of teachers and in the quality of teaching skills, rather than by concentration upon the formal structures of the educational system, which until now have been the chief targets of educational reformers of all kinds.

One of the disappointments of the past third of a century has been that while the world has passed through a process of technological change without precedent, particularly in media with the development of the transistor radio, television and other devices for communication, the impact on pedagogy has been minimal. To some extent this is inevitable, because the essence of good teaching is that it is a personal relationship between teacher and taught, and this cannot in any sense be substituted for by technological aids. At the same time, the development of a new technology of communication has of course profoundly affected the context within which education takes place. The major way in which the modern civilization based on technology has disseminated itself throughout the world has been in fact not by formal educational techniques but by the impact of the technology itself, particularly through the mass media. This process will accelerate, not decelerate, therefore the context in which educational innovation takes place will be of profound importance in this respect.

This suggests that the debate on reform may well take place within the context of a population growing more sophisticated about the aims and purposes of education, both formal and non-formal, and yet unconsciously assimilating the purposes of education through what might be called in hyperbolic terms a non-formal education situation which it does not recognize as an educational situation at all. It is likely therefore to concentrate a debate about education on issues which are not actually central to the functioning of that system. This relates also to the fact that the whole of society is caught up in these sweeping changes of which it is only partially conscious, and each different group in society—social, sexual, racial and occupational—reacts in a different way to these changes. They will all be demanding different things of the education system, seeking to preserve those elements which they feel ensure that they have a particular gain to be made or a particular position to be held, and attempting to destroy those which they see to some extent as a threat to their own position. The net sum of these attitudes towards change may well not be in any sense a coherent programme of educational change and reform. The question raised is of great importance and significance, and indeed points to the need to try to pinpoint the way in which education fits into the general context of social and economic change, a process which is only partially understood, and which is inherently difficult to know, given the fact that the basis of economic change is now the rapidly advancing technology, a technology with its own inner logic and which, in changing the material basis of life, changes the cultural and social patterns of life in ways which those who are participants see in occasional ebbs and flows as they try desperately to keep afloat in the turbulent streams in which they find themselves.

It may well be, therefore, that the period of high hopes in educational reform which appear at the moment to have diminished very substantially, may be regained when major groups in society begin once more coherently to demand sets of realizable achievements which involve changing attitudes and techniques and skills held by, particularly, children and young people who could get them through the formal educational system. In such a context it may well be that the particular changes which are called for would become part of a coherent pattern of great significance.

There is, to this observer, a striking feature of the changes of the past third of a century. The initial period of inertia gradually yielded to a sustained period of major change and reform which caught the enthusiasm and imagination of many millions of people, particularly teachers, throughout the world. This has been followed by a period of disillusionment and the shift of the centre of the debate away from educational reform towards consolidation or towards a concentration upon other areas of society which it is felt can be more manageably reformed. There has also been a major shift away from heroic ideological concerns with the total restructuring of the world towards more piecemeal social-engineering attitudes which are concerned with setting defined limits to a particular change, and seeing that the particular change should be achieved efficiently and effectively. This paradoxically has been accompanied by a growing devotion of many millions of people to the purposes of educational reform, and with their own children they are determined to achieve the highest possible standards in the education which they wish to have provided for them. It therefore follows that much of the alleged disillusion with education must be more superficial than real, since when people decide in their own lives or the lives of their own children what they wish to do, that decision reflects perhaps more the reality of their attitudes than do the pronouncements to which they occasionally give vent; the latter express perhaps more the impatience that they have with the slowness of change than with the purposes for which change itself has been accomplished. It follows, therefore, that future reforms will not be applied to a static situation, nor to a situation where the educational system is demoralized, but rather to a system which has changed more rapidly than ever before, and to one where the change has in fact been endorsed by very widely influential sections of the population who find in the lives of their own children the satisfaction with educational achievements which verbally and politically they may deny. Similarly, it will be the case, therefore, that the attempt to accelerate change or to alter its direction may well run into a simultaneous opposition by those who are in fact satisfied by the system but who vocally say they are dissatisfied with it. This also takes place in a context where there has not only been a shift away from education, but a shift away from easy solutions in a wide variety of fields. There has been, for example, a growing disillusion with the therapeutic result of much medical progress, despite the fact that the achievements of modern medicine have been beyond all doubt incomparably greater than could ever have been foreseen by those who invented the modern drugs which are now available to eradicate diseases which have been scourges of mankind throughout recorded history.

Thus, in all walks of life this parallel process of enthusiasm for the actual, together with an antipathy to the theoretical basis of change, seems to be one of the crucial factors which is dominant in the relationships of change in the future to the educational reform and evolution in the past.

It would seem necessary for a realistic look to be taken at the actual achievements of education in the past thirty-five years, both numerically and also in its content; it would seem desirable to study the way in which the reforms and changes have percolated throughout the world, and the contexts in which these changes have been seen. It may well be that such a study, profoundly difficult though it would be, would reveal unexpected successes, and refute much of the alleged pessimism and disillusion which appear to surround the efforts of those who have in fact so successfully achieved the major developments of the past thirty years.

International co-operation for educational reform

by Malcolm S. Adiseshiah

Four general propositions concerning the costs, scope, purpose and essence of educational reform in the 1980s are set forth below by way of prolegomena.

Costs of educational reform

The costs of educational reforms that need to be effected in the eighties are lower than the costs of mis-education and/or non-education which have characterized the sixties and seventies. The Washington, Karachi, Addis Ababa, Santiago and Beirut decisions to expand education unilinearly on traditional or foreign school and university models have, during the sixties and seventies, resulted in mis-education whose costs have been computed in several studies.[1] In terms of educational wastage, unemployability, unemployment and mis-employment alone, these costs have been computed at 50 to 60 per cent of annual educational expenditures. In global terms, around $100,000 million, out of yearly educational outgoings of $275,295 million, may be estimated as the cost of this wastage.[2]

The opportunity costs of the non-education of 800 million illiterate adults in the seventies and 820 million in the eighties have not been computed.[3] However, since these illiterates constitute three-fourths of those of the poverty sector who are destitute, and are about identical in numbers with those defined as unemployed and severely underemployed, the cost of not educating them in terms of lost production and productivity (apart from the non-quantifiable costs of non-participation in the political and cultural life of the country) may be estimated at about the same amount as the costs of mis-education. The costs of the educational reforms and innovations envisaged for the eighties will be

112

only about half the costs of continuing on the current path of mis-education and non-education. Hence, cost is no argument against educational reform.

Scope of educational reform

In planning for the Third Development Decade, development must be conceived of not as unidimensional growth of income or of gross or net product, but as a multidimensional process which includes the natural environment, social relations, education, consumption and welfare geared to the satisfaction of needs, beginning with the basic needs of the poor, who now number 1,200 million. At the same time, the process should humanize man — his ethnic, linguistic and cultural minorities as well as majorities — through satisfying his needs for self-expression and deciding his own destiny. [4]

Concurrently, there must be a restructuring and renovation of the scope of education. In the sixties and seventies, the school and university system was the be-all and the end-all of education. At their best school and university accomplishments fall far short of conservation of the biosphere, mass production, distribution and consumption of goods and the attainment of personal and social well-being based on individual participation and decisions.

Education in the eighties must go beyond the school and university; it should be seen as a continuous function of the total social environment. Its scope and purpose will not be merely personal attainment and acquisition but equally, if not even more, progress of society as a whole. This means that education would be the permanent obligation of the whole of society to every one of its members, who would be involved concurrently in learning, work and production.

The learning locale will not be simply the school and college (of which there are enough for the eighties if they are used for twenty and twenty-four hours a day for 365 days a year instead of the present five hours a day for 180 to 200 days). These will be supplemented by library, laboratory, workshop, animal-house and sports-ground annexes constructed in every co-operative farm and factory, in hospitals and in offices. Educational expenditures in the eighties must be directed to building these educational structures to close the gap between the world of work and the world of learning and so produce a new amalgam: the worker-student, the teacher-learner, who is a direct contributor to development as defined earlier.

Purpose of educational reform

Educational reform in the eighties will be concerned with structuring systems so as to make a start on reducing the intranational and international inequalities which have characterized the educational systems of the previous two decades. Such reduction would be a counterpart and contributor to the scenarios which have been developed by the United Nations to close the development gap — again intranationally and internationally — by the middle of the twenty-first century.

The important Leontief study[5] sets forth various scenarios in line with the aims of the Declaration on the Establishment of a New International Economic Order[6] to reduce the income gap between industrialized and developing countries (12 to 1 in 1970) to 7 to 1 in 2000. The model comprises forty-five sectors of economic activity, eight types of pollutant emissions, and five types of pollution-abatement activities, while in accordance with its terms of reference the study addresses itself to correcting international income inequality. The reduction above depends on the effectiveness of measures to reverse the effects of factors tending to inequalities within each country.

For the educator, two elements are missing from the study: the role of education in the programme of the new international economic order, and the parallel corrections in regard to internal and international educational inequalities. Education receives only indirect, sometimes offhand, references. Under conditions of growth in food and agriculture, the study speaks of an increase of land productivity in the developing countries as calling for substantial increase in 'research and development — especially education of the farmers and the like'.

These incidental and *ad hoc* educational references must be elaborated into educational reform for the eighties within the context of the dimensions of the new international economic order as set forth in the United Nations models. Such reform must concern itself with reversing, from the eighties onwards, the growing educational inequalities of the sixties and seventies between the rich and the poor countries. Four types of such inequalities may be noted: unequal distribution of educational resources, unequal growth rates of educational infrastructures, unequal educational attainments and achievements, and unequal status of educational diplomas and certificates. In the eighties, this inequality gap should begin to be closed so that, in line with the international economic model, it is halved by A.D. 2000 and ended by the twenty-first century.

Equally serious are intranational educational inequalities. Within each country, the distribution of educational facilities between town and country is unequal; the urban industrial school model is imposed on the agro-rural structures of society; education is denied to the majority of adults (ranging from 60 to 90 per cent in the developing countries); educational provision for girls and women is inferior to that provided for boys and men; and the formal school system has a class bias.

This last inequality is particularly serious. Up to 80 per cent of those who complete school and university may come from only the top 20 per cent of society.[7] In this situation educational inequality feeds on and reinforces itself. The educated élite are in a sense like the absentee landlord or a monopoly manufacturer, able to earn an income which, in the current stage of countries' educational development, includes a rental element and so continues and fortifies further the ramparts of inequality. Educational reform within a country must be part of the organization of a dispossessed majority's fight for equality and for participation in all political, economic and educational decisions.

A further facet of educational reform aimed at breaking down inequalities is equalization of educational development among developing countries. The new international economic order will fail if only a small group of developing countries carries out the necessary educational reforms. At the simplest level, if the mass of illiterates, for instance, continues to grow in the majority of developing countries, this will reduce the size of the market for industrial products and slow down the take-off and industrialization of the few who are on the point of economic and educational breakthrough. Thus the eighties must see the start of equalization of educational development between rich and poor countries, among the Third World countries and — somewhat more sharply — within each country.

Essence of educational reform

The essence of educational reform in the eighties will be its response to change. The dominant characteristic of our times is the world's dizzying rate of change, vividly described in part two of the Report of Unesco's International Commission, *Learning to Be*.[8] Internationally the seventies have seen the emergence of the super-powers and the *détente* between them; the renewed Arab-Israel war; the establishment of the Organization of Petroleum Exporting Countries (OPEC) as a decisive political economic force in international relations; the end of the war in Vietnam and that country's development as a socialist State; the breakdown of the Bretton Woods international monetary system and the acceptance for the moment of a state of international monetary chaos, high inflation rates, mounting unemployment and stagnation; and the formulation of the United Nations programme of the new international economic order, the Charter of Economic and Social Rights, the Cocotayya Declaration and the Five-Point United Nations Industrial Development Organization (UNIDO) Programme. Behind these events are advances in science and technology about which the above-mentioned Unesco Report warns that 'this progress in human knowledge and power which has assumed such dizzying speed over the past twenty years is only in its early stages'.[9] The doubling of the world population by the end of the century[10] will have massive effects on food supply, resource use and pollution, education, health and the normal development infra-structure. It will have even more critical effects in the moral and spiritual realms, by doubling our opportunities to help or to hinder, to be honest or to cheat, to play straight or to corrupt, to love or to hate.

One example must suffice of how fundamentally educational reform may need to respond to change. Developing countries regard it as an educational failure and a social blight that retention rates may range from perhaps 40 per cent at Standard V to less than 5 per cent at university level, and they bend their efforts towards increasing such rates. In the industrialized countries by contrast, the view is gaining ground that older children should be encouraged to drop out and return to the education system when they know what they want to do with themselves and for society.

The speed with which events will impose and superimpose them-selves on our world in the eighties is unique. Their nature will not conform to any of our known systems — astral, biological or economic — but be rather a series of systems breaks. Their consequences in the moral and spiritual realms, including the potential of deepening inequalities, extending exploitations and aggravating inequities, demand attention. Change has become the daily diet of our time and society to the point where the only things we can be sure of are that the eighties will not be like the seventies and that education can and will become an in-dependent social variable and, in the Third World, contribute to and reflect a growing and just society.

Groundwork for international co-operation

Two preliminary moves towards effective international co-operation in educational reform would be disaggregation and 'scenario writing'. The former would apply to education, the process, already started, of disaggregated inter-country exchange, analysis and joint action, and extend it to more nearly homogeneous units and sub-units. These may then be brought together through a complex linkage mechanism into a global model. The five traditional Unesco regions need to be broken down further, using as criteria the levels of educational restructuring, renovation and innovation attained in each country.

Educational reform, whether aimed at increased internal productivity, or renovation and restructuring in conformity with the doctrine of lifelong education, or at reducing international and intranational inequalities, or enabling education to emerge as a change agent, needs to be expressed in various alternative 'scenarios' for each group of countries during the eighties and on to the end of the century. Such educational scenarios for each region must be developed as part of overall development scenarios. At least one scenario for each of the subregions should outline reforms to reduce educational inequalities internationally by half by the end of the century. (From that point it should be possible to work back to scenarios for the eighties.) This suggestion breaks away from the projection approach of the last two decades. Instead, goals and objectives are defined in qualitative terms for the end of the eighties or of the century and from these definitions alternative educational reform paths are derived for each sub-unit.

Intra-Third World co-operation

A major missing link in international development and the world educational movement is the almost complete absence of intra-Third World co-operation. This has so far remained at the level of rhetoric or of unexecuted resolutions. The common nature of these countries' problems and solutions—in a politically explosive, socially sensitive and morally and economically inescapable area—reinforces the need for inter and intra-Third World co-operation, particularly in the basic area of programmes to correct intranational inequalities and injustices in the social and educational fields.

The disaggregated groupings and the scenarios developed will provide normal and natural bases for co-operation in educational reform among the groups and subgroups of Third World countries. Such reform calls for an international strategy consisting of a series of concerted reform policies, complementary to the regional economic integration set forth in the United Nations document on the future of the world economy, and envisaging joint utilization of common facilities and networks. Six main areas such a strategy should comprise are: democratization, technology, content, staff training, evaluation and management.

DEMOCRATIZATION OF EDUCATION

Access to education in the eighties will need to be massively increased by:
1. Adult education, especially: literacy for the 820 million illiterates who will form 29 per cent of the adult population; education to combat the unemployment and underemployment of 300 million persons;[11] and education to make a start on integrated rural development.[12]
2. Non-formal education for those who are left out or pushed out of schools or who drop out for reasons of poverty.
3. Compensatory learning for first-generation learners.

EDUCATIONAL TECHNOLOGY

The massive educational clientele of the eighties will call for the fullest inter-country use of electronic instruments and programmed books and work-sheets which will provide individualized and sequential learning sets, by broad groups of similarly placed learners and countries. Radio and television, also collectively organized, can make available to each school, and to growing adult and student numbers, upgraded education and diversified and challenging learning modules confined at present to a few élite institutions.

International co-operation could provide for the collective use of large economic and productive infrastructures based on technologically advanced communication systems, such as direct-reception satellites, banks of audio-visual programmes and co-operative production of teaching and learning materials. International co-operation could also, by a new division of labour, develop educational industries within the subregion and so reduce the large current outflow of resources to pay for imported products such as paper, pencils and pens, textbooks and reference works, audio-visual apparatus, films and video tapes, simple and sophisticated scientific equipment, laboratories and libraries.

CONTENT

Major problems affecting educational content in the eighties calling for international co-operation are the interrelated ones of unemployment, rural development and the values system. Massive unemployment prospects face countries, parents and pupils. Neither formal nor non-formal curricula provide any counter to these prospects, the former being largely irrelevant — as evidenced by falling enrolments — and the latter being functional to various forms of employment and self-employment. Co-operation between countries can help in replacing the current unemployable nature of products of the formal system by setting up agreed norms and methodologies to ensure employability.

As regards rural development, international co-operation can help develop educational models or prototypes which grow out of the indigenous agro-rural society and culture, within the framework of integrated rural development, to replace the present school model, which is derived from an urban industrial complex. Short-term initiatives in higher education might centre around a rural orientation to traditional disciplines, by introducing some relevant applied discipline related to the basic subject and having students apply their theoretical knowledge to rural situations through project work or extension.

Under this system, for instance, the political-science graduate course could include, as ancillaries, community and district development administration; the home-science course, food production, preservation and post-harvest technology, energy utilization and waste recycling; and the chemistry course, soil and water analysis, fertilizer dosage and pesticides.[13] The longer-term task, on which international co-operation can make a start in the eighties, is the development of new specialities — with concepts, frames, methods and methodologies — which arise from the resource endowments and cultural value systems of the Third World societies, in which 80 per cent of the people, 60 to 70 per cent of the work-force and 50 to 60 per cent of GNP are in the rural sector.

STAFF PREPARATION

Staff preparation will face new perspectives in the eighties. The function of the present teacher will become more that of a facilitator than of a pedagogic prodigy; that of a learner who must replace the low amount of specific information and the high degree of personal insight that he or she brings to the task by judgements and hypotheses based on continuously changing, evolving and increasing amounts of information; that of a seer who prepares himself or herself and other learners for the unknown future, rather than continuing to be a purveyor of the glorious past. The future 'tender' must close the gap between the apparent curriculum, with its rhetoric about objectivity, truth, equality, human rights and peace, and the concealed curriculum, buttressing the *status quo*, inequalities, elitism and various forms of personal and social corruption and violence.

Staff preparation to meet such future demands calls both for national leadership and for inter-country co-operation. This latter may be particularly important in higher education. In the eighties, university and college teachers will be massive in numbers and demanding in their need to respond to the explosive rate at which knowledge and information will be developing: yet at present they receive no professional preparation.

EVALUATION AND REWARDS

Present examination systems, which result in education not for learning but to pass examinations, need wide-ranging reform, leading to their replacement by evaluation systems which can become tools for learning and self-learning along paths to achievements and goals, material and intellectual, individual and social. Furthermore, the present systems' appendages of classifications, certificates and diplomas need replacing by insignia which will not, as they are now, be susceptible to being linked to non-rational and unsocial rewards, which make for growing equalities both within and between countries and to which the brain drain is not unrelated. There is perhaps no more urgent area for international co-operation than such replacements.

MANAGEMENT AND FINANCE

In educational management, international co-operation (especially subregional) should aim at evolving means of reconciling two divergent requisites. These are (a) centralized policies and strategies stemming from national or subregional aims and (b) local learning autonomy suited to the size of the educational enterprise and to the specific demands of the individual learner, the local learning unit and the district.

Decentralized and reformed education systems are costly. Hence, each country should make a fearless technical, managerial and financial audit of the manner in which existing resources—financial, material and human—are being used or misused within its educational system. Experience suggests there may well be excessive continuing commitments, much 'dead wood', traditions to the effect that change will entail increased expenditures, and potential for significant savings—of the order, perhaps, of 20 per cent of current expenditures—which could, without educational detriment, be made available for reform and innovation programmes. International co-operation, at the subregional level, might help to reveal such hidden resources and establish guidelines for their release and use.[14]

Nevertheless a regular flow of funds to finance educational reforms will depend mainly on successfully countering the balance of payments deficits of the non-oil-producing developing countries, estimated in the Leontief Model rather conservatively at U.S.$18,000 million in 1980 and reaching U.S.$80,000 million by the end of the decade.[15] A precondition for the reforms sketched above for the eighties will be the change in the world economic order envisaged in the Leontief document. This would involve: developing countries decreasing imports and increasing exports; the reduction of industrialized countries' tariff and non-tariff barriers; and lessening the developing world's outflow of 15 per cent of GDP—or three-fifths of export earnings—arising from foreign investments in it.

NOTES

1. Government of Tamil Nadu, India. *Report of the Education Finance Committee*. p. 3, 20, Madras, 1976; ILO, *Matching Employment Opportunities and Expectations: a Programme of Action for Ceylon*, Geneva, 1971; G. Watson, *Change in School Systems*, Washington, NEA, 1967; E. Faure *et al.*, *Learning to Be: the World of Education Today and Tomorrow*, p. 40–8, Paris/London, Unesco/Harrap, 1972.
2. *Unesco Statistical Yearbook*, p. 69–70, Paris, 1975.
3. Unesco, *Literacy 1969–71; Progress Achieved in Literacy Throughout the World*, Paris, 1972, 128 p.; H. Reiff, *The Role of Educational Planning in Situations of Unemployment*, Paris, 1976, 23 p.
4. P. A. Samuelson, *Economic*, p. 195–7, New York, McGraw-Hill, 1973; M. S. Adiseshiah, *Let My Country Awake*, Paris, Unesco, 1970, 214 p.; Dag Hammarskjöld Foundation, *What Now: Another Development*, Uppsala, 1975, 128 p.
5. United Nations, *The Future of the World Economy* (by W. Leontief), p. 32, New York, 1976.
6. United Nations, *General Assembly Resolution 3201 (S-VI)*, New York, 1 May 1974.
7. NCERT, *Field Studies in the Sociology of Education*, New Delhi, 1971.
8. Faure, op. cit., p. 87–160.
9. Ibid., p. 90.
10. Using the medium United Nations demographic projections.
11. ILO, *Employment Growth and Basic Needs, a One-World Problem*, Geneva, 1976.
12. Unesco, *Education in a Rural Environment*, Paris, 1974, 64 p.; Unesco, *Economic Development and the Programming of Rural Education*, Paris, 1966, 59 p.; Government of India, *A Programme of Integrated Rural Development*, New Delhi, 1976, 22 p.; Unesco/UNDP, *The Experimental World Literacy Programme: a Critical Assessment*, Paris, 198 p.
13. Malcolm S. Adiseshiah, *The University in 1975*, p. 36, 44, Madras, 1976.
14. Government of Tamil Nadu, *Report of the Education Finance Commission*, Madras, 1975, 123 p.
15. United Nations, *The Future of the World Economy*, p. 22–9, New York, 1976.

Part Three   # Case studies

The modernization of education in an advanced socialist society: the example of Poland

by Stanislav Kaczor

Dynamics of the Polish reform

The preparation and application of the reform of the educational system in the Polish People's Republic are linked with the country's social, economic and cultural development. They also constitute a response to society's educational aspirations — to new ambitions which are finding more and more forceful expression.

Under the new programmes, the introduction of compulsory secondary education was scheduled for the beginning of the 1978–79 school year. This historic reform arises partly from the progress made in Poland in the economic, educational and cultural spheres, and partly from the advances made in contemporary teaching theory and practice throughout the world.

In 1973,[1] the Commission on National Education and the Diet promulgated a decree laying down the lines of reform of the educational system. The Sixth Congress of the Polish Unified Workers' Party, analysing the trends in this field, indicated that a distinction should be made between the effects on education of modernization in all its forms, on the one hand, and the influence on the educational system of current organizing and programming techniques, on the other. The aim was to bring education into line with the needs of an advanced socialist society in the year 2000.

The Ministry of Education's activities for the years 1972–75 (and 1976–80) aimed to secure the same education for everybody at the highest possible level. Thus, compulsory education was established from infant school level to the completion of secondary education. This decision was in line with the present situation, as 95 per cent of teenagers are now pursuing their studies in high school. A number of measures were taken in this connection, namely:

Stepping up school attendance figures in infant schools, the end in view
being universal education for all children reaching the age of 6
during the 1977–78 school year;

Creation, organization and equipment of complete schools for the
people, to replace the badly organized and widely dispersed village
schools, involving the institution of a school bussing network;

Modernization of the structure, content, methods and techniques of
education, entailing improved school equipment and a greater
effort in terms of school buildings (erection, modernization,
reconstruction);

Raising the standard of teachers' education, resulting in a higher
proportion of university graduates or the equivalent;

Updating the nomenclature of professional specializations and the
corresponding training programmes to secure a better adjustment
to the needs of a modern economy.

To carry out these reforms, the educational authorities considered the
findings of research undertaken in centres under their control, or included in the activities of the higher schools and the scientific institutes of
the Polish Academy of Science.

Furthermore, in 1971, on the initiative of the Political Bureau of the
Central Committee of the Polish Unified Workers' Party, a Committee of
Experts was set up to prepare a report on education in the State. The
report was compiled and published in 1973. On many points, its
recommendations converge with those of *Learning to Be*,[2] compiled at
roughly the same period by a group of eminent experts chaired by
M. Edgar Faure.

To create auspicious conditions for correctly defining the orientations of the future system, in 1972 the Praesidium of the Government
founded the Institute of Pedagogic Research, Institute of Research on
Young Age Groups, Teacher Training Institute, Vocational Training
Institute and School Curricula Institute.

One important step for national education was the adoption by the
Second Polish Science Congress of a motion put forward by the Minister
of Education concerning the implementation of a national plan for
research on this key problem. The plan was called 'Modernization of the
Educational System in an Advanced Socialist Society'. Thousands of
researchers drawn from nearly all the Polish universities and from several
specialized institutes made an intensive study of this problem. Their first
research findings are already contributing to pedagogical development.

Main guidelines and methods of reform

Apart from the scholastic commitment, the chief features of the educational reform now in preparation are as follows:

Importance attached to lifelong training.

Opportunity for each individual to pursue his studies up to higher level.

Flexibility of the content of education and of teaching methods.

Recognition of the diversity of sources of knowledge and the means of access to them.

Greater emphasis in school on the socio-economic milieu.

Facilities granted for interdisciplinary studies.

Assessment of the interaction between knowledge and professional experience for lifelong education.

Each of these points will be dealt with in greater detail below.

Any modern system of education has to allot great importance to lifelong education for the acquisition of a new branch of knowledge or a new skill, or for the practical application of knowledge previously acquired. During the last few years, the rapid progress of science and technology has increased its importance, particularly in the professional field. The problem of further vocational training had ceased to be a 'matter for the individual' and had become one condition of the country's socio-economic progress, economic growth and cultural development. At present, the object of lifelong education in Poland is the fulfilment of the individual, over and above any considerations relating to occupational needs or the length of working life.

The Symposium on the School and Lifelong Education held at Warsaw in 1974 (attended by representatives of Unesco), investigated the problems involved in the concept and process of lifelong education. Poland is applying both the recommendations contained in the symposium publications and those of the eighteenth session of the Unesco General Conference, in which the Director-General is invited to give particular attention to the programme activities concerned with the following problems:

(i) the consequences of the principle of lifelong education for the structure, organization, curricula and methods of formal and non-formal education;

(ii) the tasks of higher education in the context of lifelong education;

(iii) the forms of organization, programmes and methods of the education offered to the adult throughout his life and while he pursues an occupation, bearing in mind in particular the role of unions and firms;

(iv) the role of the mass media (publishing, radio, television, etc.) in the lifelong education process. [3]

Opportunity for each individual to pursue his or her studies in higher education is a fundamental aim of the new system. Thus, access to the universities is also possible for non-students. The question is what sort of action should be initiated to ensure that a pupil who has completed his or her secondary studies can continue his or her education, be trained for life and work in a socialist society, and benefit from the various forms of further training in his branch of knowledge or qualifications. A selection is now being prepared of the contents of secondary education, a selection spotlighting basic knowledge concerning Man, culture, nature and society. However, the studies and experiments are not restricted to the content of education. A secondary-level pupil has to 'learn to learn' — hence the necessity of developing the intellectual and manual capacities on independent, creative lines.

In this connection, mention should be made of the flexibility of the content of education and the teaching methods. Pupils who have not been successful in certain types of studies taught on specific lines can choose other forms to suit themselves, possibly outside working hours in some educational establishment, or by correspondence. Such flexibility is only possible thanks to a system of equivalences.

One guiding principle of the new system of education is the recognition of the diversity of sources and roads leading to knowledge. This implies that knowledge and skills acquired after school education should be taken into consideration, especially vocational training or further training; so should the part played by the firm and the unions, not only in the further training needed to raise productivity but also, more and more, in the cultural sphere. In the case of agriculture, pride of place in training is allotted to instruction by radio or television, supplemented by practical work in the laboratories of the local schools of agriculture.

In Poland, the principle of linking education to the socio-economic milieu has been developed in theory and in practice, whether it is planned for children, adolescents or adults. For instance, growing importance is attached to a common educational approach in schools and firms, in the spheres of agriculture, industry, services or co-operatives. Thus the Unesco recommendations in *Learning to Be* are applied:

Efforts must be made to bridge the gap, still found in all too many cases, between educational establishments and business companies . . . for the latter constitute a key element in the over-all education system. Their role should not be limited to training workers, but extended so far as possible to training technicians and researchers.[4]

Poland considers that linking education to the socio-economic milieu involves disinterested co-operation between the entities concerned. each having equal rights and obligations; such co-operation should be established according to each party's possibilities. This conception, already introduced in the education of children, adolescents and adults, promotes mutual assistance, international co-operation and a high regard for peace. It is in line with the principles of a socialist society.

Another aspect of the reform provides for the possibility of inter-disciplinary education. This reconciles the needs of the economy and the required conditions for the safeguard of culture. It enables sound knowledge to be acquired in two broad fields: mathematical and biological, and social and humanist. Individual specializations can be built on this foundation.

Not only are the sciences being developed in Poland; steps are also being taken for their wider dissemination, with the result that research findings are more frequently geared to practical application. In linking theory and practice, science and technology, it is often necessary to break down the academic partitioning of scientific specialities, or in a word, to adopt an interdisciplinary approach.

Giving due weight to the link between education and the pursuit of the occupation concerned is just as important for the enrichment of the personality as for the improvement of professional skill.

The adoption of this principle satisfies two needs of society. One is the continuous development of science and technology, involving changes in the process of production of material goods and in everyday life. No improvement in life-style can be secured without some addition to and modification of the required qualifications. However, this is only one aspect of the problem. The other need, no less important, is bound up with the innate urge of every human being to achieve the fulfilment of his or her personality. Any individuals, adopting the rhythm, approach and content which suits them, can augment simultaneously their culture and their competence, whether they remain in the same profession or job, or wish to change them. The application of this principle is found to involve four functions: adaptation, equalization, renovation and reconstruction.

According to N. T. Nowacki, the adaptation function should help the individual to prepare to meet the demands of his job. The equalization function serves to complete his stock of knowledge to the extent required at the different professional levels. The renovation func-tion responds to changes in theory and practice. Lastly, the recon-struction function yields the elements of personal creation by the individuals concerned, who work while contributing to their own improvement. A similar conception is to be found in a Unesco publica-tion. Although the functions listed there relate to teachers, their general character is consistent with the above, namely, (1) the adaptation function, which helps a candidate to train for his or her profession, (2) the recycling function, which improves upon the instruction already acquired by knowledge of new scientific theories, (3) the specialization function, enabling certain people to prepare to undertake new responsibilities, including that of management, (4) the innovation function, which paves the way for the implementation of gradual changes in the job concerned, or in the firm as a whole.

The hub of reform: compulsory secondary-school education

In accordance with the 1973 Decree mentioned above, the basis of a reformed system of national education will be compulsory secondary-school education. The principles governing the organization and curricula of such schools have been worked out by a team of theoreticians and experts made up of the most highly qualified people from scientific circles and from educational establishments of all categories. The projects concerning the content of education were included in the curricula for the respective subjects, and discussed by representatives of all concerned. At national level, a vast exchange of views was published in the columns of the daily press, the socio-cultural reviews and the specialized journals. Tens of thousands of teachers, representatives of scientific circles, unions and youth organizations, etc., put forward their opinions in the course of the discussion. Consequently, a series of projects concerning the content of education in the compulsory secondary schools is at present being applied experimentally in schools belonging to different milieux. These trials will enable a preliminary evaluation to be made for the improvement of curricula.

The most important elements in the content of education in the compulsory secondary schools will be the mother tongue and mathematics. At the same time, all didactic and educational activity will be aimed at the development of every aspect of the individual's personality, and at preparing the students for life and work in a socialist society. This will be achieved through a study of the technical subjects required for work organized near the school, in the school itself, and in industrial or agricultural enterprises. The aim is to help young people to choose a profession which will bring them satisfaction. Much time will be devoted to 'learning to learn' independently. To this end, motivations favourable to instruction will be introduced, as well as training in self-management.

The compulsory secondary school will not be equivalent to a vocational school, but it will dispense education geared to working life. This will facilitate subsequent vocational guidance and training, and will augment the individual's chances of finding satisfaction in the exercise of his profession.

The compulsory secondary school will thus serve as a basis for the organization of vocational schools training executives for the various branches of the national economy, and for several cultural spheres. The aims of education and training in these schools will be as follows:

To provide the students with general occupational knowledge and some specialization essential for the exercise of their future occupation, as well as for subsequent further training in their branch of employment.

To impart the know-how and manual skill essential to the exercise of an occupation in the branch concerned.

To develop proper ideological and moral attitudes, qualities essential for social relations, and ability to co-operate at the place of work.

Higher education will also be reformed in accordance with the needs of society. The same will apply to non-school education, which forms an integral part of the national educational system.

The above elements served as a basis for the studies required for the construction of a new educational model in Poland. Arising from analysis of the development trends in the country as a whole, they also correspond to the contemporary trends in the development of education throughout the world, and are in line with progress in pedagogics and other educational sciences.

NOTES

1. The 200th anniversary of the creation of the first Ministry of Education in Europe.
2. E. Faure et al., *Learning to Be: the World of Education Today and Tomorrow*, Paris/London, Unesco/Harrap, 1972.
3. Extract from the Records of the General Conference, Eighteenth session, Paris, 17 October to 23 November 1974, *Resolutions*, Vol. 1, p. 24, Paris, Unesco, 1974.
4. Faure, op. cit., p. 198.

Educational reform and technological innovation: the Ivory Coast experiment

by A. N'Guessan Konan-Daure

Human, political and geographical context of the Ivory Coast

The Ivory Coast covers an area of 322,000 square kilometres. The comparative simplicity of the country's relief is in contrast with its extreme human diversity (forty-four ethnic groups), the result of a large number of migratory currents some of which still survive and which have produced four main linguistic groups. Religions include Christian, Moslem and animist. The Ivory Coast was established as a modern State and proclaimed an independent republic on 7 August 1960. It adopted its first constitution in the same year, based on the principles of democracy and human rights and instituting a presidential regime with a National Assembly elected by universal suffrage, an Economic and Social Council, a Supreme Court and a High Court of Justice. From the administrative point of view, the country is divided into departments, sub-prefectures and communes. In 1975 the population numbered 6,673,000.

Economic and social context

The Ivory Coast economy, based on a combination of economic liberalism and State capitalism, has, since 1960, shown almost constant growth thanks to the development of agriculture and steady industrialization. Disparities still exist, especially between urban centres and rural areas and between savanna and forest regions. The 'Plan for an Ivory Coast Society' which inspired the Five-Year Plan for economic, social and cultural development over the period 1976–80 calls for a number of fundamental changes, i.e. transformation of agriculture and rural life; the building up of a diversified industry strong in exports; an active adjustment of the balance between regions; changes in the civil service; speeding up of 'Ivorization'; the search for a new cultural synthesis; and reform of the educational system.

The educational system

The traditional educational system, rooted in the distant past of the societies and cultures of pre-colonial Ivory Coast, is still very much alive in rural areas, where various structures provide for the handing down from one generation to another of traditional forms of knowledge and know-how. In its early days, the educational system was much influenced by colonial policy and tended towards cultural assimilation, excessive emphasis on practical skills, and elitism. Independence made quantitative development possible at all levels; however, skilled personnel for development could not be trained to meet the needs of the country's agricultural and industrial growth, and young people were not integrated into their socio-cultural environment, especially in rural areas.

Although much money was spent on the educational system, it was no longer an efficient instrument of national development. Traditional education, seen from this point of view, showed a very high drop-out rate. A survey conducted in 1965 showed that out of every 1,000 children who had started school in 1959/60, only 297 had reached the fifth year of schooling. The cost of education was consequently high. In 1965, a pupil costing 13,200 CFA* francs per annum (i.e. 79,200 CFA francs over six years) in fact cost the country 219,000 CFA francs (2·7 times more) because of the large wastage due to the poor quality of the education offered. Drop-outs aside, the selection which takes place at the various levels means that every year, 25 to 30 per cent of the pupils are required to repeat the first five levels. The figure rises to 52 per cent in the final year, when pupils hang on in the hope of acquiring the leaving certificate and above all of gaining admission into secondary education. Teachers are not only insufficient in numbers, but often possess only a low level of qualification. Their efficiency is further impaired by a system of teaching which does not correspond to the Ivory Coast environment as it really is. Finally, school attendance rates vary very much, showing great disparities between the regions (they ranged from 13·6 per cent to 90·2 per cent in 1971/72). Similarly, teachers' qualifications left much to be desired.

---

*CFA: Communauté Financière Africaine.

Television and the new education policy

The 1967–70 plan for the Ivory Coast had brought out the weaknesses of traditional education and the difficulty of spreading fundamental education widely. The 1971–75 plan said that 'economic and social development should be subtended by a policy aiming at the promotion and training of human resources'. A system therefore had to be found which made it possible to reach the maximum number of pupils and to train capable teachers. Audio-visual methods make it possible to broadcast visual and oral models which are educationally efficient. Their use brings about a unification of teaching methods and gives teachers an opportunity of learning from highly qualified specialists. The use of television makes teaching more efficient through a technological centralization which enables a comparatively small staff of experts to back up teachers who are insufficiently qualified or not yet familiar with new teaching techniques. It thus also continues and reinforces the initial and in-service training of teachers.

Thus the fashioning of the educational message, which used to lie in the hands of each teacher alone in his classroom, is now concentrated in the hands of a planning and production team possessing all the necessary skills. To prevent this division of labour from being an obstacle to the necessary educational unity, each of the individuals involved must know that his or her personal effort forms part of the general process. This leads to the psychological problem of the role and function of the teacher in television teaching, and consequently the questions of class organization, teaching aids, and evaluation. They will be examined later. The use of television also makes it possible to unify content and give the same high-quality instruction to both rural and urban schools, thus bringing about a better balance in the distribution of educational facilities; to make immediately available, and bring up to date quickly and permanently, the findings of educational research; to make visually available materials normally inaccessible to both teachers and pupils, thus opening a window on the world and widening the children's field of experience; to teach children how to receive and understand a message in sound and picture form, which is an important source of information and of culture; to encourage inter-regional exchanges between inhabitants of different regions of the Ivory Coast, thus contributing to the development of a common culture and enabling education to act as a promoter of national unity; to motivate and liberate children so that they can express themselves more spontaneously; and to change the traditional relationship between teacher and pupil which to a large extent conditions the meaning of education.

Television can never be a substitute for the teacher but it supports his efforts by programmes which help to liven the minds of his pupils, to make them aware, motivate and inform them, and which aid in the work of synthesis and evaluation. Programmes employ different methods according to the end they have in view.

The compulsive aspect of the message makes it possible for active and adapted education to affect the whole environment and thus help to bring about a kind of osmosis between the various milieux. In the early years, however, programmes aimed chiefly at arousing interest and imparting knowledge. They have gradually become less compulsive, and now help to reinforce learning and promote intellectual synthesis. They also act as a stimulus to intellectual activity, the necessary condition of any profitable teaching. In the older classes, television programmes play a supplementary role in informing the children about facts and con-ditions outside their immediate environment. Some innovative programmes also encourage the children to use their own initiative.

Significance of introducing educational technology into primary education, and implications for teacher training

While television plays an important part in teaching and is irreplaceable as a means of dissemination and renovation, it is not the only resource available. However, its compulsiveness has created a point of no return in the Ivory Coast, and this has made it easier to combat the inevitable resistance to innovation which often gets the better of experimental trends which are too limited.

Television has not only accelerated the process of education; it has also made necessary a radical overhaul of the educational system. It is not a question of turning the teacher into a robot, or a mere usher, present just to press the buttons, but rather of turning someone who was, not so long ago, simply an instructor into an educator with a technical aid at his disposal which rehabilitates his whole profession. An educator who had a new instrument at his disposal but who had had no more than a traditional education himself might have found himself in difficulties, unable to use the powerful new medium sensibly. It became necessary therefore to adapt the system of training to take account of these new professional requirements.

An examination of the new situation revealed: a new weighting among the usual functions of the teacher; the emergence of new func-tions altogether; the need to relate the new situation to a systematic overhaul of the system of teacher training.

The use of a combination of many media profoundly modified the traditional linear relationship between teacher and pupil, replacing it with a triangular relationship between teacher, media and pupils. But however great the contribution that television can make, it is the responsibility of the teacher in his classroom to adjust the collective information of the television message to the needs and abilities of each pupil and each group, and to reconcile the necessity for a certain degree of planned teaching with an appeal to the children's spontaneity and creativity.

The story of a challenge

In 1967, with the object of improving fundamental education, of remedying the defects inherent in traditional education, and of democratizing the educational system, the government undertook research into the quickest and most efficient ways of bringing these changes about. This research, which formed part of the country's cultural development planning, already stressed the possibility of using television for educational purposes for the benefit of both young people and adults.

In 1968, after these studies had been examined, it was decided to employ the means made available by modern technology in the service of education. These included television, for which the Ivory Coast already possessed an infrastructure. The planning of the Programme for Television Education (PETV) covers the period up to 1980.

In 1969, the television education complex (CETV), which combines both production and training activities, was set up in Bouaké, and the first mixed teams (of nationals and expatriates) started work at the École Normale d'Instituteurs (ENI) (Teacher Training College) and the Centre de Production.

In 1972, simultaneously with the extension of broadcasting to the second year of primary education, a multi-media programme (press, radio and television) for the re-training of all practising teachers was begun. It continued until 1975.

In 1973, in accordance with the initial plan, the facilities of the PETV were made available for adult education, in collaboration with the national radio and television network (RTI) and the technical ministries concerned. The first experimental broadcasts were made. In the same year, the data-processing unit was set up to solve the problems presented by the industrial dimension the project had acquired. In 1975, the unit became the department for the organization of educational management.

In 1974, the training of the technical and art technician staff of the PETV entered a new phase with the creation at the Bouaké complex of an 'in-house' training unit, the Section for Specialization in Educational Technology (which in 1977 became the Centre for Specialization in the Technology of Education). At the same time, harmonization of the training provided by the different establishments was gradually completed.

In 1975, as planned, the 'frontal' re-training of teachers begun in 1972 was completed, and was replaced by a system of continuous training, the 'École Normale Permanente'. A section was established at the Teacher Training College to train teachers for educational organization and training centres. Syllabuses and methods of television teaching were extended to the first year of primary education throughout the country, whether or not the classes had television receivers.

In 1976, the Secretary of State's office became the Ministry of Primary and Television Education. A National Centre for the Permanent Training of Educational Staff was set up in Bouaké. Not every eventuality could be foreseen in 1968, and the logic of development has required the constant updating of the PETV so that it can achieve its aims.

The Television Education Programme and the aims of the educational system

The law on educational reform lays upon

institutions responsible for education, teaching and vocational training, the task of developing a spirit of initiative and action, providing education and training based on national development aims, and achieving the social and cultural integration of the Ivory Coast's citizens into the national community and into the main currents of world civilization. (Article 2)

The aim of general education is

to provide a scientific, technological, literary, artistic, physical and sporting education enabling pupils and students to understand the phenomena of the modern world and to adapt themselves to the continual evolution of technology so as to be able to control the environment in which they have to live. (Article 11)

Basic education, which covers the first nine school years and is preceded by one year of pre-school instruction, must be

responsive to the social and cultural realities of the country. Its aim is the awakening of the personality, the formation of a scientific spirit, and the development of thought and knowledge. It must lay particular stress on: basic subjects (French, arithmetic, science, technology, languages); the introduction to civic and practical life; physical activities and sport; relationship to the cultural heritage; relationships with the environment and with town and country. (Article 15)

It must provide a 'close connection between manual and practical work on the one hand and intellectual work on the other' (Article 16).

The law reforming the whole of the Ivory Coast educational system was passed in 1977, six years after the launching of the Television Education Programme. Nevertheless, the objectives assigned to the PETV are largely the same as those for the first five years of basic education as instituted by the reform. This is not surprising, since the work of the National Commission for Educational Reform and the successive updatings of the PETV have kept pace with each other since 1971. This emerges clearly from a study of the different stages which led to the adoption of the law on educational reform:

May and August 1971. Meetings between the President, the Political Bureau and the teachers brought out the inadequacies of the current educational system in relation to the real needs of the Ivory Coast.

August 1972. In a message to the nation, the President sounded the alarm as follows: 'Despite the efforts made so far, especially in the field of television education, it is only wise to acknowledge that our educational system is too costly for the results it produces, and has developed in a way unrelated to our economic growth rather than contributing to it. As no provision was made before now for an adequate link between the function of production and the function of training, our educational system still fails to meet the most urgent needs of a developing African country like our own'. The National Commission for Educational Reform (CNRE) was set up officially by the Political Bureau at the President's request.

21 December 1972. In a letter to the Minister for Foreign Affairs, who was also chairman of the CNRE, the President of the Republic defined the commission's terms of reference. It was to 'try to prepare a reform which will enable every child of the Ivory Coast to have a trade at his fingertips when he leaves school, and which will make it possible to improve both the level and the quality of education'.

30 July 1974. The CNRE report was submitted to the President of the Republic. It included 'a critical account of the present education system', a proposal for a 'new educational system for the Ivory Coast', and the 'preliminary draft of a general law on educational reform'.

16 August 1977. The National Assembly adopted the law on educational reform.

Content and methods of the new primary education

In addition to the introduction of television, which modifies traditional classroom relationships and establishes new ones, the educational renewal brought about by the PETV led to: the teaching of French as an instrument of communication and exchange which, during the first few years at school, lays special stress on oral expression; priority being given to modern mathematics and logic; the introduction of scientific and pre-technological education, which makes the children familiar with handling things and experimenting, thus linking knowledge of the environment with the mental operations on which rational thought is based; and great importance being accorded to activities relating to self-expression and creativeness (the plastic arts, music, poetry, etc.), linked to a knowledge of African and Ivory Coast culture and the practice of traditional craft techniques.

The educational renewal has not only brought about changes in content but has also introduced new working methods and new approaches to teaching. These include the active participation of the children themselves, allowing a large proportion of the work to be carried out in small groups, appealing to the child's spontaneity, developing the power to wonder and ask questions (hitherto often stifled by authoritarian attitudes), and encouraging independence, responsibility, creativeness, etc.

The pupils completing the television primary course are thus of a different type from those moulded by traditional methods. Not only have they learned certain new subjects, but also and above all, their behaviour both inside and outside the classroom is different.

The educational renewal introduced by the PETV bases its aims on two main principles: first, that children should be helped to be independent and responsible, and second, that education should be geared both to the environment and to the media. This has led to the adoption of methods which rely on stimulation and dialogue rather than explanation by the teacher.

Training of staff to carry out the renewal

Since 1966, teachers and assistant teachers have been trained in the ten educational development and training centres (CAFOP) which have capacity for about 2,000 trainees. Training to prepare assistant teachers for promotion is given at the Teacher Training College in Bouaké.

Inspectors of primary education and CAFOP teachers receive training at the higher Teacher Training College in Abidjan. This is at present in the throes of reform, the aim being to produce inspectors who are not mere supervisors, but active organizers and managers of an educational system employing modern techniques of communication.

Specialist staff are trained at the Centre for Specialization in the Technology of Education in Bouaké, and they go on for further training to the teaching studio of the RTI, or abroad.

Reorganization and co-ordination of training activities

During 1976–77, the desire to achieve closer co-ordination of training activities and to integrate initial with in-service training led to the reorganization of this sector. The Sous-Direction de la Formation Initiale et Continue (Sub-Directorate for Initial and In-Service Training) was transferred to Abidjan under the authority of the Direction de l'Enseignement du Premier Degré (Direction des Écoles Primaires et des Centres de Formation) (Directorate for First-Level Training — Directorate for Primary Schools and Training Centres).

The way for this reorganization had been paved by the following measures during 1976–77:

The foundation of a National Centre for the Permanent Training of Educational Staff (CNFP), combining the different departments existing in Bouaké: central audio-visual department, department for co-ordination of training in the CAFOPs, resource centre for self-education and the re-training department.

The ENI-CAFOP ensemble became an independent establishment on a par with other initial-training establishments.

The CNFP was entrusted with: the permanent training of executive and organizational staff; the permanent training, either on the spot or at a distance, of teaching staff, in close co-ordination with the CAFOPs; giving support to initial-training activities through application of the methods and techniques of self-education and the use of audio-visual methods; and helping to supply everyone in the educational system with general and educational information.

In addition to organizing regular courses for executive staff (inspectors, educational advisers, head teachers, instructors at re-training centres) and specialist staff (evaluators, documentalists, organizers of out-of-school activities), the CNFP broadcasts television and radio programmes for teachers and publishes L'École permanente (Lifelong School), a weekly pull-out inserted in the Party newspaper to which all teachers subscribe.

When the government adopted the aims and plans of the PETV in 1968, the need became apparent for the 'Ivorization' of all the operating staff concerned, since the complete takeover of the television system implied laying stress on the quality and skill of staff to be trained or given further training.

The 'Ivorization' of the various categories of staff involved in the development of the PETV is to be continued and speeded up during the five-year period 1976–80.

Multi-media production: the television education complex (CETV)

Multi-media packages (broadcasts and written materials for pupils and teachers) are planned, prepared and produced by the CETV at Bouaké, which is also responsible for sending out both broadcasts and texts. It has its own studios and laboratories and a powerful rotary press, one of the biggest in West Africa. The expert staff includes directors, editors, producers, graphic artists, photographers, and various technicians specialized in sound-recording, cutting, camera work, film developing, making television films, radio and television engineering, video maintenance, printing, etc.

The CETV is also in charge of the maintenance of the closed-circuit television system with which all CAFOPs are equipped. It works in close collaboration with the CNFP and the CSTE (the Centre de Spécialisation en Technologie de l'Éducation) in the training of educational, technical and art technician staff.

Out-of-school educational television

In May 1973, teachers were asked for the first time to make the television classrooms available to adults, in the evenings, for educational broadcasts. The subjects dealt with included problems of health, domestic hygiene, stock-raising, co-operatives and management, agricultural loans, agriculture, etc. At the same time, experiments were undertaken to find ways of organizing discussion among the groups of adults brought together in the television classes by teachers and by local officers of the development services. There are two weekly peak-hour programmes in French, *Télé pour Tous* (Television for Everyone), presented in such a way that group organizers can pass on the oral content in the language of the region concerned.

Maintenance of receivers

Receivers are made to meet the special requirements of education. A contract has been signed with a specially created Ivory Coast company, the Compagnie Africaine de Télévision (CATEL), which is in charge of installing receivers and making regular checks on them. The sets made for the PETV have a box behind them in which are all the principal electronic components, so that in the event of a breakdown, all the regular servicing officer need do is replace the box. Any necessary repairs are carried out at a central workshop in Abidjan. Although they carry out repairs, the servicing officers try to prevent breakdowns, which is why they visit the schools systematically. Some sets (20 per cent) work on electricity, others on alkaline batteries with a life of 2,000 hours (roughly equivalent to two school years).

Educational management in the PETV

One of the things clearly shown by the experience of the preparatory year before the PETV was launched and of the first two years of its functioning was the need for strict control over the various parts of the system. The organization and the management methods are based on the industrial model. A central department for the organization of educational management is responsible for working out a system of internal information for the Ministry of Primary and Television Education, and for using the resulting data to establish a method of management applied in terms of separate objectives. The ultimate aim is to find the best way of managing available resources, and the department is also at the disposal of the Ministry of National Education.

Evaluation

In order to check how effective radio and television broadcasts are, audience research 'from life' among both pupils and teachers is called for. Such feedback becomes an absolute necessity in the case of a programme being transmitted for the first time. To obtain immediate results among pupils or teachers, there obviously has to be some flexibility in the transmission timetables, and this necessitates close collaboration between evaluators and producers from the time the programmes are first planned.

Medium-term evaluation is geared towards pupils and consists of periodically checking the quality of what they learn. The results may be used by teachers to check their pupils' progress and the effectiveness of their own work. They may also be used as a means of communication with parents. The authorities, too, may use them as a basis for making decisions. Those in charge of production may take them into account when planning future schedules. This type of evaluation should tend towards a formative appraisal whereby the teacher assumes responsibility for assessing his pupils, using instruments more sophisticated than any traditional form of interrogation can be.

The kind of evaluation with which we are concerned here seeks to answer the question, what proportion of what is taught is really assimilated by what proportion of the school population involved?

It takes time to develop ways and means of arriving at such evaluations and three years are needed at every level. The first year is devoted to analysing classroom material (books and broadcasts), and also includes a preliminary test. The second year includes a dry run based on a more or less representative sample. In the third year comes a final test based on a representative sample.

Under an agreement between the Ivory Coast and Belgium, the evaluation service carries out its appraisals in collaboration with the laboratory for experimental education in Liège. Studies have been carried out in various fields, including teachers' attitudes, activities promoting self-expression and creativity, the re-training of teachers, the evaluation of effectiveness in mathematics teaching, the evaluation of television pupils in the sixth grade, aspects of cognitive development, results achieved with beginners in reading, language and mathematics, and so on. Between March 1974 and October 1977, six courses were organized, attended by 300 evaluation officers (inspectors, educational advisers, and CETV producers), and ten students underwent long-term training at the laboratory in Liège. Stanford University, with the aid of the United States Agency for International Development (USAID), collaborates in the evaluation of out-of-school education. Economic evaluation is carried out in co-operation with the Department for the Organization of Educational Management.

Expansion

Numbers have risen from 447 classes with a total of 20,500 pupils in 1971/72 to 10,063 classes with a total of 425,289 pupils in 1977/78, i.e. the number of pupils increased twenty-one times. In the first year of primary schooling, there are about 77 per cent television pupils; the rest are 'traditional' pupils. The total number of children receiving education (both traditional and television) rose from 415,000 in

1971/72, when the PETV started, to 672,000 in 1977/78, while the number of teachers undergoing training rose from 800 in 1968/69 to about 2,000 in 1977/78, a mean annual increase of 8·4 and 10·8 per cent respectively.

Improvement of internal efficiency

Among the main objects of the PETV is the improvement of internal efficiency through lower drop-out rates and a reduction in the number of repeaters. Ultimately the promotion rate for the first five years of first-level education will reach 94 per cent (at present it is about 88 to 89 per cent in television education). The last year of primary education presents a special problem because selection for entrance to secondary education creates a bottleneck and produces an appreciable increase in the proportion of pupils repeating classes. Pupils under the age of $14\frac{1}{2}$ are allowed to stay on at school and may thus sit the secondary-school entrance examination two or three times. In 1975/76, the proportion of 'traditional' pupils repeating this class two or three times was 40·9 per cent. As pupils get younger because of the improvement in internal efficiency, an increase in the repetition of classes must be expected if on the one hand there is no rise in the rate of access to secondary education, and if, on the other, post-primary structures are not introduced.

It should be noted that pupils in areas not covered by television broadcasting are not neglected. The gradual extension of renewed education was begun in 1975/76 in the non-television classes of the first year of primary education, both public and private. In 1980/81, all primary education classes, with or without television, will use the materials and methods of television education. The shortage of teachers has been the main obstacle to universal school attendance, and to meet this need, the government has decided to increase the number of training establishments. The recent rise in teachers' salaries has also helped to produce more candidates.

Some progress after the active effort of this period to improve the qualifications of teaching staff may be seen in the following percentages of highly qualified personnel:

	Teachers	Assistant teachers	Instructors	Assistant instructors
1970/71	12·8	69·9	15·6	1·6
1977/78	34·7	61·9	3·4	0

Teachers enter training after the terminal class (*baccalauréat* level). Assistant teachers do so after the BEPC (Brevet d'Études du Premier

Cycle primary leaving certificate). Instructors are no longer being recruited.

In addition to the ultimate achievement of universal school attendance, there is the immediate aim of reducing regional disparities. The National School Catchment-Area Commission has accelerated the establishment of schools in three regions with the lowest attendance rates. Since the building of primary schools is normally the responsibility of village communities, the government has decided to help poorer groups by granting them large subsidies.

*Improving the quality
of teaching*

The educational renewal introduced by the use of school television has borne fruit in an undeniable improvement in the quality of the teaching provided. Provisional results applied to the first cohort involved, that of 1976/66, give a rough idea of what has actually been achieved in the field.

Children in television classes have in fact practised a new kind of communication, resulting in great spontaneity in relationships between teacher and pupils and between the pupils themselves. They have not been trained to receive information passively, nor to memorize things mechanically. Their usual mode of acquiring knowledge is independent work, performed most of the time in small groups or individually. They express themselves correctly in French and are most at ease when expressing themselves orally. Some weaknesses survive in written work. In modern mathematics, the objectives have been reached. Together with oral expression, the field of logic and mathematics is the one that has produced the most satisfactory results. In the study of the environment, many practical objectives have been achieved, including learning to observe, to compare different points of view, to show a critical spirit, construct and interpret graphs, tables, etc.

*The second generation of PETV output in
the light of the educational reform*

PETV production has now completed its sixth year, and the experience acquired so far should lead to a second generation of multi-media production that is more realistic and closer to the aims of the educational reform. It has been decided to allow a necessary pause for reflection and to institute a stabilization phase, beginning now and lasting three years, during which broadcast and written material will be sent out without fundamental changes.

This period will be used to arrive at a general appraisal of production and to prepare for a general overhaul of programmes for use in primary education. If necessary, there will be fewer productions, but what there is will be of high quality, effective and really helpful to the teacher in the classroom. The programmes will be more compatible with the programme of action and with the content and methods of a renewed fundamental education. The teacher of 1978 differs from the teacher of 1972, and the dogmatism and frequency of some broadcasts, useful in the early days of the programme, are less suitable for its next stage.

This pause for reflection is also being used to pursue the 'Ivorization' of creative and production staff. Apart from the contribution of certain high-level experts, the remodelling should be the work of Ivory Coast nationals. Hence the importance of training problems; to help to solve these, CAFOP training is to be extended to two years.

The main concern of the programme has been to maintain constant links between the shaping of the new education and those who are at the receiving end, and thus to adapt preoccupations to the needs of national educational policy.

Self-reliance in educational reform in the United Republic of Tanzania

by Paul Joseph Mhaiki

The Arusha Declaration[1] states that one of the principal aims of the TANU[2] Party is to see that the Government of the United Republic of Tanzania mobilizes all the country's resources towards eliminating poverty, ignorance and disease. One of the obligations of every member of the Revolutionary Party (CCM) is to strive constantly to acquire more education and utilize it for the benefit of all. Article 28 of the TANU Biannual Conference 1973 gives the responsibility for good school attendance in primary and adult education to village and ward leaders who must take negligent parents to court if necessary. Difficult cases may be referred to the district or regional leaders.

Directive No. 10 from the President's Office calls for workers' committees and participation by workers in decision-making, and it emphasizes workers' education for efficiency and self-reliance in industry. The Prime Minister's Directive 1974 orders enterprises to regard education programmes at the work place as a part of work. The President's calls for adult education in 1970 (Adult Education Year) and in 1971 spell out the importance of educating adults for self-reliance. The Musoma Declaration in November 1974 proclaimed universal primary education by 1977 and urged renewed efforts towards implementing education for self-reliance, especially in secondary schools and higher education. The concept of education as work aroused secondary schools to undertake production projects more seriously and to structure the schools around practical subjects.

The biannual TANU party conferences have repeatedly recalled the objectives of education for self-reliance, and have from time to time assessed performances and then set new targets to be achieved. The Ministry of National Education, as the executor of the policy of education for self-reliance, has organized conferences and seminars to interpret policy, work out programmes, prepare syllabuses and teaching manuals, set up institutions, administer and evaluate programmes and make necessary changes in order to achieve self-reliance.

'Education for Self-Reliance has to increase man's physical and mental freedom to have control over themselves, over their own lives and over the environment in which they live. The ideas imparted by education should be liberating skills.'[3] There have been successes, and there have also been challenges in putting abstract ideas about self-reliance into practical programmes despite problems of money, manpower, materials, buildings and transport.

Primary education

In the context of education for self-reliance, curricula have been reformed to enable primary education to be village-life oriented instead of white-collar and higher-education oriented, as in colonial times and before the Arusha Declaration. Even the first Five-Year Development Plan did not change this orientation, since its emphasis was on expansion of secondary education and higher education with the aim of self-sufficiency in manpower by 1980. However, attention was focused on primary education in the second Five-Year Development Plan in 1969. This provided that every child entering Primary I should finish seven years and abolished competitive examination in Primary 4. This decision raised the school-going population by 46 to 50 per cent.

Besides government efforts in providing buildings, manpower and materials, much of the plan was implemented by self-help. The local community had to contribute in putting up the walls of the classroom while the government would provide funds for the roof, floor, windows and school materials. Self-help schemes included the building of primary schools, teachers' quarters and dispensaries, and sometimes welfare centres, Party offices, markets and storage places. Out of government estimates of 22 million Tanzanian shillings, the people actually contributed 19 million mainly for classrooms, primary-school teachers' quarters and dispensaries. In some areas enthusiasm was so great that primary schools and dispensaries mushroomed so fast that the government could not provide teachers or materials for the new schools.

The second major policy stressed in the second Plan, in keeping with the concepts of self-reliance, was that primary education was to be complete in itself, preparing children to live in the village as progressive farmers. For this, they need to be of age by the time they finish school. Hence the primary-school entry age was raised to 7 or later so that school leavers would be 15 to 18 years old and able to participate in farm work. Consequently, curriculum reform was necessary with emphasis on agricultural knowledge and skills. Farm work and production, political orientation and cultural training form a large part of the curriculum, academic work being complementary to practical projects and skills.

Experience has shown that it is necessary to have a two-year vocational training section in a primary school in order to impart important skills needed in the villages (i.e. carpentry, masonry and domestic science). These courses have proved very useful, since these skills are badly needed in *ujamaa* (Tanzanian Socialism) villages where people construct permanent houses and want roofs, doors, tables, chairs, etc., made. Domestic science for the women is very much called for to raise the standard of life in the villages.

Resolution 29 of the TANU Biannual Conference 1973 specifically says that as part of education for self-reliance, pending a national programme, students of classes VI and VII should be taught skills that will be useful in the villages, such as constructing brick furnaces, making tiles, painting, agriculture, keeping village statistics, and arranging and conducting meetings. In practice, the major problems have been found to be lack of teachers with adequate skills and of tools for use in schools and for work outside. Training and seminars for teachers and supplies of tools and equipment are badly needed.

While the government was trying to implement the objectives of the second Five-Year Plan in education and to solve the problems involved, the political climate changed rapidly. By 1974, before the end of the Plan, it was politically decided that universal primary education (UPE) was to come by 1977. Although work has already started on ways and means of obtaining the necessary manpower, classrooms, teachers' quarters and school materials and of ensuring attendance, the strategies to implement this decision had to be defined in the Five-Year Development Plan scheduled to start in 1978.

Decisions taken to implement various stages of education for self-reliance at the primary stage have been difficult and courageous. Reform of the curriculum has met with criticism and resistence on the part of the élite, of parents and of teachers. Heavy implementation responsibilities have been laid on the village and town communities in respect of self-help schemes and of ensuring good attendance. Self-help is expected to cover the difference between the unit cost of a classroom or a teacher's quarters of 28,000 Tanzanian shillings and the government payments of 5,000 and 7,500 shillings respectively. This has caused problems in some areas. By 1972 the government was decentralized, and this made the financing of primary education a regional affair. As regional budgets differed, financial resources for primary education began to differ also, and some regions faced serious problems owing to inadequate funds. Inflation and measures to beat it, such as restriction of imports, had severe effects on availability of school materials. Hence the need for making local materials as a measure of self-reliance was realized more and more, but even with the few that were available, the problems of distribution and of transport from the capital, Dar es Salaam, to distant villages in the regions have not always been easy to solve.

The Ministry of Education is aware both of the various problems facing primary education and of their solutions. Besides making people politically aware through adult education, it is necessary to strengthen the relationship between school and community in order to ensure good attendance. This had become particularly important by 1978, when the government had provided facilities to ensure that all children of school age could go to school. The Ministry is aware that, with universal primary education, it cannot rely on imported school materials, and so the making of local materials is being emphasized to make sure schools are adequately supplied. The plan is to start regional school materials stores. The Swedish Government has been willing to assist in starting a school-equipment factory. Textbooks are a major need for effective teaching, and to ensure their availability the Ministry has revived the inspectorate, whose duties include the preparation of school textbooks and teaching manuals in the major subjects, along with evaluating primary education methods and giving advice to schools they inspect.

Secondary education

After independence, manpower self-reliance and the filling of all major civil-service posts with Tanzanians was an important target. Hence in the first Development Plan, one objective was manpower self-reliance by 1980, and to this end emphasis was laid on expanding secondary and higher education.

President Nyerere's Education for Self-Reliance has very specific references to the type of secondary school which is compatible with *ujamaa*. As in the primary school, education should be complete and prepare a student to be an effective member of Tanzanian society. Similarly, the secondary school should modify its curricula and prepare workers with knowledge and practical skills required by manpower in different situations of service.

In the ten years since the Arusha Declaration, the concept of manpower as consisting of those prepared by secondary and higher education has undergone a radical transformation. Today, with *ujamaa* established in the villages, and decentralization extended to the latter, the secondary school trains personnel to work not only in town offices but also in the villages, where theoretical knowledge alone is useless. Practical skills, nationalism and commitment are the greatly needed assets. The reforms have been hesitant and slow but sure. The departure from an academic-oriented curriculum to a practical one has been slow, but by now a pattern of a practical secondary curriculum has emerged. This will have four possible emphases: agriculture, domestic science, commerce and technical. Each has specific objectives and prepares students for specific functions after secondary school.

The student who completes the twelfth grade in a secondary school, specializing in agriculture, should have acquired knowledge and skills equal to those of a field agricultural auxiliary in the Ministry of Agriculture. Some of those qualifying can join the Ministry of Agriculture Training Institute in order to qualify as agriculture officers. Others can join agricultural companies. Students who show special ability in science will be able to go on to Form 5 and later to university. Those of professional level in agriculture and other related fields will come from this latter group. Those who do not find posts are expected to become self-employed in agriculture.

Students taking domestic science should become versed in nutrition, cooking, textiles and dress-making. Those who complete twelve years of secondary school can be employed in hotels and industries, and as rural development officers in the villages, or as domestic-science teachers in primary and secondary schools. Others will go to home economics institutions, and later serve in institutions and ministries. The more able will go on to Forms 5 and 6 and university.

Commerce is divided into three subjects: stores, accounts, and secretarial studies. The student is expected to gain sufficient proficiency in one of these subjects to begin working at the end of the secondary course. All students in this course are expected to take national business economics, which comprises commerce and economics. At the end of the course students are expected to have knowledge and skills equivalent to those of a Stores Officer Grade II, an Account Assistant or a Typist Grade I in the government service. Most of those qualifying are absorbed into the official and private sector.

Technical education consists of carpentry, masonry, painting, electrical engineering, mechanics, smithing and plumbing. At the end of the twelfth grade, a student should be able to function as an artisan in one of these subjects. Students with special ability can go to technical colleges or continue on to Forms 5 and 6 and later university.

All secondary schools and teachers colleges try to be self-reliant in food. Hence each school or college has production projects such as animal-keeping, vegetable-growing, maize production, brick-making, dress-making, etc. In 1976 production from self-reliance projects in schools reached a value of 7·7 million Tanzanian shillings, covering 40 to 50 per cent of their recurrent costs.

The foregoing is an ambitious curriculum reform in secondary education. Naturally, the constraints are many. This kind of educational innovation requires heavy expenditures on equipment for teaching, tools for practical work, books, materials and libraries. Money is short, and even when it is available, supplies may not be available when needed. When an academic system changes to a practical one, the reorientation of teachers also is challenging and time-consuming.

Adult education

In the United Republic of Tanzania, education has very much been the instrument of change and development. For the concept of *ujamaa* to take root, and to bring about socialist development and change in society, education had to involve adults. A good system of adult education has been developed after more than eight years of operation. The approach has been functional adult education and lifelong education, the aim to give adults an awareness that development in production, health, housing and food is in their own hands. To expand an adult's consciousness of himself and of his environment, and therefore of his power over himself, his environment and society, the ideas and skills imparted should liberate adults from poverty, sickness and ignorance.

Adult education of this kind was launched by President Nyerere in 1969 in his end-of-year speech, and his declaration of 1970 as Adult Education Year. He has been a constant supporter of adult education and has brought the whole TANU political party to follow him. The performance of adult education in the regions has been a major report item to the biannual Party Conference and this has in turn mobilized and encouraged the people, the government and the teachers. Article 27 of the sixteenth Biannual Conference authorizes the adult education organizers in the villages and wards to report to the district and regional authorities all government and political leaders who participate or do not participate in adult-education programmes. The interest of some foreign countries, such as Sweden, has been attracted to assist in adult education by giving funds, materials, advice and experts, while Unesco has given its support to experimental functional adult education.

To meet the need for adult education, the government had to set up administrative structures, provide materials, train teachers, establish institutions and work out curricula guidelines. A Directorate of Adult Education was created in the Ministry of National Education, and regional district, village and classroom adult-education committees were formed comprising people from all walks of life.

An education programme involving 10 million people must necessarily be very expensive and no government in a developing country can have sufficient funds to provide accommodation and transport, print books and train and pay teachers. The programme's success has therefore depended on the spirit of self-reliance. Adults had to put up their own classrooms; existing facilities such as court-rooms, party offices, co-operative buildings and, above all, primary schools had to be shared with their usual occupiers. This sharing made it possible to integrate various communities with schools. Not only did the adults come to their local primary school to learn; they also used the school farm to learn agriculture, the school playground to perform dances, the school workshop to learn carpentry and building projects at the school to learn masonry, while their own children assisted in teaching them reading and counting.

The teaching was carried out after school hours, by regular teachers, by primary and secondary pupils and by a large army of voluntary teachers, unpaid or with a small honorarium. As experience accumulated, more and more teachers were trained and appointed as organizers, first in the regions and then in districts, wards and finally villages. With the Declaration of Universal Primary Education by 1977, a strong motivation was provided for youth volunteers to teach in adult classes. Young people who had diligently taught for a year in adult classes were eligible for training as regular teachers in primary schools. Today regional district organizers have motor vehicles, ward organizers have motor bicycles and village organizers have bicycles for better performance of their work. An adult-education organizer and teacher has won government status. The work itself, besides being technical, is highly political and requires strong leadership qualities.

The efforts of the Ministry of Education have been supported by specific adult education bodies such as the Institute of Adult Education, the Mwanza Functional Literacy Centre and the Adult Education Press. The Institute of Adult Education, with branches in every region, has played a great role in conducting courses of continuing education type, in training adult education organizers, in running a correspondence course and in organizing mass campaigns directed towards peoples' awareness of specific life problems.

One such campaign was in 1969 to familiarize the people with the content of the second Five-Year Development Plan and get them to collaborate in its implementation. The 'Choice is Yours' parliamentary election campaign in 1970 was conducted in order to make people participate in electing suitable parliamentary candidates. The 'Every

Ten Years' campaign in 1971 aimed to make people politically conscious of their independence, while 'Man is Health' in 1972 and 'Food is Life' in 1974 were run to make people more aware of the problems of health and nutrition.

The institute runs a correspondence school for adults to provide continuing education for those who graduate from the mass adult-education programmes in subjects like political education, health, agriculture, accounts, English, etc. It also offers job-oriented subjects such as accountancy and economics and academic subjects such as history and geography. Further, with the need for many more teachers for universal primary education, the correspondence section trains teachers by correspondence and radio.

The Functional Literacy Centre develops functional literacy methods applicable to the whole country, develops reading and teaching materials and, by radio, keeps in constant touch with teachers on adult-education methods. It runs a rural newspaper for adults, for which it has a press, and assists in establishing library centres in the villages in collaboration with the library service, which operates a mobile library service to the villages. The National Union of Tanganyika Workers (NUTA)[4] and the National Institute of Productivity (NIP) are charged with responsibilities for workers' education in industries and offices. The Ministry of Education runs a printing press that puts out adult-education textbooks and supplementary reading materials in Kiswahili, the national language.

When the basic work of adult education has been done, the learners must be led to further horizons. To this effect, there is the Correspondence Institution and now the Ministry of National Education has opened a Folk Development College in every district. Kivukoni College has a branch college in every region. The University of Dar es Salaam itself has changed into an Adult Education Institution by the decree of the Musoma Declaration, 1974. Those who qualify to go to the university have to undergo national service for a year, then work for a year or two before being admitted as mature students. The national service itself carries out considerable adult education.

The Ministry of National Education has completed an assessment of adult education performance in 1975 and 1977. Illiteracy which eight years ago stood at about 80 per cent has now been halved and stands at about 39 per cent. Political awareness, while unmeasurable, is very high, while housing and food have shown great improvement. These achievements have been made despite many obstacles, especially during these years of world inflation. Money to finance various projects has been difficult to come by. Reading materials, especially in Kiswahili, have been scarce. Voluntary teachers, on whom the programme has depended heavily, have not been trained. The sheer size of the country has imposed special problems of transport and distribution of materials and of feedback and easy evaluation. It required considerable determination to undertake this programme, but the results have been very good.

Teacher training

The Ministry of National Education has set itself the target of training all teachers. Before 1974, training was confined to Teacher-Training Colleges, but since 1975, owing to the urgent need for teachers, this has been extended and now takes place in colleges, in villages and in secondary schools. There are currently thirty-two teacher-training colleges with a capacity of some 9,500 and an annual output of about 4,500 teachers. The bigger colleges provide teacher training for secondary-school graduates. Four colleges train teachers who have finished Form 6, and all the smaller colleges train teachers who have completed primary education. Four training colleges specialize in science and mathematics and three in combining ordinary teacher training with military training. The university's Department of Education trains secondary-school teachers and adult-education organizers. The spirit of self-reliance and the participation of the teacher in school production programmes are much stressed. The colleges themselves set an example by running chicken, cattle and vegetable farms and by trying, so far as possible, to be self-reliant in food.

The political decision at Musoma to have every child of age 7 and over in primary school precipitated great demands for teachers in a very short time — hence the concept of training teachers in the villages. Young people who have finished primary education and who have taught adults for a year are recruited and put into primary schools. There the head teacher gives them an orientation about teaching for a few weeks and then they teach, supervised by the other teachers. Every weekend they undergo training in the school by these, while at the same time they are enrolled in teacher-training courses by correspondence and radio, run by the Institute of Adult Education. During the school vacation they attend teacher-training centres.

In 1976, the Ministry of National Education decided to start training Form 3 and 4 students in all secondary schools as teachers so that they could assist teaching in the primary schools in the vicinity of their secondary schools. This is another way of preparing future teachers. Everyone is called on to teach and every profession has a teaching component. The programme came into operation in 1977/78 and involved considerable adjustments in the secondary schools' timetable; secondary-school teachers had to be oriented to fit in with the changes.

This ambitious teacher-training programme to meet expanding educational needs has problems that confront it all the time. The training institutions are not numerous enough, all are overcrowded and they suffer from staff shortages. There are not enough textbooks and school materials, especially those of a technical nature. With the increase in numbers of teachers being trained in the villages, transport and distribution of correspondence, availability of radio sets and audibility of programmes pose special problems.

Higher education

The University of Dar es Salaam aims to meet requirements for highly trained manpower. Since 1970, when it became a national independent university, it has been increasingly able to follow the philosophy of education for self-reliance. More and more faculties have been opened and fewer and fewer students are being trained overseas, especially for the first degrees. Most of the faculties have opened M.A. and Ph.D. graduate courses. In 1977, the first graduates in engineering and pharmacy were produced. In the Faculty of Agriculture, the Veterinary Science Department was opened in 1976, and the Departments of Agriculture, Education and Extension and of Food Science and Food Technology were opened in 1977. The Faculty of Engineering is preparing also to open the Departments of Process Engineering and of Chemical Engineering and an Institute of Production Innovation, while the Medical Faculty is preparing to open a Department of Dentistry. The university has to expand quickly in order to meet the needs of a self-reliant United Republic of Tanzania.

The university is not behindhand in the policy of self-reliance and 'education is work'. Engineering students made ladders and charcoal stoves as part of their studies, and carried out consultancy work with the Ministry of Construction. The Faculty of Agriculture cultivates 3,000 acres of land and in 1976/77 planted 150 acres of cattle fodder. There are plans to expand self-reliance projects in areas such as animal husbandry, the university bookshop and consultancy services in various fields.

The Examination Council

In 1967, the East African Examination Council was formed to conduct academic, technical and other examinations in Uganda, Kenya and the United Republic of Tanzania. That year, the policy of education for self-reliance was announced. It emphasized the necessity that education be related to the conditions and needs of the country; hence examinations must be designed to fit the education provided. Four years later the government made the bold decision to establish a National Examination Council to replace external examination.

The Examination Council got a very special challenge from the Musoma Declaration of November 1974. This demanded radical changes in the assessment of students. The current system of assessing students' performance by a written examination only was unfair. Students should be assessed not only on written examinations but also on daily classroom work, while diligence in work outside the classroom should also be taken into account. Production work should be counted as an essential part of education. Hence, the Examination Council prepared a system whereby these aspects of education are assessed and since 1976 count in determining the final success of a student. This was another step implementing education for self-reliance.

Education for self-reliance has resulted in the transmission of definite and important *ujamaa* values. Aversion to exploitation of man by man or of one group by another has become deeply rooted. The idea of some people living in luxury while others go hungry has become repellent. Co-operation and participation in decision-making have become habit. Political consciousness among students, teachers and the communities is very high. It has taken a long time for manual and productive work to win respect, but this kind of self-reliance is being accepted as an essential part of education. Communal leadership in the running of the schools prepares students to be citizens who participate in the development of their communities.

By the reform of curricula, students are brought face to face with the development problems of Tanzanian society and are being prepared to solve them in the service of their communities. Changes in curricula are meant to change attitudes in students and teachers, and production projects in the school show such changes. Primary-school teachers have been the most overworked of public servants and yet have worked with such commitment that they have won the respect and praise of all Tanzanians. Changes in curricula and expansion of education programmes mean very big expenses, beyond the ability of the average Tanzanian parent to pay, yet programmes have been carried out in the spirit of self-reliance by students, parents and teachers. In 1974/75 self-reliance efforts of schools were valued at 7·7 million Tanzanian shillings and this was only a beginning.

Case studies

NOTES

1. The Arusha Declaration is the policy paper stating the political and development objectives of the United Republic of Tanzania as a socialist State pursuing the policy of socialism and self-reliance.
2. Tanganyika African National Union, which is the political party of the United Republic of Tanzania founded in 1954: it fought for independence which was achieved in 1961, and merged with the Afro-Shirazi Party of Zanzibar to form a new political party known as CCM (Chama cha Mapinduzi).
3. Julius K. Nyerere, *Adult Education and Development*, Vol. VII, No. 4, Winter 1976–77 (International Council for Adult Education).
4. National Union of Tanganyika Workers; in 1978 it became the Juwata (Jumuiya ya Wafanyakazi wa Tanzania).

Educational reform
in Sweden

by Sven Moberg

Major post-war educational reforms

Sweden is large in area, but small in population. Of its slightly more than 8 million inhabitants, seven-eighths live in the southern half of the country. Linguistically and religiously, the nation is very homogeneous. The largest linguistic minority has long been the Finnish but in recent years a controlled immigration programme has created a number of linguistic and religious minorities from non-Nordic countries.

The Swedish educational system is 99 per cent public. Local authorities (the municipalities) have the main responsibility for the nine-year compulsory and comprehensive school as well as for the two to four years of education in the upper secondary school, which is voluntary and directly follows the compulsory system. The central government (the State) has the main responsibility for the universities and colleges together with their undergraduate programmes, graduate studies and basic research.

Responsibility for the various types of adult education is shared by municipalities, county councils, the State and a number of non-profit organizations. Operating alongside this public educational system are a few private schools at the primary and secondary level plus a private tertiary school. Voluntary programmes of popular education are sponsored by non-profit organizations. Private and State-owned companies as well as the public administration are extensively engaged in the further education and in-service training of their own employees.

The State lends economic support for education to municipalities and county councils, paying the greater part of teachers' salaries and about one-third of the cost of building schools. By laws and ordinances the State regulates much of the scope, content and organization of the education provided. Similar regulations govern the State's undertakings in partnership with those non-profit organizations which carry on segments of the education system.

Sweden has reformed all parts of its educational system root and branch since 1945. There is space here to mention only three reforms: the compulsory school, and upper secondary and higher education. The reform which overshadows all others is that of the compulsory school. Between 1842 and 1962 Sweden had a compulsory six-year (from 1937 a seven-year) elementary school (*folkskola*). After spending three, four or six years there, pupils could transfer to a lower secondary school (*realskola*), offering five-, four- or three-year courses. In 1950 the Riksdag (Swedish Parliament) decided to replace elementary and lower secondary schools with nine-year compulsory and comprehensive schools for all Swedish children and young people between the ages of 7 and 16.

After a twelve-year trial period the 1962 Parliament laid down a definite design for this basic school. Some structural rearrangements were decided on in 1968 and the compulsory and comprehensive school was finally implemented in every municipality for all nine primary grades in 1972, no less than twenty-two years after the first policy resolution was passed. (Even so there were many who felt that the reform work had moved too fast.) In 1976 Parliament decided on substantial internal changes in the school.

Education after the compulsory school, i.e. for young people over 16 years of age, was long split up among different types of school, and had a widely varying content. After enacting a minor provisional reform in 1953, Parliament decided in 1964 to merge the previously separate upper secondary streams — three- and four-year general, three-year technical and two-year commercial — into an integrated upper secondary school with different courses, all of them running for three years but with options for students in the technical branch to take an additional fourth year.

This 1964 decision was followed in 1968 by a more sweeping reform which extended integrated secondary education to include the previously self-contained two-year streams of the continuation school (*fackskola*) and the many streams of the vocational schools, with their widely varying content and length. A thoroughgoing overhaul of the curricula and syllabuses for all these new secondary streams is a cardinal aspect of the major reform in upper secondary education enacted by Parliament in 1968 and implemented from 1971 on.

In tertiary education, covering the universities, colleges, professional schools and other post-secondary institutions, three big reform packages took shape during the post-war period. The first was the outcome of decisions that Parliament took in stages in the years from 1947 to 1950. Most of the reforms focused on the content of education in the faculties of arts and sciences, but a number related also to the teaching staffs of most faculties and colleges.

The second reform period, extending from 1958 to 1964, was mainly concerned with the quantitative expansion of undergraduate programmes and the organizational framework for all universities and colleges. The parliamentary resolutions behind these changes were passed at the 1958–64 legislative session. The third reform package was approved by the 1975 Parliament and deals with the problem of quantitative and qualitative planning of all tertiary education, together with a number of sweeping organizational changes in order to achieve a structurally and administratively strong and integrated activity within each of six tertiary education regions.

The financial conditions of students during their studies have been the subject of various post-war reforms. In 1948 Parliament voted to make many more scholarships available to students at universities and colleges. A radical alteration was made in 1964, when a system of study assistance (part scholarship grants, part loans) was introduced from which every tertiary student benefits in whole or in part. For students in upper secondary schools a number of minor reforms have been carried out, providing for allowances and loans differentiated according to parental income, location of dwelling in relation to the school, etc.

The democratic process in shaping the educational reforms

The process leading to the introduction of the nine-year compulsory and comprehensive school for all between the ages of 7 and 16 began as far back as 1809. Those who then gave Sweden a new and democratic constitution, strongly influenced by the ideas of the French Revolution, envisioned a general school open to all. In 1842 a law on compulsory schooling for all children resulted in the establishment of a six-year school, mainly for the children of farmers, artisans and manual workers.

It was not until more than 100 years later that the time was ripe for a consensus of opinion on the need for radical educational reform and guidelines for a broad school reform could be drawn up. This was due partly to experiences in Europe during the 1930s which showed what indoctrination in totalitarian ideas could lead to for whole generations of youth; partly to the democratic ideas of freedom and equality derived from the French Revolution, together with socialist emphasis on greater social and economic levelling; and partly to the demands of private enterprise and public administration for better-trained and more liberally educated manpower.

The shaping in practice of the basic school reform was fairly typical of Swedish reform policy in a number of societal areas. In 1946 the government appointed an *ad hoc* committee to submit proposals for an integrated compulsory school with a democratic objective. The committee members were nominated by political parties, the labour-market organizations, the research community and the civil service. The committee co-operated widely with all kinds of interested organizations and with the mass media and its work was largely in the open.

The committee presented its voluminous findings after three years of investigation, and these were widely circulated for comment to public-sector agencies and organizations and to political bodies, at both local and regional level. These 'submission bodies' were given a deadline to make known their views. (All such submissions emanating from government agencies and interested organizations are public documents in Sweden.) The government then presented its own views in a comprehensive bill to Parliament in 1950, accompanied by fairly detailed analysis and comment on most of the statements of opinion received from the submission bodies, so as to give Parliament and its standing committees the broadest possible decision-making base.

The procedure for reforms in upper secondary education was similar. These were backed by the labour market and the political parties. Both employer associations and trade unions strove vigorously to get the secondary vocational streams to offer training more broadly oriented to active employment and affording greater scope for general-education subjects such as languages and civics.

There was some doubt among teachers of theoretical subjects and in universities and colleges about the wisdom of reorganizing the secondary school on integrated lines. However, the same democratic and social ideas which lay behind integration of the compulsory school also supported that of the secondary school. When everybody feels at home within one and the same organization, it is easier to overcome traditional and obsolescent judgements of the relative values of theoretical and of practical lines of study. Furthermore, the main trade unions, with which Swedish teachers are affiliated, rallied behind the organizational approach in the reform.

The reforms for universities and colleges exhibit a more complicated pattern of pressure groups and the exercise of influence. The first of the university and college reform packages, dating from the late 1940s, was very much shaped on the basis of expert ratings by academic professors. In those days the labour-market and non-profit organizations, as well as most political parties, took little interest in the affairs of universities and colleges.

Reform activity in the late 1950s and early 1960s was effected in a more complicated fashion. The government's terms of reference for the commission of inquiry which presented most of the reform proposals during the period 1958–64 were strongly coloured by the views which the central organization of university students expressed in the early 1950s. Moreover, the students were represented on the commission by an expert while one of their more outstanding members served on the commission's secretariat. The chairman was a young Member of Parliament who had long been in close touch with student organizations. Hence many of the reform proposals — especially as regards the intake capacities of the faculties of arts and sciences, and a forceful commitment to new, young teachers alongside the professors — were very much shaped in agreement with student viewpoints.

In other respects, the reform proposals reflected the demands and wishes of the labour-market parties for more skilled and better trained manpower. The Industrial Institute for Economic and Social Research prepared labour-market forecasts for strategic occupational categories such as engineers and architects. For skilled vocational groups in the public sector — physicians, teachers and other professionals — central administrative boards exercised great influence over the estimates of required manpower. The trade unions representing skilled manpower warmly endorsed the proposals for substantial expansion of educational capacity in highly specialized curricula.

Widespread optimism among both employers and employed prevailed in the late 1950s and early 1960s on future prospects for employees in public administration and in private enterprise, especially in respect of highly trained manpower. The politicians in most parties were ready to accept enormous increases in commitments to higher education, since they shared the labour-market parties' strong confidence in the future. Their positive attitude reflected hopes of well-paid and congenial occupations in a near future for those entering the labour market over the ever larger cohorts which, from the mid-1950s, began to pass through not only a prolonged compulsory schooling but also the two-year and three-year secondary school, and the three- to five-year courses at universities and colleges.

The first signs of a harsher labour market for young, well-trained graduates appeared in connection with an economic slump in 1967–68. By the first half of the 1970s, when the latest reform packages were worked out for the tertiary system, a striking change of mood, sentiment and opinion had supervened. The tone among students, teachers, employers, parents and politicians was no longer so optimistic. Within the student world, developments in the foreign affairs arena, especially events in south-east Asia, had created a political polarization. Impressed by the turbulent occurrences in Paris during the spring of 1968, some Swedish left-wing students also cast an eye on the process of change that was now in full swing as a consequence of implementing the second reform package of 1958–64. This shift of focus was manifested in two ways: first, in exacerbated attacks on educational policy and its spokesmen at universities and colleges and in the ranks of civil servants and politicians; and second, in bitter assaults on the student unions themselves, especially on the central organization which had played a key role in shaping the policy that was now being put into effect.

The main forces demanding further tertiary-level reforms were two political parties, Social Democratic and Centre, the big trade unions representing manual workers, and the large white-collar groups in private and public administration. They now demanded, around 1970, first, a radical change in the qualification and admission rules relating to universities and colleges; and second, an enlargement of tertiary education to include vocational training streams which hitherto were not considered professional enough to be equated with traditional vocational curricula in the universities.

Moreover, demands were raised for greater public control and influence over university and college managements, on behalf partly of society's regional and municipal bodies, and partly of the growing number of employees, technicians, administrators and others in higher education. After protracted and laborious investigations, the main principles governing new qualification and admission rules and new principles on intake capacity and organizational structure were decided by the 1975 and 1977 Parliaments. In the end, all essential aspects of the submitted reform programme were able to be carried out, under strong protests from some of the student unions but with assent from the large trade-union organizations.

Reception given to reforms

It is as yet too early to comment on the implementation of the third reform package, dealing with higher education, as approved by Parliament in 1975. As for the two preceding packages, the first reform of the basic school was very carefully prepared among teachers and active sections of public opinion. After all the commission inquiries and pilot programmes undertaken between 1944 and 1962, it was confidently believed that it would be feasible to implement the programme speedily and without formidable problems of resistance. In some respects the outcome justified expectations. The municipalities, which had primary responsibility for providing premises, equipment, school supplies and teachers, on the whole did an amazingly good job, with great political unanimity. Good premises, adequate textbooks and a sufficient number of teachers, albeit some with defective educational background, were on hand at the beginning of every academic year to cater to the steadily increasing enrolments.

Difficulties would arise from time to time in obtaining teachers for all subjects at all primary levels, especially in northern Sweden. But the system worked. No instruction had to be suspended for more than an exceptional classroom hour or so on account of a teacher shortage. Admittedly some classes had to make do, for one or more terms, with premises that were decidedly makeshift, but no instruction was stopped for lack of accommodation. Today, as far as nine-year compulsory education is concerned, virtually all the problems of physical facilities and staffing have been overcome.

In one respect, however, the municipalities have not been able to attain the goals set for the basic-school reform, namely as regards the social composition of the school classes. In principle, if the school is to raise young people imbued with democratic principles, children from different socio-economic groups should have the same right to schooling and be able to attend school together. In Sweden, however, as in many other countries, people live in areas that are highly homogeneous in income patterns and socio-economic group affiliation. Since each school has a sharply defined catchment area, schools will differ greatly in respect of the social and income-earning status of the children's parents. Attempts to redress this inequality when new residential areas are planned have met with little success, and transporting pupils by bus to counteract housing segregation has not found acceptance among responsible school politicians.

Difficulties during implementation were experienced on the part of parents, who sometimes reacted quite violently, of teachers at post-basic-school levels, and of politicians, mainly right wing. The reactions had to do with attempts to improve standards, chiefly in respect of the Swedish language, mathematics and foreign languages. Certainly there were grounds for criticism. There were not enough competent teachers and teaching aids did not meet desirable criteria in all subjects. The objections made, however, mainly concerned methodology, e.g. the role of grammar in early foreign-language teaching or classical training methods as applied to elementary mathematics. The so-called experts fell far short of reaching any consensus, and the role and contributions of practising teachers were often severely criticized on widely diverse grounds, with resultant uncertainty and dwindling efficiency.

Resistance against implementing the basic-school reform was intense but of relatively brief duration. Today, this reform and its fundamental content again command a high degree of unanimity among politicians, teachers, parents and other pressure groups. The opposition has not led to any more substantial modifications in the original reform principles. What has happened during the 1970s is that municipalities and teachers have been enabled, to a greater extent than during the earlier implementation period, to exercise their own direct influence over the content of official syllabuses and over the wording of methods directives for particular subjects.

In the reform of upper secondary education, the opposition that surfaced during implementation was mainly among politicians and those groups of university teachers who keep especially close watch on the quality of the theoretically oriented streams in secondary school. Much of this criticism has related to the content of specific subjects. Shaping the school subject of religion has involved the application of persuasion on the part of religious groups, more with respect to the basic-school syllabus than that of the upper secondary school. Further, during the latter part of the 1960s, opportunities for the pupils themselves to influence the school's inner life came to attract interest both among the pupils themselves and among the political parties. All told, however, implementation of the upper secondary school reform has not encountered any problems out of the ordinary.

Universities and colleges are more independent than primary and upper secondary schools and so political decisions by Cabinet and Parliament concerning them have been more general than those concerning schools. They have thus enjoyed greater opportunities themselves to shape the content of fundamental changes decided on by the government and to put different interpretations on the latter's decisions. The first two reform packages were largely carried out before the big campus tensions erupted at the end of the 1960s. On the whole, implementation, especially of the quantitative reforms at most faculties and professional schools, was remarkably smooth and flexible.

Three main factors have contributed to implementation, without unduly vehement or wounding disagreement, of numerous and profound educational reforms during the post-war period. First, there is Sweden's religious and linguistic homogeneity. Second, the long political stability in Parliament has helped make it possible to plan and implement long-term public policy, a matter of cardinal importance where education is concerned. Third, both employers and employed, acting through strong central organizations with a keen interest in improving both general education and vocational training, have given the politicians in all parties powerful support for wholehearted educational reforms at all levels.

Naturally enough, the strongest opposition has been found within the educational system itself. During the 1960s, events in central subject fields at the senior level of the basic school, and in the theoretical branches of upper secondary education, were slowed down by strong teacher groups with arguments about quality. During the late 1960s and the first half of the 1970s the restraining forces concentrated their energies on the university faculties with open access, where they were represented among professors and students. This opposition, however, acquired only limited influence among the political parties.

Consequences of reforms

The initial effects of educational reforms implemented are felt in the educational system itself and in central and local government finances. The impact on the community at large first becomes noticeable within families, and then in the labour market. Upheavals in the educational system at first permeate other sectors of the national life only slowly; indeed, changes may even go unnoticed.

Within the educational system itself, the major consequence so far has been the quantitative development that has taken place. During the past twenty-five years, enrolments in upper secondary and tertiary education have increased from an insignificant proportion of the compulsory school's volume to around half of the combined student population. The increase in expenditures has been even more dramatic. Education's share in Sweden's gross national income has gone up from 2 to 3 per cent to about 10 per cent, even though total income itself has greatly increased. Financially, education has now become the biggest sector for both central and local government but unmet demands call for even heavier disbursements.

During certain periods the huge educational expenditures have had a powerful impact on other sectors. The building and construction industry has been strongly affected, positively and negatively, by variations in the volume of educational building. The concentrated academic semesters and lengthy interruptions around Christmas and during the summer months are more and more affecting the rest of society as the sector keeps on growing. The labour market particularly has experienced problems, connected with variations in temporary work. In the longer term, however, the educational reforms will considerably raise both general and vocational education standards in the labour market and there is a widespread consensus that this contains the seeds of great improvements in productivity.

A new life-style among large youth groups is so far the most visible consequence for parents and other members of the older generation. Just how much of this new life-style directly ensues from reform of the educational system has yet to be shown. It stands to reason, however, that longer schooling, with its concomitants of developing friendship and changes in study-places, together with increasing international contact through the demolition of language barriers, must contribute considerably to changes in life-style.

Some reflections

One lesson learned the hard way is that far-reaching reforms of content in the educational sector cannot be carried out unless corresponding reforms are at least mounted at the same time in other societal sectors. Educational changes must harmonize with changes in the labour market, in urban and regional planning and in other sectors.

In this respect the formulation and implementation of the Swedish educational reforms were in some ways premature, as is exemplified by what happened when the compulsory school was made comprehensive. The first six years, based upon a system with form-teachers, were made comprehensive from the beginning of the reform, while the years seven to nine continued with different streams and with subject-teachers. The result was that, during the last three years, the old selective school system was, in practice, maintained. An overwhelming majority of children from well-to-do homes chose the theoretical streams while those from workers' and farmers' homes chose the practical ones. This influenced the pupils' further choice of education or work after leaving the compulsory school and the principle of comprehensiveness was threatened.

In 1968, eighteen years after the start of the reform, a complete comprehensive system through the entire compulsory school was introduced. However, the result of this change among the three last year-groups has not been particularly encouraging. Many children, especially those from workers' and farmers' homes, found the new curricula too theoretical, which led to bad results and disciplinary difficulties. The dilemma is still present: in 1977 Swedish society was not yet fully ripe for total comprehensiveness in the compulsory school.

One unsolved problem with educational reforms is how to produce enough teachers dedicated to training themselves in the spirit of the new ideas before the reforms go into effect. Sweden was somewhat late in developing new curricula at teacher-training colleges, for the pre-services and in-service training of primary and upper-secondary school teachers. As for universities and colleges, the higher the educational level, the worse trained are the teachers. However, a bold commitment to staffing universities and colleges with a great many young auxiliary teachers was of great value to implementation of the reforms.

Elements endangering the quality of education were strongly stressed in public debates in the second half of the 1960s. Those responsible for the reforms did not plan far enough ahead to clarify the import and nature of the disparate achievements, at different educational levels, which were bound to ensue from setting new goals for the various school types. If access had been available, ten years ago, to the results of studies published in the 1970s, under Unesco's auspices, recording the achievements of young persons studying at different levels in the schools of different countries, a great deal of time and energy could have been saved and put to better use, by both defenders and critics of the reforms.

Another problem that Swedish educational policy-makers and educators have never satisfactorily solved involves relations with the large groups of parents whose children will be given a longer and sounder education than the parents themselves received when they were young. Thousands upon thousands of parent–teacher meetings were held during the 1950s to give information about the expansion of the new compulsory and the new secondary school, the universities and the colleges, and about what these reforms would mean for children and young people. The meetings were attended mainly by well-educated parents especially anxious to learn about the reforms, while few other parents bothered to come. Thus, instead of closing the gap between families in respect of ability to orient their children to changes in educational patterns, the information campaign would appear to have widened the gap even more. Other sectors of society tell of similar experiences. In effect, efforts to enlighten benefited only those who were already well-informed. Radio and television were not used until a late stage to provide systematic information about the reforms.

A concluding reflection might seem to be somewhat paradoxical. Education has proved to be of thoroughgoing, indeed decisive, importance for the individual citizen and for society. As a rule anyone who has benefited from a solid education has received a handsome return from his or her own efforts, as manifested in a comparatively assured livelihood. Both in economic and welfare terms, society has been able to progress fairly swiftly and equably, thanks in large part to a well-trained labour force. In other words, education has been macro-economically profitable.

In the decades to come, however, the substantial educational reforms in which Sweden invested so heavily during the 1950s, 1960s and 1970s will carry less weight for the individual and for society. The kind of education an individual receives will no longer imply the same crucial social and economic differences as it did in the past, nor will the national economy's dependence on changes in the educational imputs be so great as during the post-war period. Hence, reform will have taken the drama out of education's role.

Higher education in the Union of Soviet Socialist Republics: development problems and concepts

by Ivan Ph. Obraztsov

Higher and secondary school teachers form the most numerous professional group in the Union of Soviet Socialist Republics today. The fact that education has now become general is an indicator of the economic, social and intellectual development of different countries and nations. Of course, this is not by chance: it is closely connected with the scientific and technical revolution, with the growth of material production and with the rapid development of all social life.

Great attention is paid in the U.S.S.R. to the problems of education. One of the major aims of this developed socialist society is the formation of harmoniously developed, thoroughly educated and socially active persons — the citizens of the U.S.S.R. The system of higher education plays an important role in the achievement of this aim for it is the means of educating and training the Soviet intellectuals.

The characteristic feature of changes in higher education in the U.S.S.R. in the preceding period was the great increase in numbers of higher-education institutions in the country and the increased numbers of teachers, students and graduates. In 859 higher-education establishments the number of students in 1976 reached nearly 5 million, 2·1 times the number in 1960. Graduates from the higher-education establishments have risen to 734,600 a year. The number of students coming from the working class and the peasantry has increased, reaching today 60 per cent of entrants.

Thanks to the care of the Communist Party and the Soviet State, the system of higher education in the U.S.S.R. has become one of the most advanced and democratic in the world. It has great resources at its disposal. More than 400,000 scientists and educators are engaged in teaching the students. Curricula and programmes are improving. The training of specialists in molecular biology, the protection of the environment and atomic and electrical techniques has been increased.

Professors and teachers have concentrated their efforts on constantly improving all branches of work in higher school education in the light of the demands of the twenty-fifth Congress of the Communist Party of the Soviet Union (CPSU). The most important of these is to increase the standards of training and political education of the specialists produced. The staff have at their disposal a wealth of forms, methods and means to permit them to make the educational process more effective.

At the same time, scientific and technical progress, which manifested itself in an unusual acceleration of the rate of increase and renewal of knowledge and in a shortening of the time taken for scientific ideas to be put into practice, creates a number of problems in the field of training specialists with higher education. Chief among these are: the gap between the training subject and the state of science and technique; the increasing rate of obsolescence of acquired knowledge; and the growing requirements in education and for its improvement. In these conditions it is not possible to solve all the problems merely by making changes in higher-education curricula and courses.

The experience of the higher-education institutions of the U.S.S.R. shows that, when the specialist training of students takes place in scientific research or production enterprises, comprehension by students of the new problems and trends of scientific investigation exercises are an important influence on the subject and character of the knowledge they acquire. This has the advantage of securing a kind of continuous succession, by which the educational process encourages the development of the existing branches of science and technology.

In this respect, the problem facing higher-education institutions is that of improving this relationship by familiarizing future specialists with scientific activities, thereby increasing their productivity and creativity during the training process.

Three fundamental forms of organizing the educational-scientific process have reached a significant stage of development in the U.S.S.R. These imply a close connection between study and research, and application of its results to the building up of communism.

The first involves the organization and broad development of research within an institute.

The second is founded on use of the bases of research, such as institutes, design offices and industrial institutions in different fields, with specialized departments. It permits a successful combination of fundamental general education and specialized training.

The third is characterized by a close connection between institutes and industrial enterprises, based on joint agreements about the use of laboratories and production bases. These permit students to reach higher levels and enable them to solve specific problems related to their future activity.

New combinations of educational, scientific and production processes in united scientific-production or educational-scientific complexes stimulate scientists to solve pressing problems in science and technology. They offer possibilities for accelerating the pace of scientific and technological progress.

Reorganization of an educational process requires more activity classes and less formal study by the students (up to thirty to thirty-five hours a week). Thus, special stress has been laid on the student's learning on his own, with the teacher mainly acting in a supervisory capacity.

While organizing and improving the system of higher education, we do not restrict it to the narrow limits of the country's current needs for specialists. Orientation to these needs alone would cause the education system to lag behind and that would soon have serious consequences for society.

The necessary modern requirement for the system of higher learning is an orientation towards the future, with due account taken of those social-political problems which our society has to solve and of the main underlying purposes of industry, science, technology and culture. These considerations make new and great demands on those in the specialist fields of higher learning.

Today, under the influence of these considerations, a new and complex criterion for evaluating social specialist qualifications is being evolved, in accordance with the conditions of a developed socialist society and the requirements of today's stage in the revolution of science and technology. This complex criterion takes the form of a theoretical pattern of a specialist with a broad profile, and this is the pattern on which the plan for the education and training of new specialists for the national economy is based.

This pattern provides for the training of specialists who are masters of the principles of Marxism-Leninism, who clearly discern the political purposes of the Party and the country, and who have a broad scientific qualification. We consider a broad-profile specialist to be one who has developed creative powers, who has profound fundamental knowledge and the habit of working without assistance, who has ability and a desire for continuous self-education and who has mastered scientific methods of research. He is an innovator and a skilful organizer who is able to reveal, formulate and solve new problems in communicating with people, to appreciate collective experience and critically to evaluate attainments. A broad-profile specialist is a man of high culture, of great erudition, and a real intellectual in a progressive socialist society.

As this pattern shows, the aim towards which the activities of Soviet higher education are directed has never been to convey extremely narrow specialized experience and to train one-sided and narrow professionals.

A creative specialist is not a technocrat but rather a broadly educated person who understands the social significance of technological progress.

In terms of Marxist teaching about man, one-sided emphasis on technology coupled with professional narrow-mindedness damages the general cultural development of personality and contradicts the main social task of progressive socialism — forming the harmoniously developed personality of communist society.

That is why we put in the forefront the problem of the broad humanization of science and of the improvement of the humanitarian training, particularly in relation to technical training.

The significance of humanitarian training lies in increasing the role played by the human factor in material and intellectual production which, as it develops, demands the maximum use of all the intellectual and cultural potential of our society.

For this purpose the curriculum has long included courses acquainting students with the history of the development of thought and culture, that is, the study of the history of science and culture and of the history of philosophy.

Since mastering this knowledge should be closely connected with developing a dialectical materialist understanding of nature, society and creative thinking, humanitarian preparation becomes necessary.

The organic unity of science and higher education in this epoch of scientific and technological revolution — that is, the unity that relates the process of producing new knowledge with that of training future specialists — negates the concept of isolation when considering the development of scientific research and the system of higher education.

Research on the most important scientific and technical problems of our time requires complex programmes, which involve different fields of knowledge and various scientific groups. There are conditions which particularly favour the creation of such groups in the system of higher education.

First, a research team made up of scientists in the higher education system is skilled and capable enough to solve a complex problem including the study of its social, political and other aspects. Second, the work of such a team can be built up on the basis of planning all stages through fundamental and applied researches, design-experimental researches, scientific-technical assistance in the organization of serial production and exploitation and finally, the training of specialists. Third, a research team includes scientists from different institutes and can be territorially dispersed. It is therefore possible to apply effectively the method of planning and management by objectives of scientific researches.

The cultural development of a well-educated specialist is also of great importance. This is also one of the most important concerns in the improvement of teaching procedures. Knowledge in itself is not the token of highly cultivated thought: knowledge of the laws of logic and of scientific cognition is one of the conditions of creative work but not the only one.

Experience of the rich emotional, moral and aesthetic world of man is a most animating and refreshing force in making logical thinking creative. The more varied and the deeper its connection with artistic imagination, the more productive logical thinking becomes.

Einstein used to say, 'Dostoevsky gives me much more than any scientific thinker does, even more than Gauss', thus emphasizing the importance of art in the development of the creative abilities of a man who not only understands but also feels life, nature, and public phenomena and who considers creative activity to be the purport of his life.

Education has stopped being a privilege or a duty of a certain age group: it seeks to embrace society as a whole and to accompany man throughout his life. Education is considered nowadays to be not only training for life but also the essence of life, characterized by incessant acquisition of knowledge and ceaseless reappraisal of ideas.

There are two principal trends in changes in the educational process, towards democratization and towards continuity and flexibility in the process itself.

Democratization of the higher-education system means that it will no longer confine itself to meeting the requirements of a certain age group for a definite period. On the contrary, it will expand its activities for the benefit of other population groups.

This is why democratization can be regarded as an important contribution to the development of man and society. Educational institutions of higher education have been transformed from passive depositories of knowledge into active instruments for the development of society. The development of East Siberia and of the Far East would be more difficult without the centres of higher education. The flexibility of higher education means that it is able to provide the country with the kinds and amount of labour resources it needs for its economic growth, and it is for the national economy to use these resources to the full and with the utmost efficiency.

Hence, reliability in the estimates of the needs of the developed socialist society and of its members for education, and for higher education in particular, becomes so important. The main condition for getting reliable estimates of the demands of economy is the working out of a correct methodological approach to its definition.

In a socialist society, the interests of the society and of the individual are congruent.

The development of education here is a planned and controlled regular process, based on public ownership of the means of production and on the basic advantages of the social system of socialism resulting from it. The initial principle of the methodological approach to planning, forecasting, and controlling education is Lenin's statement: 'We have received a rare opportunity to establish the terms necessary to produce radical social changes.' It is quite clear now what can be done in five years, and what would take much more time.

Under the conditions of a socialist system of management, definition of the requirements for education and of means of their satisfaction depends on the State interest. Socially indispensable requirements include the levels, forms and content of education which will provide society with optimum solutions to its ideological and political, social, economic, scientific and technical problems, within a planned or predicted period and the limitations of its internal and external conditions, resource provision possibilities being taken into account.

So the developed socialist society as a public State makes quite definite claims for its citizens in the field of education. On the other hand, every member of this society adds to these his own claims, in the sense of being given the possibility of satisfying his need for education — a right he is entitled to, according to Article 45 of the Constitution of the U.S.S.R.

In this connection it should be noted that the socialist State establishes and controls a minimum limit for the public educational level required — at present general secondary education. The citizens of our country can achieve this minimum in a wide network of educational institutions, of schools providing general education, professional and technical schools, and technical colleges.

Satisfaction of the need for a higher educational level at certain specific periods in history is defined by the level of the society's development and by its economic and intellectual potential. It is necessary to distinguish between the general need for education above the established lower level required and those needs connected with the character and content of labour.

Acquiring such education can be regarded as an extra social benefit. It is obtained through self-education as well as through a widely developed network of public universities. A feature of such education is that its completion does not give the right to planned labour employment.

Another aspect of the social need for education above the minimum level is connected with the social division of labour and determined by the economic demand of the people, taking into account the demographic situation. This demand is satisfied through a broad State system of special educational institutions.

This aspect of education (including general secondary education) is the object of centralized State planning and control, exercised over training and re-training, higher qualifications and inter-republic and inter-departmental distribution of specialists.

In order to achieve greater precision in the planning process, forecasts to determine the best forms and balances in the education system in accordance with the dynamics and structure of the development of people's economy are being worked out. The nomenclature of higher-education specialists is constantly revised with the purpose of making it more precise and more extensive.

The organizational structure of the system of higher education is being improved as an important step in providing possibilities for the permanent process of 'education—higher skill'. In this connection, the system of evening classes and education by correspondence has become more and more important as a means of training specialists, e.g. middle-level organizers and engineer-operators dealing with complicated automatic equipment. It is increasingly a major factor in improving the workers' skill, to the level of engineers and technicians. Together with the preparatory departments of day educational establishments, the system of combining work with studies contributes to bringing the social structure of students into line with the social and class structure of the socialist society. In the future, the organization of the system of training specialists by combining work with studies will be progressively developed. At present, one can see a tendency towards combining evening classes with work at a plant and to replacing education by correspondence by the 'day correspondence system' of education.

In addition, education institutions should be situated near the homes of the working people.

This is a far from complete list of problems and tasks facing higher education in connection with scientific-technical progress.

Solution of these problems will not only intensify the links between higher education and the demands of the popular economy of the country but will also make an important contribution to the satisfaction of social and personal demands in the developing socialist society and the improvement of material and cultural standards.

The Soviet Union is working towards this end by systematically and persistently combining the achievements of the scientific-technical revolution with the advantages of a socialist society.

Education reform in Peru

by César Picón-Espinoza

The Peruvian Revolution and educational reform

THE REVOLUTION

On 3 October 1968, there was a *coup d'état* in Peru. At first, many saw this as just one more *coup* among the many in the country's history. However, it was soon realized that this was a different kind of coup, as the 'Revolutionary Government of the Armed Forces' took strong, specific measures, aimed at changing the entire social structure.

Among these were: (a) nationalization of the 'Brea and Parinos' oil deposits controlled by the International Petroleum Company; (b) reform of the banks; (c) a reform of business and commerce; (d) a major land reform; (e) an important new programme of social property, coexisting with forms of private and public ownership; (f) a strong foreign policy aligned with Third World countries.

During its first phase (3 October 1968 to 29 August 1975) this revolutionary government introduced its very own ideology, rejecting capitalism as 'the cause of Peru's underdevelopment and dependence' and rejecting communism as 'totalitarian'. The Revolution was defined as 'humanistic, independent and nationalistic'. The 'non-capitalist and non-communist' position was stressed during this first phase; the government's aim was to develop a 'social democracy with full participation', which would imply a transfer of power—economic, political, and social—to popular-based organizations. In practice, the Peruvian Model was directed towards 'a non-totalitarian socialism', integrating the best traditions of liberal and Christian thought.

Within this historical context there was an obvious need to reform the educational system, to tackle the problems of this system, both quantitatively and qualitatively. These problems included: increasing illiteracy; disregard for poor, marginal children; lack of adult-education programmes; an academic, intellectual elitist tendency; lack of truly Peruvian content and of content relevant to social reality; inadequate recruitment and selection of teachers; and a rigid, bureaucratic system with administrative inefficiency and financial mismanagement.

THE EDUCATIONAL REFORM

In September 1969, less than a year after the revolutionary process began, an Educational Reform Commission was established to propose a total restructuring of the national educational system. The creation of this commission was an important step, involving prominent professionals from various fields. The multi-disciplinary nature of the commission meant that the problems of education would not be considered only from a pedagogical viewpoint (as they had been in previous reforms) and that they would be studied in the global context of Peru's overall problems.

The work strategy followed by the commission included an analysis of the national situation and, within that context, a profound analysis of the educational question, based on contributions from various people and institutions who had carried out previous studies. Out of these analyses came a theoretical framework, the structure for a new educational system, and a strategy for its implementation.

The ideological formulation of a new educational system in Peru has become widely recognized, and has attracted international interest. It breaks with conventional ideas of education, and tries to apply systematically a broader concept of a permanent education relevant to the Peruvian social reality.

The educational reform had three major objectives:

1. Education oriented to work training, integrated with the national development plan.
2. Education aimed at transforming the structure of Peruvian society.
3. Education that affirms national identity and independence.

Positive aspects of the Peruvian educational reform

EDUCATIONAL RESPONSIBILITY OF THE POPULATION

Since 1972, the Peruvian population has become deeply conscious of its educational responsibility. In contrast with the past, when education was in the hands of the Ministry of Education, the schools and the teachers, today there is a new concept of education among many sectors of the population. Many current popular expressions reflect this new consciousness, e.g. 'education, the task of everyone', 'one learns all through one's life', 'education is revolution'.

THE COMMUNITY EDUCATION NUCLEUS

The *núcleo* model, created by the reform to encourage the active participation of the people in the educational process in their own geographic settings has, in spite of its limitations, promoted the participation of parents, teachers, community organizations, and diverse government entities in the various educational tasks of the nation. In this way, the 'community education nucleus', despite weaknesses in its structure and operations, has become a catalyst for participation of the community in the educational process.

The *núcleos* are contributing in various ways, with results that differ according to the particular circumstances of each area. They are encouraging the maximum use, for educational purposes, of the facilities and materials of both educational and community institutions; utilizing the human resources of the community, on a voluntary basis, in educational activities; and sharing in a growing co-operative effort between government and non-governmental institutions in educational tasks. All this takes place within a broader framework of action directed towards the development of basic community organizations.

DEMOCRACY AND HUMANISM IN THE NEW EDUCATION

The special attention that the new education gave to women, to rural populations, and to the *Pueblo Joven*, or urban slum areas, as established by the policies and strategies of the revolutionary process, has contributed to a new consciousness of the nature of the problems of marginal groups. Some of the educational achievements of such groups reflect a genuinely humanistic and democratic education, undertaken to eliminate discrimination in terms of educational opportunities.

'INITIAL' EDUCATION

The first level of the new system is pre-school education, aimed at all children up to the age of 5. This programme is, without a doubt, a feature of the new Peruvian education with the greatest potential international import, because it differs from the traditional focus, on the primary and pre-school stages, which disregards the importance of the first years of childhood.

Through formal and non-formal education of families and communities, there are growing numbers of children reached by this 'Initial Education' and given, during their early years, invaluable experience and stimulus to the development of their potential. In the implementation of initial education in recent years, priority has been given to children in rural areas. This is only the beginning of a long process of development of this form of education; none the less, its impact up to the present has been extremely favourable.

INNOVATION IN HIGHER EDUCATION

Higher education has three cycles: the first cycle is professional education provided in post-basic institutions and leading to the *bachillerato*; the second cycle is the *licenciatura* programme, followed in universities and in other institutions authorized by law; and the third cycle involves advanced studies, leading to the *doctorado* and undertaken at the National Institute for Higher Education and in the universities.

The first cycle of *Educación Superior* is especially innovative. Through this programme, Peruvian students who have completed the ninth grade of basic education, through either *Educación Básica Regular* or *Educación Básica Laboral*, have the opportunity to pursue a professional career in the humanities, science and technology.

The impact of this programme is being felt strongly among Peruvian youth, who are realizing more clearly many of its advantages:

1. The studies lead to a *bachiller profesional*, soon to be regulated by a special law.
2. Within a short period (three or four years) they can become professionals and enter the work world—within which they can continue their studies in the second cycle of higher education, either in the field studied in the first cycle, or in another.
3. The areas of professional training in the first cycle are selected carefully and resulting programmes are the joint efforts of the education and other socio-economic sectors.
4. A good working atmosphere has developed in the *escuelas superiores de educación profesional*, where both men and women behave qualitatively differently from the traditional patterns of university life.
5. The *bachiller* is in itself a professional degree that enables those who earn it to work in the fields of the humanities, science and technology, with full professional responsibilities. It thus differs significantly from the traditional qualification obtained at technical trade schools.
6. The *bachiller profesional*, thus conceived, is a response to specific needs arising out of the development and transformation of Peruvian society.

CHILDREN'S RESPONSE

Children of 6 years and older who are in the first grades of *Educación Básica Regular* are assuming new forms of behaviour not found within traditional education. Their creative potential is being challenged both materially and socially; gradually they are discovering their national culture and learning to respect it; they are learning to use simple tools that allow them to continue learning on their own and with their families and friends; they are being trained in co-operative group work, while still affirming their individual personalities; they are constantly encouraged to make their own decisions, thus developing their capacity for critical reflection; they are introduced, gradually, to the work world through practical work activities in the classroom and more and more frequently, through real work experiences outside the classroom.

ADULT EDUCATION

Great importance has been given to the implementation of adult education programmes in Peru. There are three of these: *Educación Básica Laboral* (Basic Workers' Education); *Calificación Profesional Extraordinaria* (Special Professional Training); and *Extensión Educativa* (Educational Extension), the latter oriented to the population of 15 years of age and above.

Adult-education programmes and services have been developed considerably, both quantitatively and qualitatively. While there used to be only night schools, almost exclusively in urban areas, and some technical-training programmes for workers in factories, there are now adult-education programmes in various settings; in factories, in agricultural co-operatives and societies, in mining companies, in the fishing industry, in commercial offices, etc. The present Educational Law requires all work centres to establish a *Unidad de Instrucción*, or Instruction Unit, an organizational model that stimulates the participation of the workers in the programming and development of educational services.

Governmental institutions actively participate in close co-ordination with non-governmental organizations, in developing the national adult-education programme, which has made considerable achievements with regard to the education of women, of the rural population, of marginal urban communities, and of ethnic and linguistic groups from the mountain and jungle areas.

ADMINISTRATIVE DECENTRALIZATION

The Ministry of Education, of all the State institutions, is the one that has made the greatest progress in decentralizing its administration. The administrative structure exists at several levels: national, regional, zonal and nuclear (community education nucleus). Each level has its own clearly defined functions and enjoys a relative autonomy. Obviously, for this structure to function effectively, the active participation of the people is needed. Experience in this respect has not been wholly positive, as is shown later.

NATIONAL CO-ORDINATION

Intra- and inter-sectoral co-ordination of educational activities has seen a remarkable development in recent years. Co-ordination is no longer conceived of as a simple process of giving mutual support and of carrying out sporadic joint activities. The new concept calls for a co-ordination of administration at all levels, and is aimed at achieving an ideological and methodological congruence in order to reach common goals within the general framework of national political strategies. Bringing together representatives of both governmental and non-governmental institutions, multi-sectoral co-ordinating bodies have been established at many different levels of the administrative structure of the Ministry of Education.

Negative aspects of the reform

Negative aspects of the educational reform include over-attention to theory, inadequate policies and programmes, and lack of suitable planning, research and management. These defects have limited successful implementation and satisfactory results.

THEORY

In the first years of the reform, energies were concentrated almost exclusively on the development of a theoretical framework. This theorizing slowed down considerably the development of an educational technology and of the logistical support needed to implement the reform effectively and efficiently. It also contributed to a distortion of the clarification process. The latter involved an examination of the general situation of the Peruvian society before the Revolution, in order to understand the current process and its future goals. However, this examination was not always carried out within the framework established by the Revolutionary Government. There was an obvious political infiltration, distorting the legitimate aim of the process, as defined by the reform.

INADEQUATE POLICIES AND PROGRAMMES

From the start, the government's policy for improving the situation of teachers was unclear and vacillating. Even though a high-level commission worked intensively on a project in this regard, its proposals were never approved by the policy-making body. This situation created a tension which still persists between the government and SUTEP, a union formed by the teachers.

Re-training teachers in the early years of the reform placed major emphasis on the ideological framework and on participation, disregarding educational technology and the logistical operations of educational services. Only in the last two years has the orientation changed, but it has now become more rigid, suppressing the creativity of the teachers.

Up to the present there is still no personnel policy for the different administrative levels of the Ministry of Education. There are some vague norms, but selection of personnel is usually made intuitively or based upon social and family connections. With the exception of the educational planning personnel, most technical and administrative personnel have little opportunity for training.

Educational technology was examined carefully from a theoretical viewpoint during the first years of the Reform. The transfer of technology was studied in the light of national experience and of the experiences of Third World countries. However, this study reached no concrete conclusions relevant to national goals, and only in 1977 was a national policy for educational technology proposed.

The national adult-education programme is the only one that has made significant efforts to integrate education with national social and economic development plans. Such an integration demands the participation of all the different levels and programmes in the educational system in order to meet the needs of communities, particularly the most marginal and deprived groups.

LACK OF PLANNING

During the first phase of the Revolution, the major goal was to develop 'a social democracy with full participation'. Participation was also proclaimed a basic principle of the educational reform. Unfortunately, there was no clearly defined national strategy to implement participation at the level of local organizations. Experiences of meaningful local participation were neither stimulated nor understood by the technical and administrative organizers of the programme. The transition plan failed to assess the real possibilities and resources of the educational system, on the one hand, and of the revolutionary process and its dynamic changes on the other. This failure entailed continual readjustments of the plan.

RESEARCH

Even though the reform stressed the need for the scientific study of social reality, the only effort made during the first years was the so-called *diagnóstico situacional*, or diagnosis of a social situation. This suffered certain limitations: it was one-sided, a separate diagnosis being made for each level; it was disorganized and repetitious; and communities were made objects of research instead of participants in it. A series of interesting research projects was undertaken by INIDE, the National Institute for Educational Research and Development; however, it did not include priority problems and the research results were not known in time to be of use to programme decision-makers and administrators.

MANAGEMENT

Implementation of the reform understandably required an addition of personnel at the Ministry of Education. But this tendency has increased in recent years, leading to overstaffing of the central offices, while community educational centres remain lacking in personnel. Although smooth and rapid functioning of the technical and operational infrastructure is critical to the implementation of the reform, construction of school buildings and equipment has to be approved through rigid bureaucratic procedures, making the process slow, improvised and inefficient. Further, even though the national budget allots a large amount to educational development, financial resources continue to be insufficient for the demands.

DISCOURAGING RESULTS OF THE NATIONAL LITERACY PROGRAMME: IMPLEMENTATION AND RESULTS

The theoretical framework and the basic objectives of the literacy programme were very ambitious, many objectives being developed in a very short time. The desired outcome was not made clear, and thus the literacy process was interpreted in various ways: sometimes as a way of assimilating illiterates into the Spanish-speaking society; at other times, as a consciousness-rousing process; and often, as the mere teaching of reading and writing. The selection of literacy teachers was based upon limited academic criteria and a vague sense of a revolutionary spirit that in reality represented a distortion of the original concept of the Peruvian Revolution. The strategy of the programme called for a massive social mobilization, but such an effort required strong administrative leadership. Lacking this, the programme could not satisfactorily attain its objectives.

One of the objectives of the new Peruvian education is training for work, an orientation that has been highly developed theoretically but has not been put into practice. It is not included in teachers' re-training programmes and its implementation requires minimal equipment not yet available in educational centres. To attain this objective a more realistic strategy, one which utilizes the resources of the community for educational purposes, is needed.

The reform supported strongly the development of non-formal education programmes at all levels of the system. The only significant efforts in this direction have been made in the programme of *Educación Básica Laboral* or Basic Workers' Education, and in the Initial Education Programme. If this form of non-school education is not developed at other levels, the growing needs of a vast portion of the population will not be met.

The future

POLICY

On 29 August 1975, the second phase of the Peruvian Revolution began. The principles remained officially the same, but the methodology changed. The approach became more pragmatic; changes are to be continually made, but 'rationally and methodically, avoiding unnecessary disruptions'.

Since February 1977, a national policy to continue the reform 'in the spirit of the Second Phase of the Revolution', has been in effect. Though still based on the 1972 General Educational Law, it is becoming evident that this new policy is aimed towards more formal (*escolarizado*) educational programmes.

Integration of cultural, scientific and educational development processes, integration of education with national employment policy and clarification of the university reform within the framework of the general educational reform have been significantly absent.

There is clearly a need for a strong policy aimed at improving the situation of Peruvian teachers. Without a change in the attitude of the teachers and without their commitment, the implementation of the educational reform is very limited, even if there are other major social changes supporting it. This demands a continuing, integrated retraining programme for teachers, enabling them to participate more fully in the reform.

STRATEGY

The current strategy used in the reform is seen as a 'gradual deepening of the revolutionary process, with authority'. This strategy has resulted in a return to centralized control by the Ministry; the elimination of some high-ranking Ministry officials and technicians; and bureaucratic control that limits the creativity of administrators and teachers.

In developing a long-term strategy, the following are important: clear definition of the present situation, including evaluation of the implementation of the transition plan; priority for marginal groups and deprived regions of the country; operational procedures (based on the current policies of the Revolutionary Government) to make education an instrument of social structural change and national development; integration of adult-education programmes with plans for the social and economic development of the country; a closer co-ordination within the educational system throughout the country, and between education and other sectors; and the development of a new strategy for a more funda-mental permanent educational process in Peru, with special attention to non-formal education.

ADMINISTRATION

The plan for regionalization of the country and of its industrial development has not yet been implemented and this makes co-ordination difficult. When implemented, this plan would facilitate the integration of educational development with the development plans of each region.

The community *núcleo* model has proved very effective in promoting participation of the community in the educational process. With regionalization of the country, the *núcleo* could become the basic unit not only of the educational system but of the entire government structure.

The Ministry of Education must become more flexible and efficient. This will require a total restructuring of the educational infrastructure and of the Ministry itself.

EDUCATIONAL TECHNOLOGY

The approval of a new policy on educational technology is encouraging. Such technology should profit from scientific discoveries relevant to education, should be congruent with the purposes of the Reform, and should fit the cultural, social and economic reality of Peru.

Educational technology includes four main elements: curriculum and its development; teaching methods; teaching aids (books, tapes, etc.); and evaluation of the students and of the general educational process.

In the future stages of development, consideration should be given to: diversification of the technology programme, growing out of the regionalization plan; differentiation of levels of educational technology, according to the concrete needs and resources of each local operation; use of the technological experience of various governmental and non-governmental institutions outside the Education Ministry; and adap-tation of significant experiences of other countries, especially in Latin America.

It would seem wise to establish an Office of Educational Technology in the Ministry to work with various levels and programmes.

FINANCE

Financial responsibility for the reform was originally placed in the hands of the national community. However, without a national strategy, this proved difficult to exercise, and the State ended up by assuming major responsibility, practically providing free education.

The General Educational Law (1972) demands that more centres provide financial support to education programmes for workers and their families. There is a need for enforcement of this law, for a more realistic strategy, and for more control, promotion and evaluation of the educational services offered by the work centres.

Possibilities of internal financing should be actively explored. Local educational centres, work-training programmes and other educational services should be encouraged to generate their own financial resources and to move towards self-sufficiency.

As for external financing, present lines of credit, particularly *Crédito Húngaro*, appear unsatisfactory for technical reasons. More aggressive policies should be developed in order to attract other external sources of finance; the good international image of the reform could be exploited for these purposes. Two major limitations must be taken into account: international operations are restricted by centralized internal bureaucracy and there are very few technicians qualified enough to carry out such operations.

Credit from the International Bank for Reconstruction and Development (IBRD) or the Inter-American Development Bank would necessitate restructuring Ministry operations to avoid a loss of both time and money. Main needs are to decentralize operations to 'educational Regions and Zones'; to develop specific projects, with appropriate training of the teachers concerned; and to have a defined policy for education as a component of productive work. Some progress has already been made on the first of these, but the others still await attention.

RESEARCH

A major evaluation of the reform has been undertaken, but the results appear not to have been seriously considered yet. If studied, they could contribute to the formulation of policies and strategies for the future.

Given the priorities of the Reform, research should be used to: identify specific cultural features and develop education relevant to these; determine priority work areas, and develop training programmes in relation to employment needs; build integrated developmental education programmes for marginal social groups; develop an educational model as one part of the integrated development of rural areas and of marginal urban areas; identify the interests and educational needs of local communities, through participatory research; analyse significant experiences in the field of educational technology; build models for implementing non-formal education, especially in the fields of initial education, *Educación Básica Laboral* and the first cycle of higher education; and develop models for the gradual auto-financing of educational services, especially in the field of adult education.

Educational reform and available resources: an example from the People's Republic of Benin

by Jean Pliya

A real policy of popular educational reform

Merely to work out a genuine policy of educational reform is not enough; such a policy must then be applied efficiently, without losing decision-making sovereignty when faced with a choice of priorities. This is only possible when reform is related to available resources and policy cuts its coat according to its cloth. In 1973–74, under the impetus of the Revolutionary Military Government, Benin carried out a revolutionary transformation of the country's educational system, involving the participation of all levels of the population.

Hitherto, instruction, education and culture have been at the service of foreign domination and exploitation. . . . It is urgently necessary for us to set up a democratic and patriotic educational system which will facilitate the teaching of modern science and techniques in the service of people.[1]

The reform accordingly offers a clear definition of the general principles of democratic organization and puts forward new structures for the various levels of education, so as to harness them to the task of integrated independent national development. The reform defined the content of education and established timetables, methods, types of certificates to be awarded, and the various methods of financing.

Since 10 September 1974, when the National Council of the Revolution adopted the national programme for a new education, Benin has had to confront the problems of applying the reform within the limits of its available resources; one of the major principles of the Benin Revolution is self-reliance. The reform applies to all kinds and levels of education and to all stages in the upbringing of a patriotic Benin citizen.

The Benin educational system before the reform

The ideological aims of the colonial system of education gradually brought into being a structure which in 1973, just before the reform came into force, consisted of both a public and a private sector. French was the language of instruction. The three levels of instruction — primary, secondary and higher — were the same as those found in other French colonies. The present university dates from 1970.

Main problems before the application of the reform

The first problem to take note of is the rapid growth in the number of primary-school pupils. During the ten years previous to the academic year 1974/75, the average annual growth rate was 11 per cent but wastage was high; just over 50 per cent of those who entered the six-year primary stage actually completed it. There were still considerable disparities between regions, the enrolment rate varying between 23 per cent in the north and 70 per cent in the south, while the figure for the country as a whole was 40 per cent. It was estimated that over half the teachers in the public educational system were qualified, but the proportion was much lower in the private schools.

The number of pupils has grown much more rapidly in the secondary level than in the primary: here the average annual rate of increase during the last five years was 21 per cent. There was only one teachers' training school, whose two-year course for primary-school teachers provided only one-third of the country's needs. It also trained twenty teachers each year for lower secondary education. There was no training establishment in Benin for upper secondary teachers and little research into teaching methods.

Technical and vocational training was not only inadequate in quantity but also insufficiently adapted to the needs of the labour market. Moreover, it was very expensive, the cost per pupil being six times greater than that in education in general. The return on this form of training was also low, with the great majority of pupils going on to administrative posts because business firms preferred to recruit from among those who had served an apprenticeship. Technical and vocational training was mainly concentrated in the south of the country, where there was a serious shortage of teachers. There was no contact between technical training schools and industry. Agricultural training was selective, and designed to provide civil servants to work in agricultural administration.

Growth in higher education far surpassed that at the other two levels. The mean annual growth rate between 1972 and 1976 was 38 per cent. There were about 1,150 Benin students studying abroad. Expenditure on education varied between 4 and 4·5 per cent of the GNP between 1965 and 1970; in 1973 it rose to 6·88 per cent. The education budget increased faster than the national budget as a whole, though the school enrolment rate remained below 40 per cent!

The excessive growth in educational expenditure was not the only distortion to be seen in matters of financing. There were large disparities in the allocation of expenditure as between the various educational sectors. Higher education, though still in its early stages, absorbed 14 per cent of the education budget, an alarming situation which explains the impossibility under the previous sytem of extending the educational infrastructure as a whole, of increasing the number of grant and scholarship holders, of supplying schools with adequate equipment, and of improving working conditions for pupils and students.

Speedy and effective solutions to these problems were clearly necessary if the important social demand for education was to be met. The main problem stemmed from the colonial and neo-colonial structures and from the insufficiently co-ordinated expansion measures embarked on between 1969 and 1972.

The new education: main objects and structure

For the new education to conform to Benin's policy of national independence, it has to fulfil certain basic requirements. It must be: designed to free society from the exploitation of one individual by another; democratic and popular, bringing together the rural and urban worlds and abolishing elitism; compulsory and free, so that everyone has equal opportunities and access to instruction; and public and secular. This implies the decolonization of existing structures and methods, and their reorganization in accordance with the national ideology. Hence the need to work out positive relationships between teachers and pupils; to co-ordinate Benin's own educational system with those of other African countries, while respecting Benin's own proper interests; to relate intellectual training to civic, physical, military, political and ideological education; and to recruit educators who are servants of the people, ready to respond to their technical, political, civic and social needs.

The concept of educator has been extended beyond the traditional limits so as to make use of all possible intellectual and technical abilities.

Education is no longer expected to impart merely abstract and theoretical knowledge, but rather a practical training adapted to the environment and to productive occupation. Thus the new education should form part of the social environment as a whole, and act as a central driving force for political, economic and social development, in other words for development in the widest sense of the word.

The content of education should be such as to guarantee a sound scientific training, give access to lifelong education at all levels, and encourage specialization. 'It is therefore necessary to draw up and adapt syllabuses in terms of the age of those who are to make use of them, and of the requirements of production and social and economic development, and in such a way as to guarantee employment outlets at the end of each stage.'[2] This describes an educational system which produces immediate returns, since every scholastic establishment is also a unit of production, with every child who enters it only leaving it when he has acquired a trade.

The democratic execution of this educational policy is the exclusive responsibility of the State, with the people themselves performing the essential tasks through mass organizations and official institutions. It is necessary to combine all efforts on a national plan, while determining the respective contributions to be made by the State and by the different communities, and by parents, pupils, students and teachers. The existing infrastructures must be used to the full, and education provided at minimum cost and without increasing the contribution borne by the deprived masses. The national character of the enterprise also means that the State must take over all the elements involved, and in particular control over external aid.

There remain the cultural and human aims of the reform, designed to strengthen national unity and accelerate social evolution. These include the gradual introduction of Benin's national languages into its educational system, first as subjects in themselves and then as vehicles of knowledge, and the preservation of national cultural values in so far as they are fundamental and compatible with economic and social progress and development.

The new structures

There are two main levels of instruction and a structure providing for para-, peri- and post-school education. The first level is subdivided into nursery school (lasting two years) and basic education (lasting five years). At the end of this stage the child is directed towards:
The polytechnical complex, first level (lasting three years and recruited either from basic education classes, or from the Centre Populaire

d'Éducation, de Perfectionnement et d'Initiation à la Production
(CPEPIP—People's Centre for Education, Further Training and
Introduction to Production)); or

The polytechnical complex, second level (lasting three years and
recruited from intermediate stage 1 and from the CPEPIP); or

Intermediate stages 1 and 2 (each lasting three years), which correspond
to the old secondary stages. They cover both general and technical
education.

The second main level of instruction corresponds to the old higher
education and includes specialized institutes for training managerial
staff and research.

CPEPIP provides educational activities for those engaged in
productive occupations, including literacy courses, initiation into
production, educational leisure activities, and sports.

Timetables, methods and examinations

Timetables need to be adapted to the physiological and psychological
capabilities of Benin children, thereby producing a suitable balance
between practical and intellectual activities.

The method used should be essentially active and dynamic and
based on a study of the environment. It should aim at socializing the
child so as to integrate him into his environment and at the same time
provide him with the means of transforming it.

The traditional type of examination will gradually be replaced by a
new kind of evaluation conferring a certificate or diploma at each level
of instruction and based on compulsory continuous assessment.

The financing of the reform

The initiators of the reform suggested the following methods (in
descending order of priority) of financing it: contribution from the
national budget; contribution from parents (in the transitional phase
only); contribution from communities (by means of personal service by
individuals and allocations from local budgets); voluntary and national
subscriptions; national and foreign loans; self-financing of schools as
units of production; contribution from State companies; rational use of
existing structures; contribution from private companies; foreign aid. 'It
is true that foreign contributions can help towards the realization of
some of the aims of Benin education, but such contributions can only
supplement the national effort.'[3]

The first attempts to estimate the cost of the new education produced such enormous figures that the reformers took fright. It was therefore necessary to be realistic, though without using financial considerations as an excuse for sabotaging this vital enterprise. Priorities were defined in terms of political realism; short-, medium- and long-term objectives were fixed in relation to the national plan; this was particularly necessary as in 1973 the reform had not yet been conceived of in terms of the country's economic and financial possibilities.

The basic principle is self-reliance, in the first instance. But Benin's own capabilities depend on the country's economic production and human potentialities. The new education must not appear to be something foreign, parasitical and disproportionate, but rather an essential factor in development activities, both encouraging development and receiving stimulus from it. If the new education is to lead to 100 per cent school enrolment, the State must discharge its responsibilities in the financing of infrastructure, facilities and running costs, and in making available additional opportunities through better exploitation of the nation's resources. It is also imperative that workers should be guaranteed respectable purchasing power, and that the new education system itself should participate in its own financing.

Common sense thus leads us to the idea of making a start in terms of the means at our disposal, aiming primarily at objectives likely to make a rapid contribution to the steady expansion of the educational system itself and to the country's economic and social development. Above all, we must guard against increasing the existing imbalance between educational expenditure and the national budget as a whole.

Early application of the reform

The first areas affected by the reform were basic and intermediate education, though in various ways higher education has been increasingly concerned.

The following immediate aims were decided on in 1974:

The take-over by the State of all private schools in the primary sector; qualified teachers were incorporated into the government service.

Revision of educational syllabuses and timetables.

Introduction of practical instruction and further development of technical and vocational training.

Integration of education into the environment.

National commissions were set up to work out plans of application, to define methods of approach and to point out likely problems. Thus the National Commission for Syllabuses and Timetables drew up new syllabuses first for basic and then for intermediate education. History and geography syllabuses for these two stages of instruction were adapted and freed from undue foreign influence. A new school calendar was adopted, corresponding more closely to the agricultural seasons in Benin.

But without capable teachers prepared to carry out the reform there could be no hope of positive results. Benin did not possess the necessary structures for the re-training of teachers, for the training of technical and vocational teaching staff, or for the training of nursery-school teachers. The Institut National pour la Formation et la Recherche en Éducation (INFRE—National Institute for Educational Training and Research) was founded for this purpose and already organizes courses and seminars for new teachers and re-training and refresher courses for those already in the profession. But most teachers cannot benefit by these arrangements. The new conception of the educator, which sees as a potential teacher anyone who is competent in his own work and environment, calls for stringent organization.

One of the major difficulties in applying the educational reform is the lack of textbooks and other teaching materials corresponding to the new syllabuses. Hitherto such aids had come almost exclusively from France: they were expensive, and their content was unsuited to local conditions. To fulfil the aims of the reform, it was decided that teaching materials and school textbooks should be produced in Benin itself.

The phase during which the new basic education was tried out provided for the establishment of pilot schools. These were to adapt the new structures, apply the new syllabuses and introduce national languages and practical training. These first attempts at applying the reform brought out clearly the problem of financial resources, for the cost of this operation has been considerable.

*Introduction of practical training and
development of technical and vocational training*

From September 1974, school co-operatives were widely introduced, first in basic and subsequently in intermediate and secondary education.

Students at the National University of Benin are divided up among various university co-operatives. These are a major factor in the reform—the integration of education into the environment and the functioning of scholastic establishments as units of production will depend on them. By 31 December 1975, 834 school co-operatives had been registered by the school production service;[4] those linked to agricultural production were by far the most numerous.

Thenceforth every scholastic establishment was a unit of production. At the time of the national production campaign launched in January 1976, it was decided that every establishment must produce enough to cover 20 per cent of its running costs. It was necessary to equip the co-operatives to start with, providing them with cultivable land, agricultural tools or the stock-in-trade necessary for crafts or animal husbandry.

Seminars and training courses were arranged to enable education to make an effective contribution to the economic and social development of the environment. Priority was given to the creation of polytechnical complexes (first level, second level and university), so as to meet development needs which could not otherwise be adequately catered for because of the shortage of skilled manpower. The combination of practical and theoretical training is designed to place pupils in the same conditions as regards labour and production as those that would obtain in the factories or firms in which the pupils may eventually be employed. Business firms should see the advantages of employing young workers who can help to improve both returns and the quality of production.

The cost of the reform

The cost of the reform depends on how it is put into effect in terms of time and space. This has been determined on the basis of surveys carried out during the experimental phase.

Though the final result must be awaited, it is worth analysing the financial measures decided upon in the last three years in order to reconcile the requirements of the reform with the available resources, since it is not much use having an accurate estimate of the overall cost of a project if the means of putting it into practice are lacking.

In accordance with its declared principle of self-reliance — of 'depending first and foremost on its own capabilities' — the Government of Benin has considered various ways of better utilizing national resources, the self-financing of scholastic establishments, and efficient co-ordination of foreign aid.

The State's role in the financing of the reform

In basic education, direct public expenditure doubled in the space of ten years. Political measures necessary to reduce this expenditure included: abolition of subsidies to private schools, in 1975; better use of the expenditure through a better distribution of teachers; from September

1974 on, recruitment of young revolutionary teachers who work for comparatively low pay; and priority to intermediate education, thus responding more closely to the needs of society.

The abolition of subsidies to private schools in 1975 reduced the share of intermediate education in public education expenditure from 32·4 per cent in 1974 to 29·6 per cent in 1975. But the cost of scholarships and grants remains high, accounting for an average of 50 per cent of expenditure at this level. As a way of meeting the dual problem of shortage of teachers and of funds to pay them, the Service Civique et Patriotique has been set up to recruit students at the end of the first stage of their studies at the National University of Benin; these students teach in schools providing general or technical intermediate education. In higher intermediate education, the value of scholarships has been temporarily reduced and, as an experiment, pupils are no longer admitted as boarders. New classes have been introduced which are less expensive to run than those at the high schools; the contributions of parents and of the private sector have been increased; and wastage has been reduced by better staff management.

No priority has yet been given to agricultural and vocational technical training, despite the fact that the reform is now under way. Technical instruction has not yet been incorporated into the system introduced by the reform, though the revenue received from the special apprenticeship tax could well be used for this purpose.

Higher education does not call for any major national effort in connection with the reform. But the fact that most pupils tend to continue their studies means that the number of scholarships is constantly increasing. In order that as many as possible should benefit from scholarships and grants, these were reduced in value; however, the rising cost of living has forced the government to reverse this decision to some extent.

To provide the funds necessary for the new education policy to function, a special new education account was created by decree in April 1975, funded from: the suspension of allowances and various perquisites formerly enjoyed by employees of State and semi-public companies and of industrial and commercial public enterprises, and by politicians, civil servants, army officals and others required to travel about the country; the reduction of various special post allowances and overtime payments enjoyed by employees of the State, of local communities, and of State and semi-public companies; and a reduction in the rate of student grants.

This special account is responsible for paying the salaries of the young revolutionary teachers previously mentioned, the expenditure involved in organizing, equipping and running schools and other scholastic establishments as units of production, and the expenditure involved in preparing and publishing teaching programmes and school books.

A National Stationery and Book Company has been created to centralize the purchase, sale and distribution of school books. Thus the State has given a lead in suggesting practical solutions to the problem of how to finance the new education.

Family participation in the financing of reform

In basic education, pupils' families contribute to the various costs involved in school attendance and in use of the canteen; they also give help in providing buildings and furniture. Since 1972, the parents' contribution has increased proportionally faster than the increase in the total cost of basic education.

In intermediate education, the parents' contribution varies between 20 and 30 per cent of the total expenditure. Each scholastic establishment has a governing board, and here the parents share in decisions affecting the lives of the pupils. The parents themselves decide how much their contribution should be, the rate varying from one establishment to another.

Participation of decentralized communities
in the financing of the reform

Legal and administrative regulations make provincial communities responsible for the financing, building and furnishing of general intermediate schools. Other local communities, represented by district leaders and political authorities, are responsible for the management of local taxes, by which village groups and pupils' parents supply the needs of the school and its unit of production, especially in the matter of buildings, equipment, administrative and even teaching staff.

Village groups undertake to make part of their contribution in the form of services, for example as unpaid labourers or instructors in national languages or practical subjects. Craftsmen, industrialists and technical executives are all willing to teach, as are development officials (such as those working in health, agriculture, the veterinary service, the social services, etc.), shopkeepers and other members of the community. Village groups undertake to make land and facilities available to the school, over and above the occasional raising of financial subscriptions for special purposes.

School units of production

From now on the school units of production are supposed to finance up to 20 per cent of their own running costs, by means of the school and university co-operatives. While awaiting the initial endowment due from the special new-education account or village groups, members of the co-operatives have spontaneously agreed to subscribe towards the basic outlay necessary for setting up training and operating infrastructures: for example, the purchase of tools, implements and livestock, and of fundamental requirements such as fodder, fertilizers, insecticides and building materials.

In the polytechnical complexes the units of production aim at obtaining practical returns on the pupils' hours of practical work, earning profits in order eventually to reduce the cost of technical and vocational training.

With this in mind, the idea of what is meant by production has been extended. While agricultural production is the chief preoccupation of the country as a whole, the school and university co-operatives select their own kind of production according to whether the school concerned is urban (in which case activity is geared towards crafts, garden produce, the raising of domestic animals, industry and commerce) or rural (in which case attention is concentrated on rural crafts, stock-raising, farming, industry and commerce).

The university co-operative has its own fields of cereals and its own livestock. It equips and runs a photography workshop. Its theatre group presents plays and traditional dancing. Its sports teams organize matches. All these activities are helping to finance the new education. The co-operatives of the general intermediate schools vie with one another in inventing countless productive activities which reflect a lively new spirit, though without detriment to the political and intellectual training the schools impart.

Foreign aid

Outside help thus acts as a supplement to Benin's own efforts. Foreign aid is not greatly in evidence in basic education, but is clearly seen in intermediate education, almost entirely in the form of teachers at the higher intermediate level. Foreign help is reflected most of all at the level of higher education. International organizations such as the World Health Organization (WHO), Unesco, the Association of Wholly or Partially French-language Universities (AUPELF), and the United Nations Development Programme (UNDP), and countries such as

France, the United States, Canada, the U.S.S.R., Romania, the
Democratic People's Republic of Korea and Algeria give help in the form
either of scholarships, equipment and books or of participation in
building. The technical staff of these countries help Benin as teachers,
researchers and educational instructors of various kinds.

In the expectation of more such multilateral and bilateral aid, the
following main sectors have been designated: training and re-training of
teachers; production of teaching materials; setting up of polytechnical
complexes; setting up of special institutes of higher education;
rationalization and modernization of educational administration; and
organization of a system for the improvement and equipment of
educational premises.

However, there is no question of letting such foreign aid interfere
with the attainment of the fundamental aims of Benin's policy of
educational reform.

Conclusion

Benin's educational reform is still in its early days, but in several respects
it has already emerged from the experimental phase into that of general
application (as, for example, making each school a unit of production).
The reform can only succeed in so far as educational policy forms part of
a policy for the overall development of people and resources, and in so
far as it reflects our present level of economic development, which is
based on agriculture. It was in this context that the reform was conceived
and worked out, and in this context that it is beginning to be applied.

Benin is classified among the twenty-five poorest countries in the
world, and the cost of the reform and of education itself, when compared
with the national budget as a whole, may make the project seem utopian.
But in the political context of national independence, and of socialist
determination to mobilize people for their own liberation and to give
them the civic and political training they require for awareness both of
their own potentialities and of the needs of development in general, the
future is hopeful.

It is still too early to assess the results of Benin's educational reform.
Suffice it to say that the country's intention of financing the reform out
of available resources is a good sign, even though there remain serious
problems deriving from the influence, still difficult to counteract, of
structures and habits inherited from the colonial and neo-colonial past.

At all events, the new education is the cornerstone of the whole
edifice of the nation and Benin's best hope of salvation; both the people
and the government are determined to increase their efforts in this

direction. In so doing, they aim to increase their resources sufficiently to meet the great challenge of a revolutionary new education which will act as prime mover in the social, political and economic development of the Benin people.

NOTES

1. Extract from *Discours-Programme du Gouvernement Militaire*.
2. *Programme National d'Édification de l'École Nouvelle*, p. 39, Cotonou, ONEPI.
3. Ibid., p. 74.
4. *Rapport de Synthèse des Coopératives Scolaires*, p. 1, Cotonou, Ministry of Primary Education, 1976.

Educational reform and decentralization: an example from Madagascar

by André Razafindrakoto

Decentralization is one of the basic political objectives of the Democratic Republic of Madagascar, not only in the educational but also in the economic, social and cultural sectors. The end in view is the abolition of the injustices and inequalities which the Malagasy people have inherited from the past, for there are still flagrant inequalities between regions, between town and country, between social classes and between individuals.

Situation before the Revolution

Madagascar suffers from two kinds of problems, those deriving from the colonial past, and those deriving from the neo-colonial period. During the first of these two periods all the structures of the country, and in particular the economic structure, were organized in terms of France's own economy on the one hand, and on the other of the interests and privileges of colonialism.

The neo-colonial period of Madagascar's first years of independence (1960–72) did nothing to improve matters, since the old structures were retained. If we examine the situation before the Revolution. we find an imbalance in the distribution of activities, and wide disparities between the regions (Antananarivo, Diégo-Suarez, Fianarantsoa, Majunga, Tamatave and Tuléar). The unequal development of the regions was reflected in various ways, especially in population, production and school attendance.

There were four types of primary education in Madagascar, differing markedly from one another in terms of location, conditions of entry, syllabus, level of teachers, and possibilities and procedures for access to secondary education. The four types were as follows:

The officially recognized schools, which strictly observed French syllabuses. Malagasy children were allowed to form up to 50 per cent of the total number of pupils. The period of instruction lasted five years, and the medium of instruction was French;

The lower schools attached to establishments for secondary education and forming an integral part of them. Syllabuses here were much the same as in the officially recognized schools. Pupils were prepared for entrance into the secondary part of the establishment to which they were attached;

The State primary schools, open to Malagasy and foreign children alike. The syllabuses were essentially based on the French ones, and little store was set by the Malagasy language;

The rural schools of the first primary stage or cycle, found chiefly in country areas. The medium of instruction was Malagasy, the course lasted four years, and syllabuses emphasized the study of the environment and prepared the pupils for productive occupations.

The type of school a child went to depended on the parents' place of residence (city, town or country) and on their social status (financial position, social contacts, etc.). The resulting inequality of access to education as a whole was particularly evident in the fourth type of school, where the structure did not allow pupils to proceed to the second stage of primary instruction (fifth and sixth years), or, consequently, to secondary education. In the other three types of establishment, this transition was automatic. The enrolment rate for primary education ranged from $35 \cdot 1$ per cent of the school-age population (6 to 14) in the Tuléar region to $58 \cdot 7$ per cent in the Antananarivo region.

General secondary education was based on that in France as regards syllabuses, methods, timetables and examinations. The content was theoretical and selective, and since it had no connection with the social and economic needs of the country, the pupils it turned out were not equipped to form part of the production circuit. This applied both to short-course establishments (where the period of instruction was four years and where there was no possibility of passing on into a long-course establishment) and to long-course establishments (seven years, leading to the *baccalauréat*).

The process of 'Malagasization' could only be superficial, since pupils were prepared only for French-type examinations and certificates. Moreover, the output of secondary education was very low, with a large number of drop-outs.

Similarly, technical and vocational training failed entirely to meet the needs of the individual, and still less those of Malagasy society. The subjects taught were taken from French syllabuses, and although it was expensive, this kind of training attracted few pupils.

The university had the same problems. All the faculties were in Antananarivo, with the exception of the Centre Universitaire at Tuléar, which could deal with only a small number of students.

Teacher-training schools were quite well distributed throughout the country, but there were considerable differences in the level of studies and in the status accorded to those who completed the training. This was due to the different types of primary education, described above. Higher teacher training and research into teaching methods were to be found only in Antananarivo.

As for educational management and administration, decision-making powers were completely centralized, especially in the case of secondary education, technical and vocational training, and higher education. There was also an almost total lack of planning.

Aims of the policy of
general decentralization

Decentralization is regarded in Madagascar as one of the essential conditions for strengthening national unity. The centralized system of the past must be scrapped in all its aspects — administrative, political, cultural and economic.

The decentralization policy aims at organizing administration, the economy, education, business, information and the law on a socialist foundation and in accordance with the aspirations of the masses; and at being effective in every sphere, including power, property, knowledge, know-how and the imparting of know-how.

In order to realize these aims, defined in the Charter of the Malagasy Socialist Revolution, published on 26 August 1975 and adopted by the people as a whole by the referendum of 21 December 1975, the Constitution stipulates that: 'The Democratic Republic of Madagascar, unified and decentralized, guarantees and favours activities and operations conducive to development on the part of territorial communities.'

These decentralized communities are, in ascending order: the *fokontany*; the *firaisampokontany*; the *fivondronampkontany*; and the *faritany*.

The *fokontany* is the basic decentralized community, and the others consist of groups made up from units of the preceding kind. Decentralization thus operates at four different geographical levels.

The *fokontany* General Assembly, and the other decentralized communities' people's councils, direct local activity at their respective levels, aiming especially at cultural, social and economic development and civic responsibility.

Each of the decentralized communities exercises revolutionary power in its own territory. Thus, while observing the methods prescribed by democratic centralism and by the laws and regulations in force, each community:

On the administrative plane, is in charge of the public services;

On the legislative plane, establishes the Dinas (regulations accepted by the community);

On the legal plane, exercises the powers invested in it by the laws on the dispensing of justice;

On the plane of security, shares in the defence of the country as a whole and in the maintenance of law and order;

On the economic plane, works for the development of the country's socialist economy, and in particular organizes co-operatives;

On the political plane, elects its representatives; and

On the social plane, acts in whatever way is conducive to social well-being and the social and cultural development of its members.

Educational aims

The fundamental aims of Madagascar's education policy are democratization, decentralization and 'Malagasization'.

The democratization of education means giving every Malagasy, without exception, the same opportunities: access to a basic education, and further education and training in accordance with his or her abilities and with the needs of the nation.

Decentralization applies to decisions concerning the distribution of scholastic establishments throughout the country, and to certain aspects of their management.

'Malagasization' means bringing the content and methods of education into line with the requirements of the Revolution, i.e. with the building of a socialist and genuinely Malagasy State. The languages of instruction are official Malagasy, regional variants of Malagasy, and French.

One of the popular demands of May 1972, which led to the end of the regime marking the first years of independence (1960–72), concerned the overhauling of the Malagasy educational system. The schools were closed at that time of year, so pupils, teachers and workers organized seminars to put forward a new and coherent system.

In April 1973, at the request of the Malagasy Government, a mission consisting of five experts from the Unesco Secretariat took part in the deliberations of a Malagasy Interdepartmental Committee charged with evaluating the educational system and working out possible strategies for a complete reform based on general government policy. Interdepartmental subcommittees were set up in each region. The results of these studies were used in experiments carried out by the Ministry of National Education, with a view to adapting what had been discovered to the new Malagasy structures. The Ministry then put forward a plan for reform, broken down into specific projects, with technical and financial contributions from the United Nations specialized agencies.

General application of the reform of the educational system

Immediately after the change of regime in May 1972, the administration and management of education were restructured on both the theoretical and the practical level. The French Director-General of Academic Services was dismissed together with the technical assistants who dealt with educational planning.

A directorate was created for the Planning and Orientation of Education, and this directorate, in collaboration with operational teaching directorates (Primary, Secondary, Technical and Vocational), put forward to the higher authorities a plan for reform of the educational system in accordance with the country's fixed objectives. The directorate works out practical syllabuses and specific projects, and co-ordinates the activities of the various national and regional bodies. It works in close collaboration with the Bureau d'Études des Programmes (BEP—Curriculum Review Office) and the Organe Technique d'Élaboration des Programmes (OTEP—Technical Board for Curriculum Development). These two bodies are responsible for adapting syllabuses and educational methods to social and economic conditions, at every level of the educational system; working for better liaison between pedagogical research and practical teaching, so as to improve the quality of the educational system; organizing the production of textbooks, cards and teaching aids, and the re-training of teachers, etc; and organizing the improvement of syllabuses and teaching methods on the basis of findings made by bodies which the Ministry has set up at grass-roots level among teachers.

A Publication and Audio-Visual Service (SEPAV) has also been set up, responsible for editing, publishing and distributing texts and cards produced by BEP and OTEP. The efforts of on-the-spot teachers are reinforced by radio and television broadcasts prepared by the organizations responsible for teaching aids.

Reform of primary education

At the beginning of the 1973 school year the government decided to unify primary education:

Transitional syllabuses were worked out to be used in common by all types of establishments. These syllabuses took into account the needs of the Malagasy economy and the social and economic conditions of the country, and accorded great importance to practical education.

All foreign teachers were dismissed.

All students at teacher-training colleges holding the *baccalauréat* were directed into State lower secondary schools.

A single entrance examination to lower secondary education was introduced, applying to all pupils without exception.

The number of places available for entry into secondary education was increased, partly by dividing in two all the sections in existing lower secondary schools and partly by setting up new schools.

A common programme for training teachers was worked out for those already undergoing training.

Recruitment of new teachers for training was halted until overall reform could be carried out.

A National Commission for Curriculum Review (CNEP) was convened during the 1973 school year. All regions, types of education and branches of learning were represented on the commission, which was responsible for working out transitional syllabuses for all types of education. School syllabuses, instead of originating centrally, were established by representatives from all the regions. These syllabuses were applied during the transitional period covering 1974 and 1975.

While the basic education reform was being prepared, the following considerations were borne in mind: the guide-lines and recommendations of the Interdepartmental Committee; the restructuring of rural life, begun in April 1973; the national development plan, which appeared in April 1973 and covered the period 1974–77; and the suggestions made by the Conseil National Populaire de Développement (CNPP — People's National Development Council) in April 1974.

Among the fundamental principles of the educational reform adopted by the government was the right of every individual to education, which meant making education accessible to the population as a whole.

As for the application of the reform, the National Development Plan (1973) provided for the reform to be introduced gradually at all levels, but gave priority to the reform of primary education.

Within the framework of the reform's application, regional commissions were set up to make suggestions to a national commission which in turn presented a project to the Ministry. The results of this study were adopted by the government.

The reform of primary education, known as 'basic education', rests on the principle of decentralization. The aim is to have all Malagasy children of school age attending school within three years. To avoid obliging the children to travel, basic education is modelled on the *fokonolona*, the basic community of the Malagasy people. So in three years each *fokonolona* (about 14,000 people) has to be provided with at least one school. Educational decentralization thus constitutes a fundamental aspect of democratization.

Decentralization is also reflected in the building of new schools at the level of the *fokontanys* (the territories in which the *fokonolona* communities live), and by the gradual assumption by the *fokontanys* of financial responsibility for the new schools, with contributions when necessary from the State budget.

For the moment, the construction of schools for basic education is the responsibility of each *fokonolona*, the State contributing when the local community is unable to cover the whole cost itself. It might be thought that making the *fokonolonas* responsible for building schools would hold back improvement in school attendance, but such is not the case at present. Experience has shown that the enhanced awareness created by the State and by the communities themselves has carried public opinion with it.

It should be noted that basic education syllabuses were established by teachers actually at work during the transitional period. The curriculum project put forward at grass-roots level was discussed and improved at the highest levels of the decentralized communities. A meeting was then held at national level to give final form to syllabuses and cards, which were then to be submitted for government approval after examination by the Ministry of Education.

As far as school syllabuses are concerned, decentralization takes the form of adapting the national curriculum more closely to regional conditions, taking account of the economic context and identifiable geographical variables. For example, in the case of manual training, use is made of readily available materials such as sisal, raffia, and so on.

Instruction in the traditional cultures of the region takes account of local flora and fauna, as do object lessons and lessons in gardening.

Since a child's mother tongue is part of his environment, the language of instruction is Malagasy. French is taught as a foreign language from the second year onwards. Production, another element in the child's environment, occupies an important place in the reform of the educational system.

It is obvious that the reform of primary education requires a large number of new teachers. Teachers already functioning under the old system receive in-service training. The State also calls on young people holding at least the BEPC de l'Enseignement Secondaire (Lower Secondary leaving certificate) to work as teachers instead of doing national service in the armed forces. These young men and women receive three months' initial training in the Centres Pédagogiques (teacher-training centres).

A network of professional refresher courses has been made available to all teachers engaged in basic education. Pedagogic advisers have been appointed at the level of the decentralized communities, and sections set up for the self-training of teachers.

Each of these sections holds a monthly meeting of all the teachers, some sections concerning themselves with research into teaching methods, others with the problems of integration of school and environment, constructive criticism of school syllabuses, or the production of teaching texts and cards. These sections have also been entrusted with linguistic research with the aim of enriching the Malagasy language. In a region where the main occupation is fishing, for example, they register the vocabulary of fishing and make it available for the national commission responsible for the establishment of vernacular Malagasy. They also collect oral traditions at the level of the local communities.

Last, it should be noted that since 1975 certain examinations have been regionalized.

Reform of secondary education

As we have seen above, the reform of primary education is the most urgent, but it was impossible not to provide for improvement at other levels also. Thus, at the beginning of the 1973 school year, common syllabuses were worked out for lower secondary education. To begin with, the distinction between State lower secondary schools and the first cycles or stages (junior grades) of *lycées* or high schools was abolished. All pupils now sit the examination for entrance into lower secondary education.

Teachers with a bachelor's degree who were teaching in junior lower secondary classes were transferred to upper secondary classes, and these were increased in number.

The CNEP put forward recommendations concerning the use of Malagasy as the language of instruction in lower secondary education, and 'Malagasization' began in 1976 in the first lower secondary year. It is gradually being extended year by year to the higher classes. In addition to the adaptation of syllabuses to the social and economic realities of the country, and the adoption of Malagasy as the language of instruction, the main innovations have been:

The opening of new secondary establishments throughout all the regions;

The setting up of a Commission Pédagogique d'Établissement (CPE— School Pedagogic Committee), equivalent to the self-training sections in primary education, which holds regular interdisciplinary meetings of teachers in the same establishment in order to avoid compartmentalization as well as regular meetings of teachers of the same subject in order to improve methods of instruction; and

The introduction of a new subject, 'practical education', the main object of which is to get both pupils and teachers to put their knowledge into practice.

Practical-education syllabuses are flexible, drawn up in terms of the social and economic realities of the region where the establishment in question happens to be, and worked out jointly by teachers and pupils. This subject also enables the various establishments to engage in productive work according to region: some raise pigs, others cultivate rice and vegetables, etc. Some concentrate on the manufacture of small items of physics apparatus.

Reform of technical and vocational training

Technical and scientific training are two forms of education of which the country has great need. In fact, the success both of the Republic's economic development and of the revolution depend on them. In this field, innovation consists chiefly in the setting up of schools which also function as units of production. The aims here include:

Gradually lightening the burden of the State by educating pupils to accept responsibility, by training them to enter at once into productive activity and to play a part in the development of their own school;

Enabling pupils to enter productive activity as soon as they leave school;

Enabling pupils to keep up with the evolution of technical and scientific knowledge even after their secondary education is over; and

Producing well-qualified and directly operational technicians at the end of both lower and higher secondary education, imbued with a spirit of research and creativeness which is translated into practical production, and able both to reintegrate themselves into the community they came from and also, by working and producing as members of that community, to transform it from within.

Every technical school becomes a centre of production, combining suitable instruction with practical work. With this in mind the curriculum of the technical secondary schools has been slanted towards projects of particular interest in the present context: they include the making of tools and instruments, the processing of basic products, communications, the human environment, and the making and maintenance of school equipment.

Regular meetings of teachers have been introduced in all establishments engaged in technical and vocational training.

In this type of teaching, decentralization has consisted in:

Allocating subjects among the schools in terms of the social and economic realities of the regions they belong to and taking into account the objectives fixed for production;

The establishment of technical secondary schools in every region beginning in 1975 with one for the principal town of each *faritany*.

Higher education

As with the other levels of instruction, there has been a transitional restructuring of higher education. This is based on the introduction of training networks designed to prepare students for their future employment.

Here it was necessary to solve the problems raised by the concentration of all the faculties in Antananarivo (these included living accommodation, restaurants and lecture rooms). Measures were taken to decentralize the university at the beginning of the 1977 academic year, when a regional university centre was set up in each *faritany*. The decentralized communities were consulted on the choice of training networks to be offered in these centres. Whereas holders of the *baccalauréat* were previously obliged to go to Antananarivo to attend university, students must now go to the region where their chosen network of training is offered, thus avoiding duplication. A publicity campaign was necessary to persuade students to accept this policy.

Educational management and administration

Since 1976 the Ministry of National Education has included six provincial directorates, the object being to decentralize the power of decision-making. In the field of basic education, decentralization has already begun as regards management of teaching staff (recruitment and posting) and management of funds for capital investment.

As regard national service, the Ministry fixes the number of conscripts to be trained in each specialized centre. The *fokontanys* with candidates possessing the BEPC whom they wish to recruit as teachers may propose them to the Education Adviser of the Sous-Préfecture, who sends them to be trained in the centres. Otherwise the necessary number of teachers may be recruited, in accordance with standards fixed at national levels, by the education advisers, the heads of school districts and the provincial directors. When they have finished their training, conscripts are assigned to posts by the provincial director responsible for the planning of new schools.

The projected national budget for education is worked out by a national commission on which all the regions are represented. When the budget has been voted, the allocation of funds is carried out in consultation with the provincial directors.

The funds for capital investment allocated to a province are managed by the head of the province concerned, who may modify the proposed programme to take account of the identified needs of the province, up to a maximum of 30 per cent of the total allocated. He may even make transfers as between one item in the budget and another. This constitutes the beginnings of budgetary decentralization.

Whereas in 1976 the heads of the provincial education service were responsible for basic education only, the powers of provincial directors of national education now extend to the management and supervision of secondary and technical education.

Prospects and conclusions

A national commission, continuing the reform already undertaken in the sphere of primary education, is to make proposals for the reform of the other types of education (secondary, technical, vocational and university).

The provincial directorates will soon be changed into regional academic centres responsible for running all types of education and in particular for adapting syllabuses to local conditions, providing in-service training for all teachers employed in the region and producing teaching materials suitable for the region.

In conclusion, it should be noted that Madagascar is still in the transitional stage of applying its decentralization policy, which is a long-term project. October 1977 marked the beginning of a period of change in which the decentralized communities were to take on their own respective powers. The administrators (provincial heads, prefects, sub-prefects, heads of cantons, etc.), who represented the central power, were to transfer their responsibilities to the representatives of the decentralized communities. So the application of the decentralization policy cannot be properly evaluated for some time to come.

Educational reform, constraints and obstacles: the Algerian experience

by Abderrahmane Remili

General background to reform

On the morrow of the achievement of Algerian independence, the economic and social situation inherited from the previous 132 years was disquieting in several respects. In the first place, a colonial economy prevailed, modelled to fit in with the French economy, and geared to the satisfaction of a privileged minority. The usual characteristics of underdevelopment could be noted: rudimentary industrialization, low productivity of subsistence farming, low individual incomes among the majority of the population, limited dissemination of modern techniques, and acute dualism.

Weak and non-integrated as it was, this economy was also highly dependent, commercially, technically, financially and manpower-wise. Furthermore, it had to support a heavy burden attributable to the effects of a war which had lasted seven and a half years, caused immense losses in life and property, and led to profound upheavals in the life of the various sectors of the population.

The dead hand of the past lay no less heavily on education and training, inasmuch as the colonial authorities had done their best to dispossess the Algerian people of their culture, their values and the attributes of their real personality without, in return, providing the benefit of western education for the population. The educational system then prevailing was intended to secure the schooling of the European minority, and to meet the modern colonial sector's requirements of skilled manpower; accordingly, it paid scant attention to the economic sectors composed of the mass of the Algerian population, living in a state of destitution.

Algeria could not fail to be profoundly marked by such a crushing legacy, but at the same time the nation's liberation, wrested at the cost of extremely heavy sacrifices, had the virtue of galvanizing the people's energies and steeling the national will to independence, democracy and socialist development. The policy resolved on by the nation aimed at the socialization (in various forms) of all sectors vital to development and participation (of ordinary citizens as well as producers) in the management of the administrative, economic and socio-cultural structures. Apart from the introduction of participation structures, the socialist revolution in Algeria was marked by the enormous efforts involved in the planned construction of a strong, independent economy, accompanied by the gradual socialization of the means of production and the assumption by the State of direct or indirect responsibility for the output of producer and export goods. At present, over 80 per cent of industrial production has been 'socialized', more than 60 per cent of modern agricultural production (with the application of the Agrarian Revolution), 60 per cent of transport and 50 per cent of services.

At the same time, efforts have been made to reduce the gap between those who govern and the governed, and between those who make decisions and those who must execute them. The Algiers Charter is very explicit on this point:

. . . Socialism cannot be defined exclusively as the nationalization of the means of production. It is also, and more particularly, defined as self-management, which is the real solution to the dual contradiction of private property and the gulf between control and execution.

A policy of decentralization and democratization has been constantly pursued on methodical and progressive lines, with the active participation of the masses, democratically and efficiently organized, especially at communal and departmental level and in business enterprises or collective farms (self-management). In actual fact, it was the desire to have real responsibilities shouldered at grass-roots level which inspired the general orientation of the reforms concerning local communities, which were to become the instruments of economic and social development.

The strategy of economic and social development

Algeria adopted as its aims to bring about the transformation of the existing forms of international specialization, and gradually withdraw from the world market, by organizing a process of development which is both self-centred (independent) and self-maintained (with no systematic recourse to external financial and human inputs).

The seven-year development prospects (1967–73) were actuated by a 'development strategy' turning on four themes: the beginnings of economic integration, an increase in production capacities, adaptation of training arrangements to the needs of the economy, and redistribution of income. These innovations drained off investments representing over one-third of the GNP during the first and second four-year plans, of which three-quarters were devoted to industrialization, agriculture and education.

The Algerian economy was long characterized, not by integration of the branches of activity among themselves, but by integration of those branches in relation to the economy of the colonizing power. It was thus necessary, after the achievement of independence, to create a whole series of new branches with a view to completing the initial industrial framework and intensifying inter-industrial exchanges, thereby initiating the process of economic integration. In the case of industry, the object is to put a stop to exports of raw products by setting up iron and steel, metallurgical, engineering and petrochemical plants to process the products on the spot. In the case of agriculture, the creation of a food-industries branch will enable the agricultural sector to be integrated in the Algerian economy. Such integration is important from three points of view: first, value added — and, consequently, distributed income — is mainly created in the processing stage; second, investment by a given branch, and the resulting increase in output, will make their effects felt not on the foreign economies, but on the national economy, owing to a higher demand for home-produced goods and the chain reactions it will set up; last, the more strictly imports can be limited to the capital goods needed to set up complementary branches of the Algerian economy, the sounder will be the balance of payments.

The creation of these new branches of the economy depended on the production or import of capital goods, i.e. the formation of national industrial capital. The major importation of capital goods explains why it was necessary, as a counterpart, to introduce a vigorous policy of export expansion, especially for hydrocarbons, to liberate substantial means of foreign payments. The major source of foreign exchange was provided by exports of petroleum products; thus, the increase in the whole economy's accumulation capacities depended on expanding output in the oil sector.

Two imperatives must be respected for the establishment of a new training system adapted to the economic requirements: democratization of education and generalization of training, the subject-matter and methods of which should be geared to the demands of the economy. This should be planned in two stages: 'transitional' vocational training campaigns to meet the most urgent needs arising out of the requirements of the plan; and remodelling of the 'training machinery' to prepare large numbers of people for jobs in the economy of the future.

In the short term, a policy of income redistribution (through taxation and subsidies) will allow the home market to be enlarged. Thus, under the four-year plan, redistribution of the national income, especially in favour of the most underprivileged, was achieved by many different means (rural investment, prices policy, subsidies, taxation, social benefits policy, structural reforms, etc.).

Reform of the educational system

While the Algerian system of education evolved considerably during the first twelve years of the new State's existence, it has not quite kept pace with the very rapid rate of political, economic and social change that has prevailed since the liberation of the country.

The effects of cultural dependence continued to be felt for a number of years after the advent of political independence, for many reasons. In the first place, education was still largely modelled on that provided by France; second, the Évian agreements institutionalized forms of cultural co-operation tending to aggravate acculturation, with the arrival of a large number of Co-operation Programme personnel to fill the gap left by the massive departure of European teachers, the possibility of opening schools and colleges in Algeria to correspond to the official French courses and undertakings by Algeria to organize 'within the limit of its possibilities, in the Algerian universities, the common basic education dispensed in the French universities, on similar conditions as to curricula, attendance and examinations'. This last provision was no doubt the most dangerous for the evolution of the national educational system, as the requirement of equivalent degrees and the prestige attaching to the latter were to handicap any attempt to achieve revolutionary changes in the system during the first few years of independence. Not until the first four-year plan (1970–73) was introduced was it possible to have an all-round view of the reforms required which was not coloured by the inherited arrangements, even though the latter had already been rejected from the ideological standpoint by the future rulers of the country before independence had been won.

Consequently, with a view to the introduction of a really national education system which at the same time remained open to beneficial outside influences, two essential aims were progressively pursued: the Arabicization of education and the 'Algerianization' of the staff, institutions and subject-matter.

Furthermore, the progress made in building a socialist society (designed to put an end to the alienation of the workers at management level) generated the need for a 'cultural Revolution',[1] to adopt the expression used by the President of the Conseil de la Révolution in his address of 10 October 1969, underlining the necessity 'of radical reform of education, a veritable revolution which we should at once begin, for it has become an urgent necessity' in order to attain the objectives assigned to education.

Accordingly, a National Committee on Educational Reform was officially established by the head of the government on 5 December 1969, its terms of reference being to conceive and draw up an overall plan for the reform of the educational system.

Innovations introduced

The work of the committee was halted because of the ministerial reshuffle of August 1970, when the Department of National Education was split in two. The new departments were the Ministry of Primary and Secondary Education and the Ministry of Higher Education and Scientific Research, each of which was to work out a programme of reform. The reform of higher education was determined in 1971; the reform proposed by the Ministry of Primary and Secondary Education was adopted under the second four-year plan.

Pending the introduction of a more general reform, the 1970–73 four-year plan instituted two major innovations, designed to be complementary: (a) specialized training to be provided in the institutes of technology; (b) machinery for lifelong education, in the form of the Centre National d'Enseignement Généralisé (CNEG).

As a first decisive break with the academic and university pattern of education copied from the liberal developed countries, the institutes of technology plan to train the drop-outs from the educational system as specialized staff for the production of goods and services. As the employers of the future technicians and specialized staff were not in a position to provide satisfactory initial job training, the staff trained by the institutes had to be operational as soon as they had completed their course.

As the first link in a lifelong education machinery now being evolved, the CNEG appears in the light of a corrective to the specialized training provided in the institutes of technology and as a safety net for those leaving the educational system, to ensure their occupational and human development and training. The centre's main functions are, first, to provide a basic general education to those whose schooling was interrupted; second, to arrange for training or pre-training activities in geographical and occupational sectors defined in the light of development requirements. At the same time, it has to reinforce and co-ordinate by various means the campaigns hitherto undertaken and, finally, produce educational broadcasts on subjects impinging upon the life of the country.

The new Algerian university system taking shape under the 1971 reform aims to be an integrated system producing graduates capable of playing an operational role. Teaching is organized on the modular system. The formulation of the programmes and their implementation are co-ordinated at the level of the whole university institution, not at the level of the institutes (the basic units) as under the conventional system. This new training scheme entails internal integration (organization and co-ordination of resources with a view to a modular form of education) and external integration (adjustment to the quantitative and qualitative manpower requirements). That is why higher education is organized around training courses and profiles. The universities tend to specialize, e.g. the University of Science and Technology, the University of Social Science. Each university, in turn, is made up of institutes responsible for dispensing education in a strictly defined field. For example, the University of Science and Technology consists of the Institute of Biology, Institute of Physics, Institute of Mathematics, Institute of Geology, Institute of Mechanical Engineering, etc. However, training in a given institute is not confined to a specific course or profile. The institutes do not enrol students for a degree course, and do not award degrees.

At the time of adoption of the second four-year plan, the Conseil de la Révolution and the government approved a reform involving the generalization of a basic nine-year education by remodelling inter-mediate education and combining it with the elementary course preceding it; the aim was to promote the institution of a common nine-year course of general education, with the gradual adoption of a polytechnic approach, starting from the top. The progressive intro-duction of this new system was designed to

eliminate, in the long run, the selection made before admittance to the in-termediate course, and gradually phase out the serious problem posed by children of 14 to 17 who are excluded from the school system and are too young to receive vocational training. . . . The fact that curricula are standardized and more closely geared to economic and social life . . . helps to give equal chances of advancement to all. [2]

Polytechnic education aims to convey the values of technological humanism, and achieve tuition uniting theory and practice, scientific knowledge and exercises on real situations . . . the object in view is to combine around live subjects and specific topics, regrouping the disciplines in complementary pedagogic units, intellectual and manual work, the acquisition of such knowledge as will be operationally effective and also most necessary in adult life, and the acquisition of various skills. Recourse to experimentation, observation, investigation, fabrication, production and assembly constitute the method-ological requirement of polytechnical education, whose final aim is to derive its driving-force from the environment, so as to enable the adolescent to fit properly into his surroundings. [3]

Obstacles at the decision-preparing stage

The intellectual climate was in no way conducive to the conception of innovations, owing to the inherited underdevelopment: inadequate theoretical and practical research in the educational sciences; limited means of diffusion to teachers and public; absence of multi-disciplinary teams able to plan syllabuses; and inadequate manuals, teaching equipment and methods conceived in co-operation with pilot schools, themselves limited in number and of unequal value.

Being unable to rely on experts possessing sufficient qualities of creativity (and capable of leading an operational team for the intro-duction of the reforms), and being also unable to call on a sufficient number of Algerian researchers to prepare the future on the basis of integrated innovations (as educational research would have mobilized staff needed for the purposes of immediate operational action), the decision-making centres (the Ministry) and the pedagogic research institutions (in particular the National Pedagogic Institute) were unable to integrate their activities in the kind of forward-looking, overall perspective which should govern the choice of innovations at the dif-ferent levels of the educational system, and in the various fields of training: the immense qualitative and quantitative advances which the education sector would have needed to achieve may be compared to the mutation entailed in the switch from craft production to industrial operation, having regard in particular to the importance which such a mutation must allot to research and development and to the preparation of production procedures, involving the use of techniques for prospective structural analyses and for planning the use of technological and human resources in the light of the overall aims adopted. Psychological im-pediments, administrative compartmentalization and difficulties in regard to employment forecasts are the three chief obstacles considered in the following paragraphs.

PSYCHOLOGICAL IMPEDIMENTS

Linked with the cultural impact of the colonial past or transmitted by the Co-operation Programme personnel and Algerian executives trained in western universities, mimetic tendencies represented the chief im-pediments to a radical revolutionary transformation of the system of education and training. They were all the stronger because the scale of the tasks to be accomplished (expansion of the educational system was relied on to ensure the success of the bid for development) precluded any major risks being taken. Even the decision-makers, convinced of the urgency of the reforms, were held back from fear of disorganizing the system.

The institutes of technology, in particular, in so far as they challenged the accepted staffing ratios (and thus the input and output of the new system to be set up), were the focus of incessant controversy. In fact, recruitment in them came up against vigorous resistance from administrators of education and employers, as the conditions of ad-mission did not conform to the traditional criteria.[4] In short, while the decision-makers agreed to try the institutes of technology as an experi-ment, they were regarded as being merely an adjunct to a system which did, in their view, no doubt require replanning, but on less urgent lines involving less sweeping changes; moreover, no such step was con-sidered necessary until it had been proved that the existing system, intensified and reinforced, would be completely unable to meet the economic demand.

To make sure that the demonstration was conclusive, two national seminars were organized, attended by specialists in education and training and by users of skilled manpower: as a result, the latter came to accept that the aims adopted in the first four-year development plan were ambitous enough to justify recourse to exceptional training methods to 'salvage' the drop-outs from the educational system by developing to the fullest the pupils of a standard half-way between the *brevet* and the *baccalauréat*, but not holding a 'diploma'.

The tension between economic and social demand was the subject of far-ranging public discussion at a series of national seminars, given very wide publicity by the mass media, which contributed additional support for the proposal to resort to institutes of technology. This enabled the institutes, if not to contribute a constant leaven of revolutionary pedagogics, at least to effect a wide breach in the defences of the traditional system, and thereby facilitate the general introduction of innovations. This was notwithstanding the inevitable conflicts between educational clienteles all with claims to priority consideration; thus the adult-education structures (literacy training and lifelong education) were somewhat neglected, owing to the pressure of the rising generation in a country where 50 per cent of the population were under 16.

This explains the inadequacy of the means available to satisfy the requirements of literacy training and further education; the socio-cultural consequences of this situation were grievous, as it compromised or, at best, delayed the grand design of the reformers of the Algerian

educational system, who wished to place the whole system in a perspective of lifelong education — the sole solution to the 'quantity–quality'
dilemma and to the conflict between technical and general education.

GROWING COMPARTMENTALIZATION OF
THE GOVERNMENT DEPARTMENTS
RESPONSIBLE FOR TRAINING

There were no less than fifteen ministries responsible for training in
1972, whereas there were only ten in 1968–69 (according to the 1969
census). This dispersion arose from the serious concern of the ministries
using skilled manpower in face of the quantitative and qualitative
inadequacy of the output of technicians and senior personnel from the
departments responsible for education. It enabled training courses to be
introduced outside the traditional channels and certain pedagogic
innovations to be tried out. One of the departments responsible for
training has a 'horizontal' function: the Ministry of Labour and Social
Affairs. Other Ministries with responsibilities in this field are the
economic departments (Ministry of Agriculture and Land Reform,
Ministry of Industry and Energy, Ministry of Public Works and Construction, Ministry of Postal Services and Telecommunications, Ministry
of State responsible for Transport, Secretariat of State for Water
Supplies, Ministry of Trade, Ministry of Finance, Secretariat of State for
Planning), departments responsible for the maintenance of national
sovereignty (Ministry of the Interior and Administrative Reform,
Ministry of National Defence) and the socio-cultural departments
(Health, Youth and Sports, Ex-Servicemen).

Lastly, we find that responsibility for restoration of the people's
culture and the highly important tasks of informing national and foreign
opinion, or guiding the press, radio and television and the cinema, were
at first entrusted to a separate ministerial department, then allotted to a
Ministry of National Guidance, until such time as these duties were
transferred to a general directorate in the office of the President of the
Republic. Since July 1965, however, these services have again constituted
an autonomous department. The reshuffle of 1970 increased its
responsibilities, as cultural development activities were transferred from
the ex-Ministry of National Education to the Ministry of Information.

The need to ensure co-ordination in the spheres of education and
training was felt from the advent of independence and a Commissariat
for Vocational Training and the Further Training of Senior Personnel
was set up, first under the Office of the President of the Republic and
subsequently under the Ministry of State responsible for Finance and
Planning. The commissariat was no doubt hamstrung by the absence of
official planning up to 1967, the shortage of key personnel and the

ambiguity of the texts governing its responsibilities. Nevertheless, it managed to introduce some useful innovations: investigations of training needs and resources, creation of technical committees for various occupations, drafting of statutory regulations, and compilation of vocational training nomenclatures and a map showing the existing resources. It was dissolved in 1967, and its attributions divided between the Ministry of Labour and Social Affairs and the State Department for Planning.

In face of such a compartmentalization of supervisory responsibility, there was a clear need for some instrument for concerted action in the spheres of education and training, especially to assess the manpower requirements jointly with the various ministries concerned, draw up the operational sequence of plans and programmes, and determine the policy to be followed in the matter of scholarships, distribution of staff and allocation of students.

A special department—the Co-ordination Centre for Institutes of Technology—was accordingly set up in the General Planning Directorate to see to the organization and co-ordination required for the installation of the institutes.

DIFFICULTIES IN REGARD TO EMPLOYMENT FORECASTS

Generally speaking, many heads of firms or their training managers show some ignorance (or insufficient knowledge) of the qualitative and quantitative requirements. This is mainly due to the following factors:

The users are unfamiliar with the problems of training requirements. In the absence of senior personnel capable of making the necessary analysis based on rational approaches and proven methods, such a task is usually entrusted to specialized foreign agencies.

In many cases, the user belongs to a newly formed sector of the national economy, or one in process of formation, which is subject to profound and extensive mutations. The structural reforms planned by the supreme authorities of the country form an integral part of a revolution that will have consequences for the various sectors which may sometimes be difficult to assess, as it will modify the productive forces and production relations.

Accordingly, the work of each individual will be redefined from the technical standpoint, and new working relationships will be introduced.

Generally speaking, the first task to be performed in connection with the preparation of the preliminary studies was often to visualize, in the light of the available information, the future structure of the sector or sectors concerned, trying to grasp as far as possible the different structural stages, having regard to the targets adopted in the National

Development Plan. This state of affairs undoubtedly limits the content, approach and form of the preliminary study. It should be added that there is no one hard-and-fast approach to the calculation of requirements or the analysis of manning tables. Furthermore, having regard to the diversity of the sectors involved and the multitude of users, the field of investigation can never be complete. Finally, the private sector is not taken into account straight away, so that the preliminary study can only cover the needs of the State-controlled sector.

The gaps in knowledge of the employment pattern were not too serious at the educational planning stage in Algeria when the first four-year plan was in preparation.

The shortage of skilled manpower for historical reasons (emigration of most of those benefiting from the educational system occurred during the colonial period) and the needs created by an ambitious development policy under the four-year plan led to such a demand for junior, middle-level and senior staff that there was little chance of error or misdirection in developing the traditional schooling system. Only those who qualified in the Adult Vocational Training Centres or at lower secondary level sometimes have difficulty in finding employment. As regards the new training institutions, it has been possible to achieve a quantitative and qualitative balance between supply and demand ('training to order') by new direct-liaison arrangements with the biggest users of manpower, who are usually grouped by economic sectors.

However, these overall approaches, and the progress made with the training system, will not suffice in the future, as the demands for skilled manpower will fall off by very reason of the mass-education policy at all levels provided for under the four-year plan.

Weakness at management level: first obstacle
at the stage of introducing innovations

It has been justly stated that 'the introduction of new educational methods would have little effect if the administration and management of education were not whole-heartedly in favour of innovations'. [5]

The inadequacy of management skills among school and university administrators has prevented the use of existing resources from being rationalized, and hindered the release of new available capacity to support and step up the expansion of the system. For instance, the studies on standardization of school buildings, which were initiated only in the Ministry of Primary and Secondary Education, were never completed, and could not therefore form the basis for instructions concerning the implementation of building programmes at the lowest possible cost.

No inventory was taken of the existing buildings and equipment, and no intensive study of school zoning was made during the first few years after the innovations were brought in.

All sectors of education and training leave something to be desired in the matter of management: 'Algerian education [needs to be] brought up to date in respect of productivity and efficacy, organization and rational management, just like an enormous firm.'[6]

The following paragraphs deal with some other obstacles to the adoption of innovations.

Difficulties in regard to the relationship between training and employment

In the institutes of technology for education, agriculture, planning and land-surveying, the trainees have finally succeeded in being put into the civil-service establishment even before completing their training in the institute; for students of those institutes where the civil service is not the accepted end in view, the demand for skilled manpower is such that there is no difficulty about getting them taken on at a high level, although appreciably below the level which graduates of old-established institutions can lay claim to as a matter of prestige.

The two-way exchange between the 'customers' and the training centre, which is institutionalized by decree, gives trained personnel security against the risks of unemployment, and allows the constant adjustment of training objectives to real requirements. Thus, supply and demand in the employment market tend to remain in equilibrium for the type of manpower trained in institutes of technology.

However, it has not been possible to systematize the 'training–employment' relationship by drawing up real training conventions (contracts between the professional milieu and the training institutions) because of psychological obstacles on the part of the institutions, the teachers and the pupils. Furthermore, the suppression of the co-ordination centre for institutes of technology prevented any homogeneous project from taking shape: the quantitative and qualitative achievements depend on the Ministry concerned, and within each institute on the director concerned. *Ad hoc*, more authoritarian pedagogics have largely ousted the attempted introduction of 'institutional pedagogics'.

Some solution will have to be found for the unsatisfactory distribution of skilled manpower on the basis of systematic comparison of wage scales inside and outside the civil service.

By preparing a national wage grid to put an end to the disparity in remuneration between the governmental, para-governmental and private sectors, it should be possible to avoid discrepancies in respect of qualifications and posts occupied. The social objectives of the projected wage policy are mainly 'to give concrete expression to the principle of "equal pay for equal work", to promote employment, training and re-training in general, and improve the workers' status'.[7]

The only level at which integration of education in the working world has been at all successful is that of higher education (apart from the institutes of technology).

The 'on-the-job' training organized is of doubtful pedagogic value, first, because of too few supervisory staff on the spot, which limits the student's chances of acquiring some useful experience on the course, and second, because of the inadequate links between the institutes, the university and the production enterprises coming under the different economic ministries.

The ivory tower which surrounds the conventional university was only partly dismantled through the opening of a few national and regional universities and institutes in the country. Their effect depended on the degree to which those in control were committed to educational reform and the other aims of the Algerian Revolution. One notable exception was the University of Constantine — a newly created establishment which was able to make more rapid progress with the pedagogic innovations recommended in the reform measures adopted, thanks to the dynamism of those in charge. For instance, the research and projects centre (CURER) of the University of Constantine contributed to regional development by participating in the collection and analysis of local economic and social data for planning purposes and by achieving the targets adopted by the political authorities (establishing thirteen socialist villages under the agrarian revolution, retimbering 16,000 hectares, instituting highly effective liaison between training, research and production, based on contracts with the political, economic and social authorities).

Constraints affecting pedagogic resources

The National Pedagogic Institute lacked the means of investigating and trying out innovations: its heavy burden of work, covering the compilation, Algerianization, Arabicization and publication of school books, and the provision of individual and collective educational facilities for a number of pupils increasing at bewildering speed, precluded any elaborate remodelling of school curricula and teaching means and methods on integrated lines.

It should, however, be noted that for certain scientific subjects, complete, integrated sets of teaching equipment were compiled and tried out, comprising teacher's cards, manuals for the pupils, and documentation and equipment for joint use in the Arabicized classes (prints, figurines, maps, lantern slides, etc.).

As regards efforts to rehabilitate the national language, there were grave pedagogic difficulties of historical origin. Twelve years after the advent of independence, despite efforts at Arabicization, French remained the common language in Algeria. Using classical Arabic, local Arab or Berber dialects, and French, Algerian society remained trilingual in proportions which varied according to the ethnic group, the locality, the socio-occupational category and the age of those concerned.

The problems set by the development of the use of classical Arabic are inherent in the 'grafting' of a rich and flexible language[8] on a milieu impregnated with the colonial heritage, and accepting considerable cultural and technical co-operation in French (for the purposes of development, especially industrial), whereas satisfactory solutions have not yet been found to deal with all the cultural implications of practical application of the recommended language policy: subject-matter and methods of Arabicization. teachers of sufficient quality.

The change involved in the introduction of the Arabicization policy in the information structures brings its own problems. Until such time as the new policy has made sufficient impression, the majority of televiewers only partly understand the broadcasts intended to inform and influence the public about economic and social development problems in Algeria. Such political awakening has its limitations. As the token of autonomous cultural development, Arabicization is an obvious necessity; but its methods of application should be readjusted to the available human resources and teaching methods, the improvement of which should be undertaken.

Furthermore, CNEG, conceived as the strategic instrument of lifelong education, found its vocation 'thwarted' for internal and external reasons:

It was to dispense lifelong education; it is at present a palliative for the shortcomings of the educational system, and duplicates that system, sometimes in its most traditional aspects. . . .

This is aggravated by the feeling here that there is a gulf between the CNEG on the one hand, and the Algerian educational system on the other, rendering all the more difficult any influence on the latter. . . .

The nature of CNEG staff—most work on a part-time basis, while the permanent members are described as not having been co-opted, but as usually working there for reasons irrelevant to the specific nature of the Centre—also helps to foster this feeling. . . .

At the same time, the initial pragmatism proved advantageous, as it allowed quite remarkable results to be achieved in the matter of growth; these were viewed as proofs of the CNEG's ability to cope with the problems with which it was faced. At present, however, it seems to raise more internal problems than it solves; and it is greatly feared that the CNEG may find itself imprisoned in an image which it did not wish to create, and which would rule out any future development more in accordance with its initial vocation and with the aspirations voiced by those in charge of it. [9]

An attempt to integrate all the dimensions of pedagogic renovation (subject-matter, instructors, teaching media, evaluation, physical layout, equipment) has been adumbrated since 1971–72, originating with the institutes of technology. No overall assessment has as yet been possible, however, there being differences of approach and practical application among the thirty teacher-training institutions.

The same applies to the technological institutes other than educational, except for the Institute of Agricultural Technology, which launched into the massive use of audio-visual equipment, involving many disappointments and rectifications, before finally introducing an integrated system from its fourth year of operation.

Financial constraints

The effort in the educational and training sphere which is clearly shown by the expansion of staff numbers involved a parallel increase in expenditure. Education is completely free at all levels, and many forms of assistance are granted in addition: scholarships, canteens, various allowances, provision of books and educational equipment, free (or reduced-rate) transport and expanded boarding facilities. [10] The total expenditure on education and training amounted to 11 per cent of the GNP in 1973. This record percentage has begun to decline slightly, and the ceiling seems to have been reached, representing an important constraint for the future in the choice of quantitative and qualitative priorities.

However, the rising trend in the operational costs of the technological institutes is counterbalanced by much greater efficiency: in the first place, the trainees become operational as soon as they have completed their training, which is based on systematic job analysis in close co-operation with the users. This training results in fewer drop-outs and repeaters, shorter courses, and the assumption by the students of responsibility for part of the training and discipline. It should also be noted that the preparatory pedagogic work carried out will make the diffusion of such teaching documentation by less highly qualified assistants a more economic proposition and the documentation will thus serve for many classes of students in the future; thus a real formation of pedagogic 'capital' is being effected. Lastly, the rise in costs is also offset by the wider range of the institutes, which are now experimenting with 'remote-control' training, especially in the form of correspondence courses.

The introduction of innovations is hindered by other handicaps of underdevelopment; the lack of facilities for manufacturing teaching equipment, especially that needed for technical initiation into scientific education, obliges Algeria to make massive purchases from abroad, with all the familiar disadvantages (cost in foreign exchange, ill-adapted equipment, lack of maintenance services, etc.).

At the same time, the disquieting situation as regards living quarters and the inadequate building capacity in the construction sector have hampered the success of innovations: insufficient housing or lodging capacity for teachers and pupils, delays in school and university building (especially in collective facilities for boarding-schools or university halls of residence, sacrificed in building programmes in favour of classrooms and administrative buildings).

The basic nine-year school may at present be too advanced an institution for the country's resources. The extension of nine-year courses to a growing number of pupils from 1985 onwards will not merely entail an increase in the cost of education which will have to be covered by the future expansion of the economy; it also implies the success of the policy of regional development and some stepping up of the growth of small and medium-sized industries.

NOTES

1. Defined as 'the means of freeing the potential energy existing among the masses; once that energy has been released, the cultural revolution uses it to transform man and his ways of thinking, society and its existing structures'.

2. *General Report on the Second Four-year Plan*, p. 240.

3. *Les Grands Axes de Développement du Système Algérien d'Enseignement*. Booklet issued by the Ministry of Primary and Secondary Education (April 1975).

4. The relaxation of recruitment conditions results in the diploma ceasing to be of essential importance for admission. The main criteria will henceforth be the motivation of prospective trainees, their real capacities and their desire to work. It is no longer the purpose of the institutes to select a small élite, but rather to recruit people showing aptitude for some specific occupation, capable of filling a job and performing satisfactorily the task allotted to them.

   However, for recruitment at level 4, corresponding to the training of technicians, an equivalent standard of training is required to that stipulated for entry to upper secondary education. For level 5 (graduate in applied engineering, head of service, intermediate school teacher), the training required corresponds to that acquired by the end of upper secondary education.

5. B. Hammiche, 'Les Problèmes Majeurs de l'Education', *Algérie et Développement*, No. 2, March–April 1970, p. 10.
6. The Minister of Primary and Secondary Education, quoted in *El-Moudjahid*, 19–20 September 1971.
7. Interview with the Minister of Labour and Social Affairs, in *El-Moudjahid*, 30 April 1974.
8. Modern Arabic terminology has given rise to numerous explanatory works by experts on the Arab world.
9. P. Caspar, *Mission to the CNEG. November 1973*, p. 8, 9, Paris, Unesco (ALG.72/015.53.02).
10. Including such facilities for primary schools in the Wilayats of the Oases and Saoura, given the clientele — nomads or sedentary families living too far from the school.

Biographical notes
on authors

Malcolm S. Adiseshiah (India) has been Vice-Chancellor of the University of Madras since 1975. A member of Parliament, he is chairman of several national and state committees and commissions. He founded the Madras Institute of Development Studies in 1971 upon his retirement from Unesco as Deputy Director-General. Prior to joining Unesco in 1948, he had been a professor of economics in Madras University and a lecturer in Calcutta University. His publications include *Let My Country Awake, Towards a Learning Society, Science in the Battle against Poverty* and *Mid-Term Review of the Plan*.

Roberto Artur de Luz Carneiro (Portugal) is at present assistant on economic and educational matters to the Portuguese Minister of Foreign Affairs. He has participated in Unesco meetings as a representative of Portugal and as an educational expert. A consultant to the World Bank for the Latin American and Caribbean region, he works mainly in Brazil. He has represented the Portuguese Administration in OECD and Council of Europe working-group meetings and projects, as well as in bilateral cultural negotiations and agreements. He worked for eight years in the Educational Research and Planning Bureau of the Ministry of Education as senior planner and researcher, head of several research units, co-ordinator of the Secretariat for External Co-operation and director of the research department. Previously he had been a lecturer at the Lisbon Technical University and the Nautical School and was director of a journal of education, following studies in engineering in Lisbon and education in France and the United Kingdom.

Stanislav Kaczor (Poland) is Deputy Director of the Institute of Professional Education in Warsaw and a member of the Scientific Committee 'Poland 2000' of the Presidium of the Polish Academy of Sciences. From 1969 to 1972, he was Deputy Director of the Department of Universities and Pedagogical Institutions in the Ministry of Education and before that, from 1954 to 1969, he taught at the University of Warsaw and in a teacher-training centre. Besides numerous articles in Polish and foreign reviews, he is the author of two books, *Semi-Programmed Texts in Workers' Studies* and *Self-Teaching for Student Teachers*. He has also written reports entitled *Comparative Analysis of Systems of Professional Education in Certain Advanced Countries*, *A System of Workers' Professional Up-grading* and *The Individual and the Group in General and Professional Training of Workers in Poland* (for Unesco).

A. N'Guessan Konan-Daure (Ivory Coast) has been a member of the Ivory Coast delegation to Unesco's General Conference since its fifteenth session. He is President of the Administrative Council of the Centre d'Edition et de Diffusion Africaines and Vice-President of the National Association for the Advancement of the Blind, besides being a member of other national committees. In addition to holding national honours, he is a Knight of the Equatorial Star of Gabon. He was Director of Primary Education from 1965 until 1977, when he became Director-General in the Ministry of Primary and Television Education.

Thierry Malan (France) is an inspector for administration in the Ministry of Education and professor of educational policy and planning at the International Institute for Public Administration in Paris. He served previously in the central administration of the Ministry of Education and the Planning Office of the Government (Commissariat Général du Plan) after studying at the École Nationale d'Administration in Paris. His publications include studies on French educational planning and administration.

Paul Joseph Mhaiki (United Republic of Tanzania) is Ambassador of the United Republic of Tanzania to France, Spain, Portugal and Algeria, and Permanent Delegate to Unesco. He was Principal of Kivukoni College (Dar es Salaam) from 1973 to 1976 and, before that, was directly responsible to the President for the training of national leaders and for rural development. His previous posts included those of Director of the University Institute of Adult Education, Director of Adult Education at the Ministry of Education and Director in his home country of Unesco functional literacy projects. Vice-President and co-founder of the International Council for Adult Education, he has made study visits to Cuba, Sweden, the United States, China, the Socialist Republic of Viet Nam, the U.S.S.R. and Japan. He has attended numerous international conferences on education at Unesco Headquarters and in various countries.

Sven Moberg (Sweden) has been Director-General of the Swedish Agency for Administrative Development since 1974, chairman or vice-chairman of various State agencies, State representative on the board of some investment companies and chairman or member of a number of State commissions, usually in the field of education and training. He was elected a Member of Parliament in 1970 but left in 1974 on appointment to his present position. He was Minister of Higher Education and Research and a Member of the Swedish Cabinet from 1967 to 1973. His previous career included service in the Ministry of Education and as an assistant professor of statistics.

Ivan Philippovich Obraztsov (U.S.S.R.) is Minister of Higher and Secondary Specialized Education of the Russian Soviet Federative Socialist Republic. He previously held the posts of Vice-Rector and Rector of the Moscow State Aviation Institute. A professor in applied mechanics, Mr Obraztsov is the author of more than one hundred publications in the fields of applied mechanics and the development of higher education. He is a full member of the U.S.S.R. Academy of Sciences.

César Picón-Espinoza (Peru) is Co-ordinator of the Master's Program of Adult Education sponsored by CREFAL-CEA, and Vice-President of the International Council of Adult Education for Latin America. He was a member of the Inter-American Committee of Education and has been his country's delegate to a number of meetings organized by Unesco, the Organization of American States (OAS), ILO and other international agencies. He was Director of the Peruvian National Service Apprenticeship and Industrial Work Centre, General Co-ordinator of the Peruvian Educational Reform, Director-General of Basic, Adult and Higher Education and President of the Permanent Board of Co-ordination for Educational Services. His publications have mainly been in the field of adult education.

William J. Platt (United States) is at present lecturing in the Stanford University School of Education. From 1970 to 1975, he was a staff member of Unesco, retiring as Deputy Assistant Director-General for Education. In 1969, he worked with the International Institute for Educational Planning in Paris and, before that, was a programme director for Stanford Research Institute and lecturer in the Stanford University School of Education. His publications have been in the fields of education, economic development, manpower economics, management science and aviation.

Jean Pliya (Benin) is Vice-Rector of the National University of Benin and has been entrusted with the implementation of the national educational reform. From 1960 to 1963, he was Head of the Minister's Office in the Ministry of Education. As an author of textbooks, he has published in the fields of geography and history. A dramatic writer and novelist, he is author of *L'Arbre fétiche* and other novels. He holds the rank of Chevalier in the Order of Arts and Letters.

André Razafindrakoto (Madagascar) is Director of Educational Planning and Orientation at the Ministry of Higher Education and Scientific Research in Madagascar. He was previously Director of Educational Planning and Orientation at the Ministry of Education, responsible for publications. Parallel to these activities, he has been a senior lecturer in mathematics at the University of Madagascar. He has taken part in Unesco seminars and meetings on education.

Abderrahmane Remili (Algeria) has occupied various senior posts in the Algerian Planning Secretariat since 1965, and has undertaken several missions as an international consultant for the United Nations and Unesco. His publications include articles on the administrative system in Algeria and on a systematic approach to training problems in developing countries.

John M. Thompson (United Kingdom) has, since 1970, been Secretary-General of the World Confederation of Organizations of the Teaching Profession (WCOTP), which he joined in 1959 as Assistant Director-General. Previously he had been an official of the National Union of Teachers of England and Wales, Administrative Secretary of the Co-ordinating Secretariat of National Unions of Students in Leiden (Netherlands) and President of the National Union of Students of England and Wales.

Lord John Vaizey (United Kingdom), professor of economics and Head of the School of Social Sciences at Brunel University (England), has served on many international bodies, held professorships in the United States and Australia, and received academic awards from these countries and from Spain. He has played an active part in public life in Britain, serving on government and local authority committees. He is Chairman of the British Irish Association and of the Enquiry into the Training of Professional Musicians, and is a Trustee of the King George VI and Queen Elizabeth Foundation and of the Ditchley Foundation. He was formerly a Fellow of St Catharine's College (Cambridge) and Fellow and Tutor of Worcester College (Oxford). His publications include *The Costs of Education, Social Democracy, The Political Economy of Education* and books on other topics.